The Personal President

THE
PERSONAL
PRESIDENT

CORNELL UNIVERSITY PRESS

Power Invested,
Promise Unfulfilled

Theodore J. Lowi

ITHACA AND LONDON

International Standard Book Number 0-8014-1798-8
Library of Congress Catalog Card Number 84-45804
Printed in the United States of America
Librarians: Library of Congress cataloging information
appears on the last page of the book.

The paper in this book is acid-free and meets the guidelines for permanence and durability of the Committee on Production Guidelines for Book Longevity of the Council on Library Resources.

FOR

Faye and Gaston Greil
Phyllis and Daniel Scharff
Evelyn and Harry Segal

who contributed far more than
they could possibly have known

CONTENTS

Preface

ix

CHAPTER ONE

The High Cost of Winning:
An Introduction to the Problem

1

CHAPTER TWO

Government and President
in the Traditional System

22

CHAPTER THREE

The Legacies of FDR

44

CHAPTER FOUR

Presidents without Parties:
The Making of a New Constituency

67

CHAPTER FIVE
The Future Is Here:
The Plebiscitary Presidency
97

CHAPTER SIX
The Performance of Plebiscitary
Presidents: A Cost-Benefit Analysis
134

CHAPTER SEVEN
Restoring the Balance
176

Index
213

Preface

The presidential election of 1984 was a personal triumph of inestimable proportions. Ronald Reagan's margin of victory in the popular vote, 59 percent, has been exceeded only four times since 1860—by Harding in 1920 (60.3 percent), Roosevelt in 1936 (60.8 percent), Johnson in 1964 (60 percent), and Nixon in 1972 (60.7 percent). Reagan's narrower margin of 1980 (51 percent) was attributable to a very substantial negative vote, by Democrats disillusioned with President Jimmy Carter. But his 1984 margin, confirmed by all the polls, was an outpouring of affection and approval.

The election did not, however, produce a landslide. Its effects were broad but shallow: broad enough to capture the electoral vote of forty-nine states but so shallow that it hardly penetrated political life below the outer crust of presidential politics. In the Senate, rather than gaining as most presidents do, Reagan actually lost two seats, reducing the Republican majority from 55-45 to 53-47. In the House of Representatives, the Republicans gained, but a mere fifteen seats—far short of the average for landslides of the past, and also short of the projected 24-30 seats that might have given Reagan back the "ideological majority" he had enjoyed briefly during his first, innovative year in office. The Reagan reelection victory of 1984—ominously—most resembles the Nixon reelection victory of 1972, with its 61 percent of the popular vote coupled with two Senate seats lost and a mere twelve House seats gained.

Only a full term of effort will reveal whether the 1984 victory was empty, not merely shallow. We can already say, however, that the Reagan victory was a personal vindication—a clear expression by

Americans that they felt Ronald Reagan's personal conduct had made their lives better than they had been four years earlier. We can also say that with all the credit goes the burden of high expectations. A very large percentage of those who voted for Reagan preferred the policies of Walter Mondale and the Democrats. Pre-election polls revealing affection for Reagan also revealed skepticism about the president's performance on economic and foreign policy and support for most major government programs even while condemning their costs. Post-election polls revealed that a large majority who voted for Reagan nevertheless expected him to break his promise not to raise taxes. For his encore, President Reagan is going to have to be lucky enough to have four more years of prosperity and peace and to make personal choices to which this prosperity and peace will be credited. The probability of both those occurring is a function of the relatively low probability of each. Even if Reagan should continue to enjoy Americans' affections, how can the estimate of his performance remain impervious to their expectations? Having enjoyed credit beyond desert for putting the world to rights, both the person and the presidency will have to accept blame for any wrong that may come. Neither verdict is just, but what is justice to masses whose social contract is consent in return for services? Promises were made, power was invested. Power was used: Was promise fulfilled?

In a single office, the presidency, the great powers of the American people have been invested, making it the most powerful office in the world. Its power is great precisely because it is truly the people's power, in the form of consent regularly granted. But there is great uncertainty about the terms of the social contract. We can know that virtually all power, limited only by the Bill of Rights, has been granted. And we can know that when presidents take the oath of office they accept the power and the conditions for its use: the promise of performance must be met. But we cannot know what is adequate performance. No entrepreneur would ever sign a contract that leaves the conditions of fulfillment to the subjective judgment of the other party. This is precisely what has happened in the new social contract underlying the modern government of the United States.

This book is about that government and the pathological adjustment of the presidency to it. The system of large positive national government in the United States was a deliberate construction, arising out of the 1930s. The urgency of the times and the poverty of government experience meant that the building was done exuberantly but improvisationally, without much concern for constitutional values or history. The modern presidency is the centerpiece of that construction. Considered by many a triumph of democracy, the modern American presidency is also its victim.

The accumulated changes in national government since the 1930s have brought the United States into an entirely new constitutional epoch. The two most important changes are the development of a large professional bureaucracy and the enlargement of the presidency, based upon a new political theory that democracy could be maintained and even enhanced as long as the capacity to govern was lodged in the White House. Woodrow Wilson characterized the regime of the 1880s as *congressional government*. The regime of the 1980s can be characterized as *presidential government*. The difference between the two involved the sacrifice of the Separation of Powers and the two-party system. What we now have is an entirely new regime, which deserves to be called the Second Republic of the United States. And, as with any regime, the Second Republic has developed a politics consonant with itself. The new politics of the president-centered Second Republic can best be described as a plebiscitary republic with a personal presidency. "Plebiscite" is a harsh term, intended to evoke the powerful imagery of Roman emperors and French authoritarians who governed on the basis of popular adoration, with the masses giving their noisy consent to every course of action. The plebiscite entered Anglo-Saxon awareness and anxiety in association with the coup d'etat that terminated the French Revolution and led to the conferring of imperial powers on Napoleon I. The association of the plebiscite with democracy at its worst was reaffirmed by the part it played in the elevation of Napoleon III in the 1850s. In the American context, the term is an exaggeration—but by how much? Already we have a virtual cult of personality revolving around the White House.

The gains from presidential government were immediate. Presidential government energized the executive; it gave the national government direction; it enhanced the capacity of presidential leadership to build national consensus and to overcome the natural inertia of a highly heterogeneous society. The costs of presidential government were cumulative. Most of the costs result from the fact that the expectations of the masses have grown faster than the capacity of presidential government to meet them. This imbalance has produced a political cycle, running on a regular course from boom to bust and back again. Just when the national government was beginning to develop a capacity to control the extremes of the business cycle, it was foiled by the phenomenon of the political cycle. The potential for political bankruptcy runs high.

This book seeks to identify the pathologies of presidential government and to understand their causes. It concludes with proposals for reform—made, however, with a sober awareness that the solution ultimately lies not in specific reforms at all but in a mature awareness of the nature of the problem.

Intellectual debts are never paid in full, but the academic balance of payments is kept in rough equilibrium by debtors to one group of colleagues becoming creditors to another. In citing my intellectual debts I promise my creditors to try to serve others as well as they have served me.

To Walter Dean Burnham I am most indebted because without his painstaking critique and detailed suggestions, the book would have been finished a lot sooner—and the result would have been a lot poorer. Michael Nelson also read the entire manuscript and not only made useful comments on it but gave me the benefit of his extraordinary command of the presidency literature. Walter La-Feber and Joel Silbey, co-teachers in courses at Cornell and in our Cornell-in-Washington program, contributed far more to the ideas of this book than they were aware. My thanks go also to Alexander Heard, Chancellor Emeritus of Vanderbilt University, whose incentives and encouragements actually got the project going.

Michio Muramatsu, my friend and colleague of the University of Kyoto, gave me an invaluable opportunity to try my ideas on receptive audiences of Japanese scholars in 1983. He arranged an invitation for me to deliver the distinguished Niijima lectures at Doshisha University and also provided me with powerfully stimulating seminars composed of professors from all over Japan and the Orient at the Kyoto American Studies Summer Seminar. I am equally indebted to my "students" in the year-long seminar held while I occupied the Chair of American Civilization at the Ecole des Hautes

Etudes en Sciences Sociales during the academic year 1981-82. Among "mes fidèles" there, those who made particularly important contributions to my analysis of the presidency include Sophie Gendrot, Norman Jacobs, Paul Oren, Annick Percheron, Marie-France Toinet, and Martha Zuber. That opportunity was made available by the generosity of the French-American Foundation of New York.

Cornell, my own community of scholars, is a unique intellectual environment, in large part because of the prominent role our students play in it. I am especially indebted to my students in Government 111, who have responded so well to my trying out novel formulations on them. Among my many valued Cornell colleagues, those whose writings and comments were of particular importance to this project include Benjamin Ginsberg, Martin Shefter, Sidney Tarrow, Isaac Kramnick, and Michael Kammen. Gary Bryner, Kathy Wagner-Johnson, and Bill Keller added their own creative dimension to the research they did for me as graduate assistants. Rose Zakour, my executive assistant, saved me from being buried alive by my accumulated commitments and responsibilities.

In the Cornell community of scholars I also include the staff of Cornell University Press. For them, a book is not a product but a medium of ideas to be treated with respect and affection. Working with Walter Lippincott, Kay Scheuer, and all the others at the Press was truly a learning experience.

I cannot, however, absolve any of these friends and colleagues from all responsibility for my mistakes, because their guidance was influential from start to finish. They, and I, are spared only by the reader's lack of knowledge of which weaknesses are mine alone. I urge the reader to give all of us the benefit of the doubt. The presidency is too important, and its problems are too pressing, to hold out for flawless analysis.

THEODORE J. LOWI

East Hill
Ithaca, New York

The Personal President

Prologue: The Grand Prix

In a now almost forgotten phonographic masterpiece, Peter Ustinov created the "Grand Prix du Roc," a dramatization of an automobile race on the Rock of Gibraltar. Ustinov played all the parts and provided all the sound effects. As the race was about to begin, Ustinov the radio correspondent (in a perfect American accent) went around to each of the pits to get comments on the race and the competition. Each interview was an ingenious caricature of the culture of the team. The interviews were concluded with a last word from the chief British driver (Ustinov in Liverpool accent):

Q: You doubt whether the race will be over by *tomorrow*?
A: Well, quite frankly, it's a bloody awful track, isn't it? Uh, I mean there's no room to overtake. . . . No passing on the cliff face: S-curves that are more like R's. . . . Whoever starts first will be at an enormous advantage, 'cause nobody could overtake him. . . . [except] in the water. Now, the water's gonna play a cardinal part in this, as I reckon . . . and I'm wearin' overshoes myself, 'cause I hate wet feet. . . .
Q: Who do you think has a chance . . . the Germans? The French, the Italians, the Americans?
A: Well, quite frankly—and again, don't quote me on this, uh, I don't think none of us have got much of a chance. . . .

You didn't have to be a racing car expert to predict no one had a chance. You only had to be familiar with the track. Yet all the crews were making complete preparations, including the skeptical British. Although the French crew chief was also pessimistic, he still felt France could win—"because all the others might lose."

1

The High Cost of Winning:
An Introduction to the Problem

Treadmill to oblivion
—Fred Allen

In 1936, as the New Deal looked back upon the most momentous period of governmental creativity since the 1790s, President Roosevelt appointed a group of experts on public administration to explore and make recommendations on how to manage what had been created. One of the most important presidential commissions ever formed, the President's Committee on Administrative Management, presented Roosevelt with its report shortly after the 1936 election. The opening sentence fired a shot heard round the Washington world ever since:

The President needs help

This is a book about the ensuing love-hate relationship between big government, the presidency, and the American people. Big government came late to America. And big government came quickly, within the space of less than three years. The American people embraced it overwhelmingly in 1936 and the Supreme Court capitulated in 1937. That, however, was only the beginning. Although the president had been the leader of the expansion, the presidency was one of its early victims. Congress had participated in the expansion, but on condition that responsibility for its success pass from the legislature

1

to the executive. The President's Committee on Administrative Management was the first of many efforts to adjust an eighteenth century Constitution to the twentieth century. The adjustment was made, but not successfully.

Presidential government turned out to be inadequate governing, and the difference between the theory of presidential government and real governing has been spanned mainly by deceit. Since 1937 there has been a constant effort sincerely to meet the requirements of the theory of presidential government, but a large gap remains, which has been enveloped in blue smoke and mirrors. In the 1880s, Professor Woodrow Wilson argued that congressional government was deceiving and that the reality underneath it was committee government. In the 1980s, presidential government is the deception. The nature of the reality and of the political adjustment that has been made to it is the concern of this book.[1]

The central theme of the 1937 President's Committee was that the new powers of the national government had to be centralized toward the president if they were to be made responsible. To bring about a balance between powers and responsibilities, certain changes were necessary and compelling. These included a fundamental change in the theory of the civil service. No longer did we need to protect appointments from political influence; we needed to recruit more positively for management capabilities. Therefore, the committee recommended that the independent Civil Service Commission be replaced with a single administrator responsible directly to the President. A related proposal called for the abolition of the independent regulatory commissions, making all the commissioners responsible to the president, serving at his pleasure. Another proposal of fundamental importance was that of removing the auditing function from Congress and its agent, the Comptroller-General, and transferring it along with the Budget Bureau to the proposed Executive Office of the President. It was further proposed that the president should be given "reorganization powers," by which he could in his wisdom reorganize, regroup, abolish, and transfer functions among agencies, subject to a "legislative veto": his reorganization proposals would be-

[1]My thanks to Walter Dean Burnham for suggesting the parallelism between the 1880s and today. My thanks to John Anderson for the powerful imagery of blue smoke and mirrors applied to presidential antics.

come law if within sixty days they were not explicitly disapproved by both the House and the Senate.

Roosevelt sent these proposals over to Congress in January 1937. The reorganization bill passed the House in August but was not taken up by the Senate until the following February. At that point it was hit by a firestorm of denunciation as a "dictator bill," which amounted to "plunging a dagger into the very heart of the democracy."[2] The critics compared the reorganization proposals to the recently rejected Court-packing plan in that both sought to aggrandize the power of the executive branch, in particular the president. Roosevelt took a number of unusual steps to quiet the opposition. He dropped several of the requests and indicated his willingness to negotiate further concessions. And since the fears of dictatorship had spread from Washington to the populace at large, he went to the unusual extent of issuing a presidential pronouncement that sounds perilously like Richard Nixon's 1974 assertion, "I'm not a crook":

A. I have no inclination to be a dictator.
B. I have none of the qualifications which would make me a successful dictator.
C. I have too much historical background and too much knowledge on existing dictatorships to make me desire any form of dictatorship for a democracy like the United States of America.[3]

Finally, in 1939, Congress gave the president the Executive Reorganization Act. It was far narrower than the original plan and was considered a significant political setback for Roosevelt's administration. The same fears that had produced opposition to reorganization powers, and had been evident in wild cheering in the House when the original bill had been returned for reconsideration to committee, also led to the Hatch Act of 1939, which restricted the political activities of employees in the executive branch. This was a bipartisan measure arising out of fears that a strong president could create a political machine based on the bureaucrats.

Ten years later a new commission on the executive branch was formed. It was intended to be different from the 1937 committee. A

[2]The quotes are from James MacGregor Burns, *Roosevelt: The Lion and the Fox* (New York: Harcourt, Brace, 1956), p. 344.
[3]Ibid., pp. 345-46.

Republican Congress (the 80th) rather than a Democratic president, created it and the president was the weak Harry Truman, and not the strong Franklin Roosevelt. There were twelve members (as opposed to three in 1937), and rather than coming from academia, the members and their staff were drawn predominantly from the business world. The chair, rather than going to an academic, was occupied by the rehabilitated Herbert Hoover. *Yet, virtually every observer agrees that the premises and the explicit views of the 1937 President's Committee on Administrative Management were reaffirmed by the Hoover Commission.* And they were reaffirmed again and again by a succession of presidential commissions and committees, under Democratic and Republican administrations, including at least the following: the second Hoover Commission under Eisenhower, the Landis Report under Kennedy, the Heineman Task Force under Johnson, the Ash Council under Nixon, and a host of task force reports under Carter. And these commissions and their reports were backed up by a virtually unanimous academic chorus singing the original 1937 song: "The President needs help."

As everyone knows, the plea for help fell upon increasingly attentive ears. While presidents were not given all the management and reorganization powers in the 1937 request, they received just about everything else they ever asked for. Take, for example, the White House Staff. The Roosevelt reorganization plan that ultimately got through Congress provided for a White House Staff of six senior aides. By the close of the Truman administration and the full restoration of peacetime government, this staff had reached over two hundred. It surpassed four hundred during the Eisenhower years and reached its peak of nearly six hundred at the stormy end of the Nixon administration. Under Ford it dropped slightly but at least a hundred were added again during the early Carter years, and the total moved back up toward six hundred under Reagan (Table 1).

Enlargement of staff has not been the only method by which presidents have gained the help they sought. The Budget Bureau has regularly grown in power and services, culminating in Nixon's enlargement and reorganization of it into the Office of Management and Budget (OMB). A tremendously large number of additions to presidential power have been granted in the area of defense and military policy, not the least of which was the creation of the Joint Chiefs of Staff and the CIA. The FBI has also served as an arm of the president

Table 1. The expanding White House Staff

Year	President	Full time employees	Employees temporarily detailed to the White House from outside agencies	Total
1937	Franklin D. Roosevelt	45	112(June 30)	157
1947	Harry S. Truman	190	27(June 30)	217
1957	Dwight D. Eisenhower	364	59(June 30)	423
1967	Lyndon B. Johnson	251	246(June 30)	497
1972	Richard M. Nixon	550	34(June 30)	584
1975	Gerald R. Ford	533	27(June 30)	560
1980	Jimmy Carter	488	75(June 30)	563
1984	Ronald Reagan	575*	17(June 1983)	592

Source: Thomas E. Cronin, "The Swelling of the Presidency: Can Anyone Reverse the Tide?" in Peter Woll, ed., American Government: Readings and Cases, 8th ed. (Boston: Little Brown, 1984), p. 347. Copyright © 1984 by Thomas E. Cronin. Reproduced with the permission of the author.

*Two former explicitly White House staff units, the Office of Administration and the Office of Policy Development, are now formally in the Executive Office of the President and not in the White House. But this misleads. These staffs are indeed White House and presidential staffs and thus are included here. The vice-president employs another 22 White House staffers and the National Security Council another 75 to 100, but these are not included in this 575 person staff of President Reagan.

through loyalty and security clearance processes, securing loyalty not only in the sense of patriotism but in that of faithfulness to the administration. Congress has been cooperative to the extent that it has added new programs to the national government without creating independent enterprises and commissions to handle them; though it never agreed to the 1937 plans for abolishing the independent commissions then existing and moving their functions to a direct line of presidential authority, it has rarely set up new activities on an independent basis in recent years. For example, although a large number of very important regulatory programs have been adopted by Congress in the past twenty years, only four important independent regulatory commissions have been established; and one of those, the Nuclear Regulatory Commission (1974), was only a reorganization of powers already held independently by the former Atomic Energy Commission. Finally, in the late 1970s Congress moved a considerable distance toward giving the president the powers over administrative personnel that the 1937 report had recommended. The independent Civil Service Commission was replaced by three separate agencies. Although two—the Merit Systems Protec-

5

tion Board and the Federal Labor Relations Authority—are independent, the third, the Office of Personnel Management (OPM), which received most of the powers of personnel management that had been handled by the Civil Service Commission, was set up with a single head appointed to serve at the president's pleasure.

The responses to the president's need mentioned so far are the palpable and specific types of help identified in or anticipated by the 1937 President's Committee Report. Not identified there but granted nevertheless by a succession of Congresses are some presidential powers of still greater significance. Most important was the grant of presidential discretion. Every new program Congress added in accord with its commitment to expanded government was delegated for implementation to the executive branch. These laws were deliberately written in the broadest and vaguest of terms in order to provide the largest amount of discretion possible to the agency and thence to the president in making the actual policies and deciding when it was in the public interest to implement them. Although the Supreme Court in 1935 declared the National Industrial Recovery Act unconstitutional on the grounds that too much discretion had been delegated from Congress to the executive branch, and although the ruling in that case was never reversed by later Supreme Court decisions, most of the important statutes adopted since World War II violate the principle without a peep from the Supreme Court.[4] As well as handing out these enormous grants of presidential discretion Congress developed a theory of "legislative oversight" as a safeguard, perhaps to placate the Supreme Court. But no knowledgeable person can seriously expect that Congress can take back in small pieces of post hoc committee interrogation what Congress gave away a priori in enormous portions.

Presidents have also been given help in the form of "emergency powers." In the early 1970s, one government study identified at least two hundred laws that give the president virtually unlimited power in particular situations defined in the law or by the president as a crisis. For example, in an emergency situation the president has the power to requisition any ship owned by a citizen or seize a foreign ship if he "finds it to be necessary to the national defense." President Nixon used statutory authority to declare a national emergency in

4In *Schechter Poultry Corporation* v. *United States*, 295 U.S. 495 (1935).

1970, calling out troops to deliver the mail during a postal strike. In 1968, to fight unfavorable balances of trade, President Johnson invoked statutory emergency powers to restrict the amount of American capital that could be invested abroad. In all these instances the president's power is available to him under *explicit statutory authorization*. Such authorization can of course be removed any time Congress sees fit, and occasionally—perhaps increasingly since the early 1970s—Congress has seen fit to do so. But a great number of these statutes are still on the books, and the principle of granting statutory emergency authorization is still very much alive.[5]

All this help and all these powers were approved as necessary or desirable by politicians and scholars—until the Vietnam War and Watergate. Very belated thoughts about the expansion of presidential power were then expressed by some of the same people who had sought the increase or who had helped write the poetry of justification for it. The most famous second thoughts expressed by former advocates of presidential power were probably those of Arthur Schlesinger, Jr., in his masterful book *The Imperial Presidency* (1973). The only important fault of this book is its publication date—it appeared about twenty years too late to contribute to an appropriate self-consciousness as to what was happening, and why.

The Grand Prix du President—and the Catch

What changed a Congress, a Court, and a public loath to give the president "dictatorial powers" into a Congress, a Court, and a public not only eager to cooperate with the president's requests for help but to go beyond them? The explanation is as simple as a change in point of view. First of all, Americans had grown accustomed to big government and no longer saw centralized power only as a threat. Even businessmen had grown accustomed to the idea. Professor Robert Lane dramatically documents their adjustment. In a study of the attitudes of business leaders toward the federal government's regulation of business, Lane shows that between 1939 and 1946 two very important things happened. First, the number of unfavorable ref-

[5]The study was published by the Office of Emergency Preparedness (Washington: Government Printing Office, no date). It is taken up in an excellent review article by K. W. Clawson, *Washington Post*, September 5, 1971.

7

erences to federal regulatory programs dropped precipitously. Second, the substance of those criticisms changed drastically, from broad ideological objections to government coerciveness to specialized "instrumental" topics stressing particular applications, adjustments, costs, and so on.[6]

Moreover, as people were simply growing accustomed to the larger national government, the theory about that government was also changing. The new theory transformed an increasingly familiar fact into a virtue. Political scientists, economists, jurists, journalists, even a few philosophers participated in a large-scale effort to establish the constitutionality of the new national state and to go beyond that to show that it was a positive good rather than merely a necessary evil. Along with the justification of the new national state came justification of the increased power of the presidency as necessary to its success. Although there was nothing logically compelling about having a big government governed by a powerful single chief executive, the association of big government with strong presidency was established, and then pursued with utmost vigor. The desire for a new public philosophy to fit the new presidential government was so fundamental that it encompassed an effort to redefine democracy itself to bring it into closer consonance with president-centered government. Far from a threat to democracy, the presidency became its life preserver. And once the association between big government, the strong presidency, and democracy was established, no amount of help for the president was too much. The American capacity for self-government rested from then on upon the president's capacity to govern.

The presidency was built up in theory as well as practice. President Truman's claim that the president is "lobbyist for all the people" is a significant early expression of what was to become standard ideology. Beginning in the mid-1950s, leading political scientists argued eloquently that there would be a "deadlock of democracy" without presidential leadership.[7] One of the most important political theorists of that period, Robert A. Dahl, more systematically defined the presidency as essentially the representative of the Real Majority in

---

[6]Robert E. Lane, *The Regulation of Businessmen* (New Haven: Yale University Press, 1953), p. 38 and *passim.*

[7]James MacGregor Burns, *Deadlock of Democracy* (Englewood Cliffs, N.J.: Prentice-Hall, 1963).

8

America.[8] And Clinton Rossiter, author of probably the first modern book on the presidency, defined the office in terms of the five roles its holder was expected to play: commander-in-chief, diplomat, chief executive, legislative leader, and opinion/party leader.[9] These are typical of the points of view held in academia, and they were the views of independent scholars, not point-men for the program of the Democratic party.

Completion of the task of redefining the presidency as necessary for the government and for national democracy followed the 1958 congressional elections and the 1960 presidential election. The most important of the authors at that time was Richard Neustadt, whose book *Presidential Power* became the bible of the Kennedy administration and, to say the least, the leading text on the subject among political scientists and journalists.[10] Neustadt's book is based on the thoroughly realistic assumptions that the American national government would not work unless the presidency was effective, and that no president could be effective unless he constantly concerned himself with how each decision he made advanced his power over the administration, the Washington community, Congress, and the people. Since the president's only real power was "the power to persuade," he had to manipulate each of his constituencies in order to use each for the manipulation of the other. This was necessary, and it was also good—even though it was not very pretty. Many embraced Neustadt's viewpoint for the selfish reason that support of his theory of presidential power would enhance the actual power of John F. Kennedy and the acceptance of his New Frontier program. But hosts of others joined in because they sincerely accepted the redefinition of democratic theory with the presidency at its core.

But there was a catch. Well before the elevation of the new presidency had approached completion, the stresses on presidential performance became overwhelming. And the failures mounted accordingly, despite all efforts to head them off by more responses to "The

[8]Robert A. Dahl, *Preface to Democratic Theory* (Chicago: University of Chicago Press, 1956). For a rebuttal, see Willmoore Kendall, "The Two Majorities," *Midwest Journal of Political Science,* 4 (November 1960), 317-45.
[9]Clinton Rossiter, *The American Presidency* (New York: Harcourt, Brace & World, 1956), pp. 4-25.
[10]Richard Neustadt, *Presidential Power: The Politics of Leadership* (New York: Wiley, 1960).

President needs help." Between 1946 and 1980 five of the seven presidents were defined as failures: each was retired from office and from politics by reason of unacceptability to his own party as well as to the public at large. Only Eisenhower was a clear exception. Kennedy is also technically an exception, since he died in mid passage. But it was because he was in such political hot water in the Democratic South, as well as facing an indeterminate amount of "white backlash" in the North, that he embarked on the ill-fated trip to Dallas, disregarding the fears and objections of some of his top advisers.

Like Peter Ustinov's racing drivers, presidential contestants make extensive preparations to enter a no-win situation. Moreover, Washington reality is actually worse than Gibraltar fiction, because, although formally there is a winner, the winner can be the biggest loser. He wins in enough of the preliminary heats, in the primaries and caucuses. He wins the semifinals at the convention. Miraculously, he puts together a campaign sufficient to win the finals in the November election and the December electoral vote. Then his political career is finished before he can fully enjoy the prize. Reelection seems only to postpone the inevitable. It is premature to judge Reagan, but for all other winners since Eisenhower the presidency has been something of a disaster. Meanwhile, losers, especially if they can remain in the Senate, can enjoy any number of years of political satisfaction and effectiveness. Indeed, some of the losers have their best years *after* their loss in the presidential contest.

Take the case of Senator Henry Jackson. Public reaction following his death in September 1983 was of the sort usually reserved for great national heroes. His career reputation for strength and wisdom was one of the better kept secrets of the U.S. Senate, and he had failed three times in his bid for the presidency—1968, 1972, and 1976. Yet his national stature grew immensely following each failure. It is hard to imagine such extraordinary testimonials being offered in response to the death of an ex-president.

Or take George McGovern, who has lived politically in far better shape than Richard Nixon, to whom he lost in 1972. The same can be said, at least through 1984, of Walter Mondale, who fared far better than Jimmy Carter, the man who nudged him out of the 1976 presidential race. Edmund Muskie and Edward Kennedy, two other losers, have also been treated a great deal better than Carter. Or compare the revered Hubert Humphrey, loser, to the reviled Richard

10

Nixon, winner,—and the respected Barry Goldwater, loser, to the rejected Lyndon Johnson, winner. Note also the apotheosis of Senators Howard Baker and Robert Dole following their unsuccessful run against Ronald Reagan in 1980.

The sobering regularity of unhappy successes in the Grand Prix du President can be reduced to laws—laws that will appear eminently commonsensical to anyone familiar with the presidential track. These are stated below as the Three General Laws of Politico-Dynamics of the Second Republic.[11] Although there is a certain elegance in the threeness of these laws, I make no claim that they constitute a closed system. And, although they are intended to be comprehensive, there is room for other laws to be added by anyone who studies the track or plays the horses. If a single point can be made of these laws, it is this: The harder presidents try to please their mass constituency, the more alienated that constituency becomes. This is the nature of the no-win situation, and it is built into the track, regardless of the nature and character of the players.

The Three General Laws of Politico-Dynamics of the Second Republic

(1) The Law of Effort
  (a) Presidents spend the first half of their terms trying sincerely to succeed according to their oath and their promises.
  (b) They devote the second half of their terms trying to create the appearance of success.
  Refinement 1: The second half is starting earlier and earlier.
  Refinement 2: The onset of the second half is indicated by White House complaints about bad press and White House efforts to plug leaks and otherwise manage the news.

(2) The Law of Outcomes
  The probability of failure is always tending toward 100 percent.
  Refinement: Given the exalted rhetoric and high expectations surrounding the presidency, a partial success is defined by the mass public as a failure.

(3) The Law of Succession
  Each president contributes to the upgrading of his predecessors.
  Corollary: This is the only certain contribution each president will make.

---

[11]The epoch since 1961 is institutionally, constitutionally, and ideologically so distinct that it deserves special enumeration as the Second Republic. See Chapter 3 and also Lowi, *The End of Liberalism: The Second Republic of the United States* (New York: Norton, 1979).

11

Ronald Reagan—What Kind of Exception?

Ronald Reagan's first three years as president strongly confirmed the Three Laws. Then something happened. Reagan in his fourth year appeared to be an exception. Some lessons can be learned from that.

Reagan began as the most programmatic president since Roosevelt. He went beyond Roosevelt in his willingness to convey before the election exactly what he was going to try to do. Virtually all his actions in 1981 and early 1982 indicate his sincere commitment to the fulfillment of his campaign promises, and he delivered on a number of them. Stronger confirmation of First Law, Part (a) could hardly be found.

Confirmation of First Law, Part (b) was not long to follow. Although the Reagan honeymoon period was unusually long, it came to a rather abrupt termination during his second year. Criticisms from Democratic leaders such as Speaker Thomas O'Neill began to mount and were soon joined by those of a growing number of liberal Republican leaders. He could no longer count on a large number of defecting Democrats to support his bills. The result, stalemate. As a signal of the onset of Part (b), refinement 2, in his administration, complaints about bad press and about leaks from high officials began to emanate with regularity from the White House, Reagan press conferences, infrequent enough in 1981, became rare afterward. A strong preference was indicated for planned appearances on radio and television, where the president could put the issues and criticisms in a better light, unmediated by the press. Plumbers (by other names) were assigned; lie detector tests on top officials were threatened. Other security measures were implemented. And Reagan turned out to be so good at creating the appearance of success that he earned the title "Teflon-Coated President." Charges of failure against his administration simply did not stick to him personally. There is almost universal agreement that Reagan is one of the best presidents ever at putting a smile on depressing news.[12]

Political stalemate was accompanied by one of the worst recessions since 1933. But public expectations remained high. And, while

---

[12]A good account of the president and the press will be found in James Fallows, "The Presidency and the Press," in Michael Nelson, ed., *The Presidency and the Political System* (Washington: Congressional Quarterly Press, 1984), pp. 264-81.

President Reagan's personal popularity also appeared to remain high, his performance rating began to drop, and drop. The profiles of presidential performance ratings in Figure 1 indicate that he was not able to escape the fate of his predecessors: He began using up his fund of public support. For nearly three years, Reagan's approval rating was almost exactly parallel to President Carter's, with Carter actually doing a bit better. At the end of the first twelve months, Carter's approval rating was nearly 58 percent, compared to Reagan's 50 percent. During months 18-20, the two of them were neck and neck, with disapprovals mounting over approvals. By January 1983, the Laws of Politico-Dynamics seemed thoroughly confirmed. Reagan had dropped to a personal low of 38 percent approval (Harris gave him a 38, Gallup a 37). President Carter was coming out of hiding, and even President Ford was beginning to look pretty good.

Beginning in May 1983, however, President Reagan began to diverge from the pattern of his predecessors. As shown in Figure 2, his performance rating stabilized and then began to tend back upward. In May his rating jumped six points, from 41 percent to 47 and then in September it jumped very significantly, from 45 percent to 56. From that point on, Reagan's performance rating moved upward and stayed up at around 55 percent, whereas Carter's, which blipped up briefly in late 1979, then continued dropping for most of his last year in office.

Virtually everyone has recognized that Reagan's recovery from extremely low performance ratings is exceptional, and most have tended to attribute it to the improved economy. But although there is no denying that the economy had improved, it provides a very poor explanation for the surge in Reagan's popular approval. In the first place, most of the economic indicators were simply returning to where they had been in 1981. Second, economic improvements were expressed in very general terms and moved gradually, step by step, without any single and palpable dramatic change. It is simply not good logic to attempt to explain specific effects (such as Reagan's spurts of improvement in ratings) with very general and diffuse causes. Moreover, although prosperity is never irrelevant to popularity, Reagan's presidential predecessors lost ground in performance ratings regardless of the performance of the economy. For example, the economy's climb during 1968 did not save Lyndon Johnson from disgrace. The recovery during 1976 did not save Gerald Ford, and, de-

13

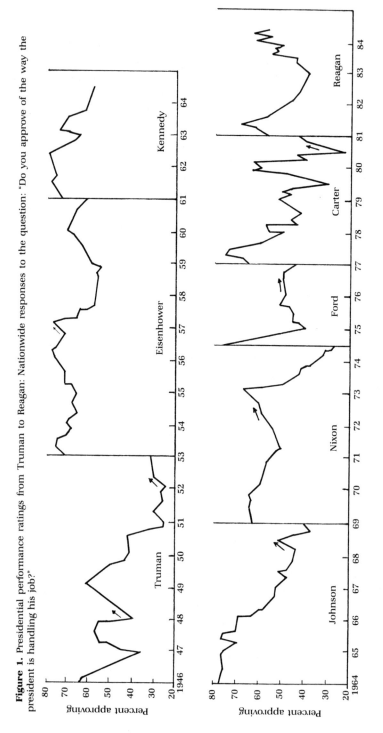

Figure 1. Presidential performance ratings from Truman to Reagan: Nationwide responses to the question: "Do you approve of the way the president is handling his job?"

Note: Arrows indicate pre-election upswings. For details of Reagan's 1983-84 ratings, see Figure 2.
Source: Data from the Gallup Poll and the Harris Survey through regular press releases.

spite the high inflation and credit figures in 1979-80, there was no sign of a recession until over a year after the suffering Carter left office as a "nonperson."[13]

Third, and more important, although Reagan's performance approval rating began to climb after January 1983 and took a couple of big jumps in May and September, his rating of performance on *specific* economic issues continued to be low. For example, during the twelve months of 1983, the polls show that 50 percent of the public continued to disapprove of his efforts to get the country out of recession, and 56 percent continued to disapprove of his handling of inflation. Moreover, he was burdened with a record-high 70 percent *negative* evaluation of his handling of the federal budget and the federal deficit. A 69 percent majority rated him negatively on his efforts to keep people from going hungry; and 73 percent of those polled in early 1984 continued to rate him negatively on "helping the unemployed, small business, farmers, and others in economic trouble." About the best that can be said for an economic explanation of the Reagan exception is that the overall economic improvement may have helped buoy his administration—smoothing out some of the rough spots in the treacherous presidential track—but it does not provide a sufficient explanation for the dramatic spurts of approval that seem to have put Reagan on a completely different track from Carter and the others.

What appears to be a Reagan exception in performance ratings can be explained in a way that reveals something important about the presidency itself. The upward trend in Reagan's ratings in the latter part of his third year and into the fourth year is, on the face of it, an exception. However, there is an explanation for that exception that not only makes Reagan a confirmation of the Three Laws but gives rise to great concern about the kinds of pressures that Reagan will be under in a second term.

The explanation for the exceptional trend in Reagan's performance rating will be found in foreign relations—or, *international events as-*

---

[13]The correlation of business cycles and political performance is a great deal stronger in American history prior to 1948. One study demonstrated that from 1928 through 1944 the party in power was returned to office in sixteen out of eighteen elections where prices were rising or were at a high plateau. Changes in administrations tended to occur when prices were declining or were at a low plateau as the election approached: Louis H. Bean, *How to Predict Elections* (New York: Knopf, 1948); V. O. Key, *Politics, Parties, and Pressure Groups*, 5th ed. (New York: Crowell, 1964), pp. 541-42.

sociated with the president. Not every international event associated with the president will push up performance ratings, but between elections international events are the only events that *will* push up the ratings.[14]

Note well that as the economy was moving upward at a smooth, albeit impressive, rate, President Reagan's approval profile was developing in a more jagged fashion. The six-point jump in May 1983 cannot be laid beside a specific domestic economic development, but it can be understood as a fairly immediate response to the violent initiation of the United States into the Lebanese conflict. On April 18, the United States embassy in Beirut was bombed and forty people killed, including a dozen Americans. On April 19, President Reagan associated himself with the event by dramatically denouncing it as a cowardly act. On April 23, he associated himself with it still further by sending Secretary of State George Shultz to Beirut to forge an agreement providing for the withdrawal of all foreign troops from Lebanon. This was the only front-page happening of bold-faced importance during the April period when the various national polling organizations were getting ready for the May reports on performance. Improvement of the economy was being made known by publication of cheery but rather technical indicators of investment, inflation, new jobs, declining unemployment, and so forth. No front-page events in industry or Congress competed in that period with the Lebanon crisis. In Washington it was, in fact, a time of frustration

---

[14]An unusually careful study of these ratings has been conducted by George C. Edwards, III. He identifies a number of significant international events that did not push up the performance ratings of the president serving at the time of the event. However, there is nothing in his study that undermines the explanation offered here. In the first place, Edwards was able to compile a long list of international events that did not significantly rally the people to the president because his criterion for significant rallying effects was an immediate 10 percent increase in approval rating. This is a very high threshold indeed, enabling him to eliminate the Bay of Pigs as a rallying event because public approval increased a shade less than 10%. This also enables him to eliminate such important moments of rallying as the 6 percent increase in approval after the U-2 debacle, the 7 percent increase following the Nixon trip to China, the 4 percent increase after the Nixon-Vietnam peace agreement was announced, the 9 percent increase after Ford's *Mayaguez* incident, and the 4 percent increase Carter briefly enjoyed after his vain attempt to rescue the Iranian hostages in 1980. See Edwards, *The Public Presidency: The Pursuit of Popular Support* (New York: St. Martin's, 1983), p. 247. Edwards offers no compelling argument for taking the 10 percent threshold for a significant rallying event. Moreover, given the fact that almost all domestic events *depress* rather than rally approval ratings, *any* increase in approval ratings has to be taken as interesting, if not significant.

16

over congressional recalcitrance, a mood that led Reagan's public statements to become more partisan on domestic issues and more grandiose and rhetorical on international ones. It should be recalled that the Lebanon crisis was in an important sense a culmination, perhaps even a confirmation, of President Reagan's effort to mobilize the American people around fear of East-West conflict, an effort begun with the "evil empire" speech of February and carried further in March with his famous "star wars" address to Congress.

The second spurt in approval of Reagan's performance in the job, in September 1983, followed the September 1 Soviet destruction of the Korean Air Lines plane. This attack outraged the American people; more to the point, it rallied them around the president.

This connection between the president's performance rating and foreign policy shows up in dramatic fashion throughout the remainder of 1983 and the beginning of 1984 (see Figure 2). Although Reagan's rating had spurted up by eleven points in September, it lost about nine in early October. Then came the terrorist bombing of the Marine compound in Beirut, killing nearly three hundred troops and civilians, followed a few days later by the Grenada invasion— pushing the Reagan performance rating back to 56 percent. When it again began to droop, the intensification of U.S. sea and air attacks on the Lebanese hinterland brought about another blip upward. President Reagan even gained from the liberation of Air Force Lieutenant Robert Goodman—although his release came in response to the efforts of Jesse Jackson.

There was one more upward blip in 1984, following the February "redeployment" of U.S. Marines in Beirut, the death of Andropov, and his replacement by Chernenko. Reagan's performance ratings moved up a full twenty points between late March 1983 and April 1984.

Thus, although the pattern of public approval for roughly ten months following May 1983 is exceptional, it fits into a pattern established by presidents long before Ronald Reagan: First, *presidential performance ratings will tend downward and continue downward unless interrupted by an international event associated with the president.* Second, *the event does not have to be defined as a success.* A disaster can rally the American people just as effectively as a triumph. Although the facts are somewhat masked by the way Figure 2 is drawn, Kennedy's performance rating jumped from 73 to 83 percent after the Bay of Pigs, and Carter's jumped from 32 to 61 percent fol-

17

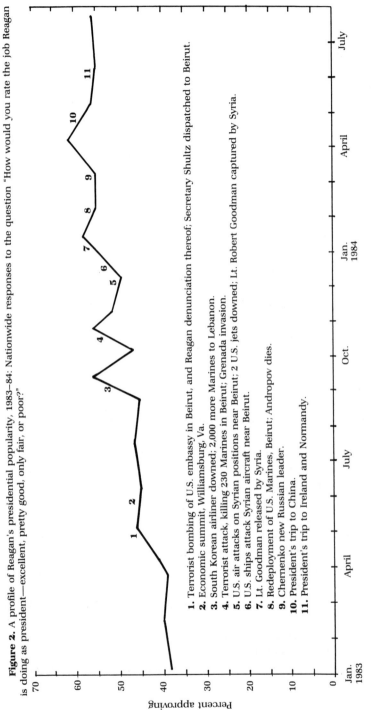

Figure 2. A profile of Reagan's presidential popularity, 1983–84: Nationwide responses to the question "How would you rate the job Reagan is doing as president—excellent, pretty good, only fair, or poor?"

1. Terrorist bombing of U.S. embassy in Beirut, and Reagan denunciation thereof; Secretary Shultz dispatched to Beirut.
2. Economic summit, Williamsburg, Va.
3. South Korean airliner downed: 2,000 more Marines to Lebanon.
4. Terrorist attack, killing 230 Marines in Beirut; Grenada invasion.
5. U.S. air attacks on Syrian positions near Beirut; 2 U.S. jets downed; Lt. Robert Goodman captured by Syria.
6. U.S. ships attack Syrian aircraft near Beirut.
7. Lt. Goodman released by Syria.
8. Redeployment of U.S. Marines, Beirut; Andropov dies.
9. Chernenko new Russian leader.
10. President's trip to China.
11. President's trip to Ireland and Normandy.

Source: Data from the Harris Survey through regular press releases.

lowing the late 1979 hostage incident in Iran. Third, *the effects of the rallying event tend to be brief.* In a short time, approval ratings return to their downward tendency until there is another foreign policy fix, or until the fourth factor is introduced, which is the national electoral cycle: A reinspection of Figures 1 and 2 will show that for each president, *voters tend to suspend judgment about presidential performance as the presidential election approaches.*

Although at first blush shaken by the unexpected rise in Reagan's performance ratings, the Three Laws of Politico-Dynamics remain intact. Reagan possesses no talents all that much in excess of his predecessors, and there is no evidence to suggest he carries with him a special secret of how to succeed in the presidency. He simply profited from a well-spaced succession of international events for which he deserved neither credit nor blame. This succession of events took him all the way to the point where he picked up on the electoral cycle, which buoyed him on into the general election of 1984.

If the reason for Reagan's popularity lies in his personal charisma, then it is close to meaningless for an understanding of American institutions, because personal charisma passes with the person. If the buoyant economy truly explains Reagan's high performance ratings, that would be more interesting because it would mean that national elections can be bought and sold and that politics is merely an epiphenomenon of economics. But, as I have already shown, the economic explanation is insufficient. The factors that have to be added are the rallying effects of international events and the approaching national election.

Because the succession of international events brought President Reagan so strongly into the electoral period, he was able to defer the last judgment of the people as implied by the Second Law. But eventually, he will be paid because he is the piper. The presidency is not long to be trifled with by standing tall, whipping Grenadians, and whipping up testimonials. As Reagan's popular support begins to decline at some point after a brief honeymoon in his second term, politics will return to war in the trenches, as it was after 1981, and the people will return to making their judgments according to performance. Reagan will not be judged more harshly than his predecessors, but he will indeed be judged harshly, because that is the way the presidency is now built. The Three Laws of Politico-Dynamics are simply a light-hearted way of characterizing the presidency within the larger political context created for it by the large powers of the office within the large, new modern state. They point directly to the problem of the presidency in the 1980s and beyond—a problem so profound that the future of national government itself rests upon its resolution. First, having given presidents maximum power to govern and all the help they have ever asked for, the public has rationally focused its expectations on them, counting on them to deliver on all the promises they explicitly made and all those explicit and implicit in the policies and programs they vowed faithfully to execute. Second, the civic training of the American people has led them, again rationally, to see the presidency as their own property. They have invested fully in it, they have witnessed the vesting of the "capacity to govern" in the office, they have approved, and they now look for delivery on all the promises as their measure of democracy and legitimacy. This is a new social contract: in return for delivery on promises, American citizens identify directly with the presidency and rally around it when the system itself is at stake—whether at a time of foreign challenge or at a time when the system is being renewed by another election.

This is the *personal presidency*: an office of tremendous personal power drawn from the people—directly and through Congress and the Supreme Court—and based on the new democratic theory that the presidency with all powers is the necessary condition for governing a large, democratic nation.

And this is the catch: There are built-in barriers to presidents' delivering on their promises, and the unlikely occasion of one doing so would only engender another round of new policies, with new responsibilities and new demands for help. A theory of democracy based upon a plebiscitary presidency whose measure of success is delivery operates according to a kind of Malthusian law, which, in turn, confirms the Second Law of Politico-Dynamics at the next higher plateau of expectations: As presidential success advances arithmetically, public expectations advance geometrically.

And this is the pathology: The desperate search is no longer for the good life but for the most effective presentation of appearances. This is a pathology because it escalates the rhetoric at home, ratcheting expectations upward notch by notch, and fuels adventurism abroad, in a world where the cost of failure can be annihilation.

Unfortunately, the presidency is part of a system in which all the parts are so interrelated that they must be confronted simultaneously. The presidency is tied to and legitimized by a relatively recent articulation of American democratic theory that in turn arises out of a particular view of the facts about modern government with the presidency at its center. I will attempt to keep the parts together, but will divide the book into three pieces, corresponding to my grasp of three quite distinct regimes in the history of the United States since its founding in 1789. These are the traditional system, the New Deal transition, and the post-1961 era, which I have entitled the era of the Second Republic. Although as stages of history they are of unequal duration, they are sufficiently each of a piece to provide a basis for comparison as well as a sense of development. In each case, I will identify the changes in the system of government first—an ordering that proceeds from the very powerful assumption that every regime creates a politics consonant with itself—such that any basic change in the structure or functions of government will in fairly short order be followed by appropriate changes in politics. Following that, the politics of the era will be examined, with a particular focus on the presidency. Then I will make an effort to analyze how those political adjustments in turn affect the capacity of the regime. Whenever the political process falls short of a successful adjustment, a change of regime becomes a distinct possibility.

Does this mean that the inadequate adjustments of the political process during the 1960s and 1970s are producing a new regime, perhaps a Third Republic? The logical hypothesis is necessarily yes. But when, how, and in what form?

2

Government and President
in the Traditional System

Far more may be done by entrusting to the citizens the
administration of minor affairs than by surrendering to
them in the control of important ones.
—Alexis de Tocqueville

America got its modern national state after 1933, at the
expense of a tradition. Developing over the previous century and a
half, practices had become institutions, habits had become customs,
customs had become morality, and the Constitution was the scrip-
ture for civic religion. The long duration of the traditional system will
help explain why the political adjustments of the modern era have
been so deeply flawed.

The American Political Tradition, 1800-1933: R.I.P.

Many observers of nineteenth century America would have us believe that it had no tradition. The Constitution itself was a rejection of
tradition and an embrace of a new American faith in the capacity of
individuals to make their own institutions and fashion their own society. Jefferson was attacking tradition when he asserted the right of
revolution. Tocqueville picked up on this as a major theme in the
1830s. He was struck by the restlessness of the typical American, who

clutches everything . . . but soon loosens his grasp to pursue fresh gratifi-
cations. . . . If in addition to the taste for physical well-being a social con-

22

dition be added in which neither laws nor customs retain any person in his place, there is a great additional stimulant to this restlessness of temper.

Equality begets in man the desire of judging of everything for himself; it gives him in all things a taste for the tangible and real, a contempt for tradition and for forms.[1]

The young Abraham Lincoln conveyed the same impression not long after Tocqueville's visit. In a speech before the Young Men's Lyceum of Springfield on January 27, 1838, Lincoln observed that after half a century the spirit of Revolution had persisted too long and was beginning to interfere with "the perpetuation of our political institutions." If those institutions were to be perpetuated, he argued, the passion that helped build the "temple of liberty" must be replaced by "a reverence for the Constitution and laws," including "a strict observance of all the laws." But even as he was appealing for respect for tradition, Lincoln was being the very American Tocqueville described: In the same speech he recognized there were bad laws that "should be repealed as soon as possible," albeit "borne with . . . while they continue in force."[2]

Yet, America already had a political tradition in the 1830s and, if duration and repetition count for anything, that tradition grew stronger in the ensuing century. The Constitution of 1789 remained virtually the same Constitution throughout a century and a half, being more strengthened than weakened by the Civil War and its aftermath. The structure of government remained the same throughout the period; moreover, that structure was almost precisely as anticipated and intended by the Founders. This is the traditional system within which national politics, including the presidency, was shaped.

The Regime of the Constitution

One of the commonplaces of the American Constitution is that it provides for a national government of strictly delegated powers. Set

[1]Alexis de Tocqueville, *Democracy in America*, ed. Phillips Bradley (New York: Vintage, 1955), II, pp. 144-45, and p. 42. The epigraph appears on p. 111.

[2]Abraham Lincoln, "The Perpetuation of Our Political Institutions," speech before the Young Men's Lyceum of Springfield, January 27, 1838. Reprinted in Lowi, ed., *Private Life and Public Order* (New York: Norton, 1968), pp. 43-44.

Table 2. Specialization of functions between national government and the states in the traditional system

1. National government functions (domestic)	2. State government functions
Internal improvements	Property laws (incl. slavery)
Subsidies	Estate & inheritance laws
Tariffs	Commerce laws (ownership & exchange)
Public lands disposal	Banking & credit laws
Patents	Insurance laws
Coinage	Family laws
	Morals laws
	Public health & quarantine laws
	Education laws
	General penal laws
	Public works laws (incl. eminent domain)
	Construction codes
	Land-use laws
	Water & mineral resources laws
	Judiciary & criminal procedure laws
	Electoral laws (incl. political parties)
	Local government laws
	Civil service laws
	Occupations & professions laws
	Etc.

forth largely in Article I, Sec. 8, the theory was implemented almost to the letter. Yet, it is one of the most universally unappreciated commonplaces.

Table 2 is a mapping of the direct consequences of the theory of "expressed powers." When implemented, the powers expressly delegated to the national government, as distinct from all the other powers "reserved" to the states, turn out to be functions or areas of policy. Column 1 gives a picture of the functions of the national government throughout the nineteenth century and well into the twentieth. Column 2 does the same for the states. Since these are categories of policy, more examples could have been added to each column, but the resulting picture would have been only a more complicated version of the list offered here.

The first impression given by the table is that the national government was not doing a great deal during the traditional century and a half, especially in comparison to the state governments. The second impression is that the national government was holding itself (or being held) closely to the functions expressly delegated to it in Article I, Sec. 8. Both these states of affairs were intended.

was made possible by the presence of patronage policies and the absence of the more divisive regulatory policies.

During the century and a half of the patronage state there were a few exceptions to patronage policies, but so few as to confirm the rule. For example, the Fugitive Slave Acts were efforts on the part of the national government to regulate the conduct of northerners in instances when an escaped southern slave came into their custody. This effort to regulate directly the conduct of citizens was such an exceptional type of policy, and was so divisive in Congress that it contributed significantly to the polarization and ultimately to the destruction of the Union. Civil War policies were also exceptional; it should be remembered how quickly the extraordinary policies of the national government during the war period were dismantled afterward. The other exceptions to patronage policies were the few regulatory statutes passed by Congress between the late 1880s and the first two years of the Wilson administration. These were few in number and, more important, were recognized by almost everyone not only as exceptional but of such doubtful constitutionality that they were built on a very narrow definition of "interstate commerce." It was not really until the 1930s that exceptions to the rule of patronage policies became so frequent as to create a new rule altogether, and that is precisely what brought the traditional system to an end.

To call the national government a patronage state is in no way intended to imply that it was an insignificant force in American history. The national government was clearly the largest institution in American society, and the sum total of its public policy activity had a tremendous influence, physically and fiscally, on the development of the United States. The patronage state could also be called a "commercial republic" in that most of the policies adopted by Congress during the nineteenth century were primarily oriented toward the husbanding of commerce, the facilitation of investment, and the productive distribution of population. However, this state of affairs was the cumulative and residual result of hundreds of individual policies and not the clear outcome of some fundamental choice of direction for the nation. Each policy was a response to an argument for the merit of a given land grant, privilege, public works project, tariff concession, and so forth. For this reason it is legitimate to conclude that, although the national government was an important institution, it was a highly specialized one—one whose significance was diminished, as its stability was enhanced, by the fact that so few fundamental social choices had to be made and implemented through public policy. In these characteristics lie the nature and character, and the advantages and disadvantages, of the regime of the traditional system in the United States.

The Politics of the Traditional System

The patronage state developed a patronage politics. No relationship between a regime and its politics was ever closer.

Although the Separation of Powers equals federalism as a constitutional principle, the actual relationships among the branches of the national government were shaped primarily by the forces of federalism and the patronage state that federalism made possible. In 1885 a bright young political science professor named Woodrow Wilson wrote a textbook on the American system which he entitled *Congressional Government*. No matter that the reality was most often committee government: National government was Congress-centered throughout the era of the traditional system, including the eight years of Wilson's presidency. In fact, President Wilson probably considered himself a victim of Congress-centered government.

The patronage state could be Congress-centered because patronage policies could be framed and almost completely implemented by Congress through its individual members as well as its committees. Each patronage policy could be carried out largely in the absence of bureaucracy. The resources to be distributed could be broken down into a large number of small units, and the main question was one of equitable short-run distribution. What bureaucracy was needed could be staffed by ordinary people. And if ordinary people could administer government, then there could be rotation in administrative offices comparable to rotation in electoral offices. This is the underlying basis of the "spoils system."

Distribution of government jobs to the faithful was not invented by Americans, nor was it limited to nineteenth century America. Nowhere else was it so systematic, however, before or since. During the decade or two of state-building after 1789, government jobs were already being treated as patronage but mainly on the appointments side, to vacancies resulting from resignations or the creation of new positions. The first presidents removed very few office holders. Jefferson held the record for removals, but many of those were persons President Adams had hastily appointed "at midnight" before the end of his term of office. It was President Jackson who elevated political rotation—appointments and removals—to a virtual principle of government. And in this he was loyally followed by his successors, regardless of party, throughout the nineteenth and into the twentieth century.[4]

The principle is what makes Jackson's contribution significant: Since government could be handled by ordinary citizens, all jobs *should* be rotated in accordance with the election outcome—and therefore all jobs should be considered vacant the minute a new administration took office. By 1900, over 60 percent of the 256,000 employees in the federal service were still in "patronage" jobs, despite the passage of the Civil Service Act in 1883. Coverage under civil service expanded fairly rapidly after 1900, to slightly over 60 percent at the beginning and 70 percent toward the end of the Wilson administration. However, the absolute growth of the number of employees in the government from 256,000 in 1901 to 480,000 just prior to our entry into World War I made it possible for political parties and administrations to live comfortably with the expanded civil service coverage.[5] Thus, the patronage regime of the nineteenth century was literally a regime of the "common man."

One of the great misconceptions in American political history is that of treating patronage and jobs as synonymous. Political jobs were an important form of political patronage all during the traditional system, but they were only one type of patronage and far from the most important. Even if one leaves aside the old saying attributed to Louis XVI, that one appointment makes a dozen enemies and one ingrate, jobs had some severe limitations as a resource for patronage purposes. First of all, only a small proportion of the jobs available for patronage were attractive to the people whose support of parties

---

[4]Good treatments of the earliest practices, culminating with Andrew Jackson, will be found in: James Lord Bryce, *The American Commonwealth* (London and New York: Macmillan, 1888), II, pp. 124-34; and Frederick C. Mosher, *Democracy and the Public Service* (New York: Oxford University Press, 1968), ch. 3.

[5]Herbert Kaufman, "The Growth of the Federal Personnel System," in N. Wallace Sayre, ed., *The Federal Government Service*, 2d ed. (Englewood Cliffs, N.J.: Prentice-Hall, 1965), ch. 1.

and campaigns was essential. Appointments of uneducated and un-skilled persons to low-paying jobs probably swayed some votes and cemented the parties' ties to new groups in the community, but such patronage was far from appropriate for the big interests that swayed whole sections of the country. Furthermore, party leaders quickly ran out of jobs, especially federal jobs, because they were unevenly distributed around the country. In contrast, patronage in substantive public policies lent itself to almost unlimited expansion. The resource base for patronage purposes could be replenished any time a majority in Congress could in its wisdom decide on a new set of internal improvements, a new round of tariffs, new territories to be developed, new land or waters to be exploited. The point is that the patronage state was built not on job patronage but on policies which produced resources that could be distributed to a variety of interests and claimants throughout the country.

Moreover, it should be noted that the relatively large amount of job patronage that existed did not produce a strong presidency. Article II, Sec. 2 of the Constitution provides that the president shall appoint ambassadors and other diplomats, judges of the Supreme Court, and "all other officers of the United States." It provides further that these require the "advice and consent" of the Senate unless Congress by law provides for the appointment of inferior officers by the president alone without senatorial involvement. Thus the Constitution gives the president ample leeway to build his own machine. That did not happen, however, in the traditional regime, which remained throughout Congress-centered and Congress-dominated. Was this the case because members of Congress rather than the president controlled the distribution of jobs in their respective constituencies? Or because members of Congress or the party dominant in it controlled the enactment as well as the subdivision and distribution of patronage policies? I suspect both are true, because patronage in almost any conceivable form is compatible with and reinforcing of existing structures of power. The Constitution was designed to make Congress the center of the power structure—why else would the powers delegated to national government be lodged in Article I, the legislative article?—and the nineteenth century was the golden age of the legislature. Nonetheless, legislative dominance was possible only under special conditions, and those conditions include the patronage state.

30

The Presidency in the Constitution—
the Meeting of Principle and Interest

In such a system, the presidency was inevitably less important. But not only the compatibility of Congress and the patronage state served to reduce the power of the executive. It was also rendered less important by intent and design. The latter point is worth a brief review before we confront the politics of the presidency in the patronage state.

Although Article II has rightly been called "the most loosely drawn chapter of the Constitution,"[6] its intent can be understood in light of the concepts of the times when the Constitution was drafted and implemented. In the first place, the vesting of the powers of the national government in Congress in Article I meant above all that the presidency would be an office of delegated powers. This intent is spelled out in Article II, Sec. 3, with the charge that the president "shall take Care that the Laws be faithfully executed." The so-called checks and balances made the executive branch capable of participating effectively in the Separation of Powers. Nonetheless, the equality of the executive branch vis-à-vis Congress was an equality only in the negative sense of counterpoise and virtual frustration. There was no creative equality between the branches.

At the time of the founding, there was, of course, great fear of executive power because of the memory of monarchy. However, the direct experience of the founders under the Articles of Confederation was the opposite. There was no executive at all. Several executive departments were created, including Foreign Affairs, War, Marine, and Treasury, but the heads of these departments were obliged to report to Congress. As Richard Pious has observed, "the departments were mere appendages of the legislature, not an executive branch." Pious goes on to make the fascinating point that according to eighteenth-century experience "president" referred simply to a presiding officer of the legislature. No executive powers as such were associated with it; presidents tended to serve one-year terms and were usually men "whose talents and reputations matched their office."[7]

The first seven presidents may have been extraordinary people who did extraordinary things. But they were exceptional in ways that

[6]E. S. Corwin, *The President: Office and Powers*, 3d ed. (New York: New York University Press, 1948), p. 2.

[7]Richard Pious, *The American Presidency* (New York: Basic Books, 1979), pp. 21-22.

31

confirm the general proposition that each type of regime creates its own politics. The period following 1789 was a period of "state-building," when the national government, by virtue of the uniqueness of beginnings, did things and performed functions that were "one time only." These included the creation of the first departments, the establishment of the system of taxation, the arrangements for recognition by foreign states and the stabilization of that recognition through fundamental treaties, the stabilization of the debt, and all other matters that had to do with the establishment of legitimacy. During that formative period there was inevitably a stronger role for the presidency and a cabinet than that actually called for in the Constitution. And there were compelling reasons to stress merit and breeding in the chief executive and in the personnel in the federal service. Even the presumption of tenure for bureaucrats seems consistent with the regime of state-building.

The presidency was being drawn into a role subordinate to Congress, however, even while the seven great founding presidents were still serving, and the quality of presidential performance declined accordingly. Even of Madison it was said that he knew everything about government except how to govern. But this should not be permitted to overshadow the very substantial extent to which the president was subordinated to Congress by intent. The same intent, apparent in Article II and its relation to Article I, can also be seen in the original design of the process of presidential selection.

Although the Constitution is silent on what we now call the nominating process, a careful reading of its provisions will show that this was nevertheless provided for, albeit not in so many words. Article II originally provided that the election of the president would be directly in the hands of electors, apportioned according to the number of representatives and senators in each state. The manner of selecting electors was left to the state legislatures, and the assumption probably was that it would be done by legislative appointment rather than by general election. However they were chosen, the electors were then obliged to meet in their respective state capitals to cast their ballots for two persons, one of whom could not be an inhabitant of the same state. All ballots were then to be transmitted to the president of the Senate of the United States, where the votes would be counted. The person with the greatest number of votes would then be declared president of the United States, provided that that number was an absolute majority, not a plurality. The person coming in second would be declared the vice president. There was no need to allow for the political parties of the candidates. If no person had an absolute majority, then the names of the *five highest* would be submitted to the House of Representatives, where the choice for president would be made, each state having one vote regardless of its size. The second in terms of numbers would be declared vice president.

These provisions broke down in 1800, because by then political parties had so well organized presidential campaigns that a tie between Jefferson and Burr, of the same political party, resulted. This tie had to be broken in the House of Representatives, and the politics of the crisis produced not only a victory for Thomas Jefferson but a duel between Alexander Hamilton and Aaron Burr, resulting in Hamilton's death. The Twelfth Amendment, covering all succeeding elections, was adopted. It provided for separate ballots for president and vice president, and in the case that no candidate received an absolute majority, the names of the top three instead of the top five candidates would be submitted to the House of Representatives. Otherwise, the same system of electors, with general election in November and electoral balloting in December, was retained.

Although the Twelfth Amendment did change the system in some fundamental ways, a consistent meaning remained that says a great deal about the original intent. It is fairly evident that the general election in November and the meeting of electors in December was meant to be a *nominating process* in which a relatively large number of candidates for president would be identified—that is, "nominated." And a relatively large number was expected: Why else provide that the top *five* be submitted to the House in the event that no one had an absolute majority? Electors were expected to be local notables in whom the voters would have sufficient confidence to permit a choice among possible presidential candidates. Each state or each section of the country would produce its "favorite son," on whose behalf the electors, in effect, would campaign the following December; and the choice would move on to the House in the case that the Electoral College failed to produce an absolute majority for one candidate.[8] Note well what is happening here. The general election

[8]*Electoral College* is an informal designation that has through history been formalized. There is no mention of such a collectivity by name in the Constitution or in the *Federalist Papers*.

coupled with the balloting of electors constituted the nominating process, and the House of Representatives must have been expected to perform the actual electoral process *because such a large number of presidential candidates could be expected to produce an Electoral College deadlock.* Accordingly, the House of Representatives would be the effective constituency of the president. Even if an unusually popular consensus candidate such as George Washington came along from time to time, the great likelihood of an election's being thrown into the House would make such an eventuality part of the contingency planning of every presidential aspirant.

Thus a very good argument can be made that "president" was an especially appropriate term for the American chief executive, precisely because a selection process culminating in a parliamentary body would make the presidency an essentially parliamentary office. Did the Founders really contemplate such a pattern? Not in so many words. One should note, however, a brief passage almost lost in an argument by Madison in *Federalist* No. 39:

> The immediate election of the President is to be made by the States in their political characters. The votes allotted to them are in a compound ratio, which considers them partly as distinct and coequal societies, partly as unequal members of the same society. The *eventual election* . . . is to be made by that branch of the legislature which consists of the national representatives. . . .[9]

This consideration of original intent reveals a theory of government in which the place of the presidency is profoundly at odds with that of today. Articles I and II were designed for congressional dominance. The great stature and accomplishments of the first three presidents suggest that (1) Congress-centered government is not incompatible with a strong president, even a great one, but (2) this conjunction would probably occur infrequently and under special conditions — war, of course, but also in a time of fundamental stress on or change in the regime.

As the state-building phase passed into the era of patronage policies, the place of the presidency declined and with it the stature and accomplishments of presidents. This had already begun in Jeffer-

[9]Clinton Rossiter, ed., *The Federalist Papers* (New York: Mentor, 1961), p. 244; emphasis added.

34

son's second term and can be seen even more clearly in those of his three successors, despite the tremendous qualifications of each. Jackson was the only exception between 1804 and 1860, and he was part of a fundamental regime change, whether he was a product of it or its creator. Great presidents all but disappeared, and the American two-party system came into its golden age along with Congress because American parties were (and still are) patronage parties, compatible with Congress, reinforcing its dominance, and by that means, perpetuating the traditional system.[10]

The Presidency in the Patronage State

Almost everyone who examines the formative period of American political history is struck by the immediacy with which political parties were formed in the national government. By the end of the first decade, the decade of state-building, well over 90 percent of the members of Congress were affiliated with one of the two major political factions and voted regularly with that faction.[11]

It is curious that national political parties did not form during the thirteen years of the Articles of Confederation but did begin to form almost immediately after the new government under the 1789 Constitution took hold. This is in part attributable to the intensity of the debates on ratification and the one-time-only decisions that had to be made during the decade of state-building. The sudden availability of a lot of patronage was, of course, also important. Another factor contributing to party formation and especially to the two-party system was the creation of the presidency and the special provisions for presidential elections.

The development of political parties strongly reinforced the constitutional tendency toward congressional dominance. Parties first organized in Congress to control congressional business. The Jeffersonian Republicans then discovered that if they went outside Congress they could influence the elections of congressmen of their choice and at the same time could control presidential selection. This they did by selecting loyal Republicans to become candidates in November for presidential elector and having them pledged to vote in De-

---

[10]Compare Herbert Agar, *The Price of Union* (Boston: Houghton Mifflin, 1966).

[11]William N. Chambers, *Political Parties in a New Nation* (New York: Oxford University Press, 1963), pp. 90-91; see also Joseph Charles, *The Origins of the American Party System* (New York: Harper & Row, Harper Torch Books, 1961).

cember for the Republican presidential nominee. Another way Congress controlled the presidency was by seizing control of presidential nominations through the system of selection called King Caucus, whereby the members of each of the two parties in Congress met separately, in "caucus," to decide upon their candidates for president and vice president and to pledge their electors accordingly. As is well documented, this method of selection converted the Electoral College into a rubber stamp for the majority party. Although party regularity to that extent reduced the probability of an Electoral College stalemate throwing the election into the House of Representatives, Congress nevertheless maintained control of the presidency through domination of the nominating process in King Caucus. King Caucus was a transitional method, however, because one of the two parties, the Federalists, declined and collapsed, and with that came the collapse of what the historians called the First Party System. The Federalist party had remained a social elite party, a party of principle dedicated to state building, and was not well adapted to dealing with the millions of "minor affairs" of which Tocqueville was speaking in the statement that opens this chapter.

Historian Richard McCormick observes that the two-party system did not begin to revive until after 1824 and that the stimulus for its revival was the contest for the presidency. He refers to this as the formation of the Second Party System.[12] Consistent with his interpretation is the development of a deep factional struggle inside the Republican party, a struggle that widened as the party spread into all parts of the country, reflecting the eternal sectional cleavages of the nation. Thanks in large part to Andrew Jackson, competition between the newly established two parties spread to nearly every county in every state of the Union by 1836. What McCormick and others referred to as the Second Party System is the party system of the entire traditional regime, or patronage state, spreading from roughly 1832 until 1932.[13]

[12]Richard McCormick, "Political Development and the Second Party System," in William N. Chambers and Walter Dean Burnham, eds., The American Party Systems, 2d ed. (New York: Oxford University Press, 1975), pp. 94-97.

[13]Ibid., pp. 97-98; and Lowi, "Party, Policy and the Constitution in America," in Chambers and Burnham, American Party Systems, pp. 248-54. See also Stephen Skowronek, "Presidential Leadership in Political Time," in Michael Nelson, ed., The Presidency and the Political System (Washington: Congressional Quarterly Press, 1984), pp. 87-132.

The nominating system that came into being with the emergence of the Second Party System was foreshadowed during the Federalist decline. Once the Federalist party's representation in Congress was sharply reduced, its congressional caucus was no longer able to speak for the party as a whole. The Federalists hit upon a means whereby representatives of districts with a Federalist member of Congress could meet with members of districts which no longer had one, and together they could settle upon their candidates for president and vice president. This method of nomination outside Congress was attempted as early as 1808 and repeated in 1812. But those efforts were rudimentary compared to 1824, when Andrew Jackson confronted the Republican party with a tremendous popular following but insufficient congressional support to gain the nomination. Under pressure, the Republicans imitated the Federalists, rejected the choice of their congressional caucus, William H. Crawford, and nominated Jackson. By 1832, both of the major parties had organized the first bona fide national nominating conventions, and the system prevailed without serious alteration for at least 120 years.[14]

Establishment of conventions as the controlling force in presidential selection gave the presidency a base of popular support—a constituency independent of Congress. It also helped salvage the Separation of Powers from an almost certain death from congressional domination of the presidential selection process. However, the new selection process did not in any significant way alter the centricity of Congress in the national government. The selection process democratized the presidency, but that meant only that the presidency became dominated by party politics just as Congress was. The presidency came to be merely the top party office; the party was the primary criterion of selection. Two important lines of analysis flow from the democratization of presidential constituencies, each of which will be dealt with briefly.

First, although democratization of the presidency salvaged the Separation of Powers, it did so in a negative sense only. That is to say, presidents were much more likely after 1832 to veto congressional enactments than they were before, but they were not more likely to present programs for positive legislation to Congress. For example, Andrew Jackson used the veto twelve times, more than all the six pre-

[14]V. O. Key, *Politics, Parties and Pressure Groups*, 5th ed. (New York: Crowell, 1964), ch. 15.

vious presidents put together. After the Civil War, the use of veto power jumped very significantly: Johnson used it twenty-nine times, Grant ninety-three times, and Cleveland in his first term over four hundred times.[15] But none of those presidents attempted to be an equal branch in a more positive, creative sense.

Second, democratization of the president's base did not improve the quality or performance of presidents. In the patronage state there was no demand for creativity or energy in the office, Hamilton's observation that "energy in the executive is a leading character in the definition of good government" to the contrary notwithstanding.[16] Moreover, the method of selection was very unlikely to produce creative or energetic figures. Since this subject will be dealt with in more detail later, suffice it to say here that all nominations by conventions during the long epoch of the traditional system were brokered affairs, lasting over several ballots, in which the ultimate presidential nominee was almost certain to be the most widely shared *second choice* of a majority of the delegates (or two-thirds of the Democratic delegates under rules that prevailed until 1936, precisely in order to guarantee that each convention *would* be brokered). The scant few exceptional presidents between 1824 and 1932 can be explained in largest part by two unusual circumstances—war and regime crisis—occurring separately or together, and involving significant, albeit temporary, departures from the patronage state. Consensus points to Jackson, Lincoln, possibly TR, Woodrow Wilson, and FDR, and each fits both the exceptional circumstances.

These two lines of analysis can be brought together for some general conclusions about the traditional system that may also shed some light on current institutions and problems.

Almost thirty years after the initial appearance of *The American Commonwealth*, Lord Bryce published the third and last edition of his classic work on United States government and politics. Though many changes had been made, the chapter entitled "Why Great Men Are Not Chosen Presidents," appeared almost without revision. Bryce opened it with the following observation:

[15]For a good review of the uses of the veto, see Raymond Tatalovich and Byron Daynes, *Presidential Power in the United States* (Monterey, Cal.: Brooks/Cole, 1984), pp. 148-51.

[16]Rossiter, ed., *Federalist Papers*, No. 70, p. 423.

In America, which is beyond all other countries the country of a "career open to talents" . . . it might be expected that the highest place would also be won by a man of brilliant gifts. But from the time when the heroes of the Revolution died out . . . no person except General Grant . . . would have been remembered had he not been president, and no president except Abraham Lincoln had displayed rare or striking qualities in the chair. Who knows or cares to know anything about the personality of James K. Polk or Franklin Pierce? The only thing remarkable about them is that being so commonplace they should have climbed so high.[17]

Bryce identified several factors which to him helped explain the phenomenon. Among these were the existence of exciting occupations and careers apart from politics; the lack of a civil service with high social status; and the absence of a tradition wherein many persons of wealth and leisure enter politics. But those factors receive a bare mention, while two others are given much more attention. The first of these is that "the methods and habits of Congress, and indeed of political life generally, give fewer opportunities for personal distinction" (Bryce returns to this point in later chapters.)[18] Strongly related to this is the fact that "party loyalty and party organization have been hitherto so perfect that anyone put forward by the party will get the full party vote if his character is good and his 'record,' as they call it, unstained." Parties seek the safe candidate. A person who is already eminent has made enemies, has taken divisive stands, and in general does not satisfy the party's preference for a candidate who "may not draw in quite so many votes from the moderate men of the other side as the brilliant one would, but he will not lose nearly so many from his own ranks."[19] In conclusion, Bryce reasoned that "the merits of a president are one thing and those of a candidate are another thing" and that when the choice comes between the two, the party will pick the candidate and let the presidency take care of itself.[20]

My analysis of the party-dominated presidency is in no way intended to be a condemnation of the traditional selection process or of its presidential products, dreary though most of them were. Its aim is only to state a set of facts whose significance requires careful

[17]Bryce, *American Commonwealth*, 1914 ed. (New York: Macmillan, 1924), I, p. 77.
[18]Ibid., p. 78.
[19]Ibid., pp. 78-79.
[20]Ibid., pp. 79-80.

assessment. I fully agree with Bryce's explanation but believe something can be added to it on the basis of the perspective of an additional sixty years. Bryce's various points (and mine) can be synthesized as follows: The presidents produced by the party-dominated selection process were very ordinary people with very ordinary reputations in the job precisely because they presided (in the sense given by Pious) over a patronage party in a patronage state dominated by a legislature. As long as the national government was doing nothing but patronage, no great demand was placed on the presidential office, for either performance or stature. In the nineteenth century, chief executives were chief of very little and executive of even less. They were commanders-in-chief without an army and chief diplomats without a unified and professional diplomatic corps and without any substantial foreign policy except the tariff. Prevailing constitutional and governmental theory was antagonistic to executive power, and this attitude was reflected in the complete absence of administrative assistance available to the president. The movement to unify administration in an executive branch with management responsibilities culminating in the president really did not get under way until after 1900.[21]

The party system and its method of presidential selection persisted as long as the patronage state remained. And it was not even condemned by prevailing theories of American government at the time—despite almost universal recognition of the dreariness of presidents and presidential candidates. This acceptance of mediocrity seems to me attributable precisely to the fact that no one attached to the presidency any theory or criterion relevant to "the capacity to govern." The major importance of the presidency during the traditional epoch was probably its influence on the maintenance of the two-party system. And that contributed to the patronage state, congressional dominance, and, ironically, the intent of the Founders.

Since FDR, every president has been exceptional, as compared to presidents under the traditional system. Every president is now a "strong president" because the circumstances calling for strong presidents are no longer exceptional. And those circumstances had made for strong presidents before the United States became heavily involved as a world power. The growth of national security needs con-

[21]Leonard D. White, *Introduction to the Study of Public Administration*, 4th ed. (New York: Macmillan, 1955), p. 44.

40

tributed significantly to the increase of presidential power and responsibility, but the institutionalization of the strong presidency had begun beforehand, with FDR and the passing of the patronage state.

The End of the Traditional System

If the traditional system was in equilibrium all during the nineteenth century, it was a moving equilibrium. The economic and social changes that would challenge the patronage state were beginning to reach great and undeniable proportions toward the century's end. A brief review of the major challenges shows, if nothing else, that the tardiness of the national government's response is harder to explain than the response itself.

Stated in their broadest terms, the important developments included the following: the mechanization of production and transportation; the concentration of capital and the rise of the corporate form of organization; the proletarianization of labor; the "nationalization" of markets beyond the confines of a single state or region; the commercialization of agriculture; and the closing of the frontier.

These changes spawned a variety of reactions. In political terms, the twenty-year period beginning around 1870 constituted an era of social movements. And from these movements there issued a cascade of demands for government action, ranging from the outlawing of monopolistic practices, to the control of rates charged by large companies, to the cheapening of the currency, to the improvement of working conditions as well as the conditions of the poor. Yet the galvanizing of social dislocation into political action and demands for public policies did little during those two decades to disturb the national government, primarily because all the enhanced political activity focused upon the state capitals. Since, as we have seen, the states were doing most of the governing, it was naturally and rationally to the states that the social movements looked for redress. Organizing to influence the national government and traveling to Washington would have been an almost complete waste of time. Madison was continuing to have the last word. Federalism was working exactly as designed.

The nationalization of political attention did not begin in earnest until the Supreme Court intervened in one of the most important de-

41

cisions in American history: *Wabash, St. Louis and Pacific Railroad Company* v. *Illinois* (1886).[22] It had become increasingly obvious that state regulation of large interstate companies, especially railroads, was inadequate. No one state could reach the whole problem, and the companies found the inconsistencies from state to state more burdensome than the regulations themselves. In 1886 the Supreme Court confronted the issue head-on by declaring unconstitutional an Illinois law which attempted to regulate the rates charged by inter-state railroads for that portion of their trip within the state of Illinois. In the words of one constitutional historian, when the Court struck down this effort as an unconstitutional burden on interstate com-merce, they "made national legislative action constitutionally imper-ative."[23]

State governments had been responding positively to the demands of the social movements of the 1870s and 1880s, and much of their most effective legislation took the name of the most prominent social movement of the time, the Grange. So-called Granger legislation at-tempted to deal with the problems of the emerging modern economy as these were perceived by farmers, small business people, and oth-ers. Once the Supreme Court closed off this avenue, a great deal of the political activity began to refocus itself from the states to Wash-ington. The decade following 1886 was a decade of the organization of trade associations, trade unions, commodity associations, and other business groupings into "pressure groups" oriented toward representation in Washington. Quite suddenly there was a cascading of demands for national legislation resembling the state Granger leg-islation of a decade earlier.

None of this is remarkable. What is remarkable is how little came of it over the next thirty years. Many were called but few were chosen. Of the hundreds of demands produced by the new, nationally ori-ented interest groups, only a few important policies were adopted; even fewer of them departed in any significant way from the pa-tronage policies of the traditional system; and the exceptions tend strongly to confirm the rule. There are the Interstate Commerce Act of 1887 and the Sherman Antitrust Act of 1890, but after those it is dif-ficult to identify important departures from the patronage state until

[22]*Wabash, St. Louis and Pacific Railroad Company* v. *Illinois*, 118 U.S. 557 (1886).
[23]Alfred H. Kelly, et al., *The American Constitution: Its Origins and Development*, 6th ed. (New York: Norton, 1983), p. 384.

the Wilson period twenty years later. And even during the Wilson administration only a few acts moved out of the patronage state pattern. These included the Federal Reserve Act of 1913, the income tax of 1913 (with a ceiling of 4 percent on income over $100,000), and the Clayton Antitrust and Federal Trade Commission acts of 1914. In the twenty years between Sherman and Clayton, and in the years following Clayton, there were hundreds of proposals but few other adoptions of acts not based on patronage policies; and these departures were rather narrowly focused upon highly specific problems: the first Pure Food and Drug Act (1906), which was very rudimentary indeed; the Hepburn Act (1906) and the Mann-Elkins Act (1910), which in some respects extended the Interstate Commerce Act; and the Child Labor Act (1916) which sought to forbid shipment in interstate commerce of commodities produced by the labor of children under a specified age.

The fact that the Child Labor Act was declared unconstitutional in 1918 points toward one of the reasons why there were so few moves beyond the patronage state despite the organized clamor: Most of the political leaders of that era shared severe doubts that policy responses to the demands of the new interest groups would be constitutional. Some leaders only pretended to be concerned about constitutionality in order to oppose legislation they were against for other reasons, but a great number were undoubtedly sincere. Either way, they believed that a strong argument could be built against the adoption of most of the proposals made. Those bills that did pass Congress were very narrow in design or were given a narrow construction by the agencies and the courts. The new regulatory laws either held very strictly to matters of interstate commerce—such as the railroads, railroad workers and merchant seaman, and certain interstate trusts; or they concerned things that the Supreme Court itself identified as innately harmful or immoral, such as sawed-off shotguns, prostitutes, stolen automobiles, and (of all things) colored oleomargarine; or they were national regulatory programs sought by big business as an antidote to inconsistent state regulations.

The patronage state survived until the 1930s. American politics had become nationalized. American values appeared to have become receptive to a positive national state. But still, it took a depression to break the tradition.

43

3

The Legacies of FDR

. . . like a dog walking on its hind legs. It is not done well;
but you are surprised to find it done at all.
—Samuel Johnson

The domestic New Deal was born in 1933 and was buried at some point toward the end of 1939. During those six fateful years, the Roosevelt administration expanded the civil service from 572,000 to 920,000 employees, a rate of increase of 58,000 employees per year. The Roosevelt budget grew from $4.6 billion to $8.8 billion, a rate of increase of about $700 million per year. In the four preceding years, the Hoover administration expanded the civil service from the 540,000 employees it inherited from Coolidge to 572,000 employees, an increase of about 8,000 per year. The Hoover budget expanded from $3.1 billion to $4.6 billion, a rate of increase of about half that of the six years of the New Deal prior to mobilization.

But where was the Roosevelt revolution? Of the $6.7 billion in the 1934 budget—the first full year of the New Deal—$2 billion was allocated to the Works Progress Administration (WPA) and $1 billion to the Public Works Administration (PWA); another half billion dollars was budgeted for the Civil Works Administration (CWA). These three programs alone accounted for nearly 53 percent of the 1934 budget, 46 percent of the 1935 budget and 41 percent of the 1936 budget. Although these programs were proposed as recovery and relief programs, and indeed did provide a lot of relief work, they were essentially expansions of the patronage state (Table 3, Sec. 1). Comparable programs that existed before the New Deal were expanded, including

44

rivers and harbors improvement, highway construction, agricultural assistance, and other "internal improvements."[1]

The national government might have responded to the Depression by expanding only those types of functions that made up the traditional system of the patronage state. That course would almost certainly have been politically unacceptable, but it is conceivable, and if it had been followed, FDR might well have brought the United States out of the Depression. Given the sorry condition of the country by 1939, he might have done no worse that way. But if he had chosen that route, even successfully, he would have left no legacy at all. The national government, in constitutional and institutional terms, would have remained what it had been all along.

But Roosevelt did not do that. He put through Congress an impressive number of bills establishing policies that were, for the national government of the United States, new and distinctly untraditional. Although these did not add significantly to the federal budget, they profoundly and permanently changed the nature of the national government.

The Regulatory State and the Redistributive State

The new policies of the New Deal can be divided into two types, as shown in Table 3, Sections 2 and 3. The first of the new types (Section 2) fits readily into the category of regulatory policies. These resemble the occasional efforts at regulation tried by the national government between 1887 and 1932. They even more closely resemble the kinds of policies traditionally associated with the state governments, because the regulatory policies of the New Deal went well beyond a narrow interpretation of interstate commerce and attempted to affect the local conditions that the Supreme Court had hitherto defined as clearly outside the limits of national government action. As constitutional historians put it, the national government discovered that it, too, possessed the police power. These new regulatory programs, often referred to as the alphabetocracy because most of them

[1]Sources of figures: Herbert Stein, *The Fiscal Revolution in America* (Chicago: University of Chicago Press, 1969), pp. 69-72; and *Report of the Secretary of the Treasury, Statistical Appendix* (Washington: Government Printing Office, 1972), pp. 12-13. Although the two sources are not identical, the differences are not significant.

Table 3. The political economy of the New Deal: Highlights of policy activity

1. *Patronage State*
   Civil Works Administration (CWA) '33
   Civilian Conservation Corps (CCC) '33
   Public Works Administration (PWA) '33
   Rural Electrification Administration (REA) '33
   Tennessee Valley Authority (TVA) '33
   Works Progress Administration (WPA) '33
   Soil Conservation Service (SCS) '35

2. *Regulatory State*
   Agricultural Adjustment Act (AAA) '33
   Banking Act '33
   National Industrial Recovery Act '33
   Securities Act '33
   Securities Exchange Act '34
   National Labor Relations Act '35
   Public Utilities Holding Company Act '35
   Bituminous Coal Act '35 & '37
   Federal Power Act '35
   Civil Aeronautics Act '38
   Fair Labor Standards Act (FLSA) '38
   Federal Trade Commission (FTC) expansion '38
   Food and Drug Act expansion (FDA) '38

3. *Redistributive State*
   Bank Holiday '33
   Federal Deposit Insurance Corporation (FDIC) '33
   Home Owners Loan Corporation (HOLC) '33
   Devaluation Act '34
   Federal Housing Administration (FHA) '34
   Farm Security Administration (FSA) '35
   Federal Reserve reforms '35
   Internal Revenue reforms '35
   Social Security Act '35
   Public Housing '39

became popularly known by the first letters of their official names, require no elaboration, because they comprise some of the most familiar actions associated with the New Deal. Even a cursory study of the items in Section 2 will reveal that they are regulatory in the sense that each seeks to impose obligations directly upon citizens, backing those obligations with sanctions. To emphasize the significance of the departure from the past that these policies represent, it should be observed that for the first time the national government *established a direct and coercive relationship between itself and individual citizens.*

46

The second new type of policy adopted by Congress during the New Deal can be understood as redistributive or welfare state policy (Table 3, Section 3). The Federal Reserve Act and the income tax are examples of this type of policy adopted earlier. But the number, extent, and constitutional status of the redistributive policies adopted under FDR once again make the New Deal a true and distinct departure from the traditional system. The list of them here should immediately convey at least two significant impressions. First, these policies are clearly different from traditional patronage policies. Second, although they are comparable to regulatory policies in establishing a directly coercive relationship with citizens, the relationship is not established in the same way. Redistributive policies do not attempt to impose direct obligations on individuals; rather, they attempt to influence individuals by manipulating the *environment of conduct* rather than conduct itself. They seek to create new structures, to influence people by manipulating the value of property or money, or to categorize people according to some universalized attribute, such as level of income or age or status of occupation.

These new regulatory and redistributive policies were not only enacted in large numbers by Congress but were accepted by the Supreme Court. All shadow of constitutional doubt was finally wiped away. At the same time the Supreme Court recognized in its own way the distinction between regulatory and redistributive policies being made here. It accepted the constitutionality of regulatory policies in the famous case of *NLRB* v. *Jones & Laughlin Steel Corp.* The National Labor Relations Act provided, among other things, that the National Labor Relations Board (NLRB) could forbid any person from engaging in an unfair labor practice "affecting commerce." The grievance in question originated in one of the Jones & Laughlin plants in Pennsylvania, and the constitutional issue was whether manufacturing, which is inherently local, had a sufficient effect upon interstate commerce in some cases to justify Congress's intervention. In the decision validating the National Labor Relations Act, the Court argued:

When industries organize themselves on a national scale, making their relation to interstate commerce the dominant factor in their activities, how can it be maintained that their industrial relations constitute a forbidden field into which Congress may not enter when it is necessary to

47

protect interstate commerce from the paralyzing consequences of industrial war?[2]

In entirely separate decisions in 1937, the Supreme Court validated the social security and, implicitly, most of the other redistributive policies. The Court relied upon the "general welfare" clause of the preamble of the Constitution and upon its own recognition that there is no limit to congressional spending power except Congress's own wisdom: "Discretion belongs to Congress, unless the choice is clearly wrong, a display of arbitrary power [rather than] an exercise of judgment."[3]

It should be clear at this point that Roosevelt and the New Deal broke with the traditional system and that the break—or double break—was widely recognized, from the Supreme Court on down. Roosevelt did not attempt to abandon the patronage state; quite the contrary, he expanded it. But alongside it he added two others: a *regulatory* state and a *redistributive* (or welfare) state. With these steps, the national government became a modern government both because it assumed powers of direct coercion over individual citizens and because, in taking on the new functions, it became a *differentiated* state—performing a variety of unlike functions. I exaggerate these distinctions by calling them *states* because I wish to emphasize that each type of governmental function tends to develop its own political process, as though each were a regime.

The distinction between the regulatory state and the redistributive state, although fundamental, is beyond the scope of the present inquiry. What is important here is that *both* new types of functions together finally brought the national government into a directly coercive relationship with the people. No longer would the state governments bear alone that fundamental burden. When the national government assumed these powers, it was on the way to becoming a new regime. The legacies of the New Deal flow from this.

A Revolution in Four Parts

Many authors have referred to the New Deal as the "Roosevelt Revolution." Journalist Ernest K. Lindley was probably the first, in a book

---

[2] *NLRB* v. *Jones & Laughlin Steel Corporation*, 301 U.S. 1 (1937).

[3] *Helvering* v. *Davis*, 301 U.S. 619 and 640 (1937); see also *Steward Machine Co.* v. *Davis*, 301 U.S. 548 (1937).

published during Roosevelt's first year in office.[4] Mario Einaudi's important work on Roosevelt addressed especially to European audiences was entitled *The Roosevelt Revolution*.[5] Thus, it is not unconventional to refer Roosevelt and revolution in the same sentence, and the term appeals to me because, like "state," "revolution" is a useful exaggeration; in a sense, I am putting certain features under the microscope the better to see their details.

Division of the Roosevelt legacies into four parts is another exaggeration—again a useful one as long as the overlap among them is recognized. Separation serves exposition but ultimately it is the combined and cumulative effect that shapes the modern presidency.

The Constitutional Revolution

Constitutional historians refer to the series of cases culminating in the 1937 NLRB case as the First Constitutional Revolution.[6] Although the NLRB case is the watershed decision, another case a few years later probably illustrates more clearly the extent to which a new, direct and coercive relationship between the national government and individual citizens had been established. The case is *Wickard* v. *Filburn*,[7] which validated the Agricultural Adjustment Act (AAA). Under AAA regulations Mr. Filburn was allotted 11.1 acres for the growing of wheat. Instead, and in violation of the act, he put 23 acres into wheat cultivation. In his defense, Filburn argued that he was too small a producer to have an effect on interstate commerce, and beyond that, his wheat was intended not for commerce at all but for use on his own farm to feed his stock. The Supreme Court ruled that although Filburn was a small farmer, and although it was true that his wheat was not intended for market, he came within the intent of Congress in the AAA because the wheat his own livestock consumed had a sufficient practical effect on the interstate market for wheat, since the wheat he grew for his own consumption represented wheat he did not purchase from the market.

[4]Ernest K. Lindley, *The Roosevelt Revolution, First Phase* (New York: Viking, 1933).

[5]Mario Einaudi, *The Roosevelt Revolution* (New York: Harcourt, Brace & World, 1959).

[6]The Second Constitutional Revolution usually refers to the period anticipated by the 1954 school segregation case but beginning earnestly in 1959 with "Warren Court" cases in civil liberties and civil rights.

[7]*Wickard* v. *Filburn*, 317 U.S. 111 (1942).

If a Filburn can be reached, economic federalism is dead. And that is a constitutional revolution. From that time onward, it became practically impossible to place any substantive limit whatsoever on the reach of government in a democracy. The Court ceased overturning important acts of Congress after 1936.[8] The most important recent application of the *Wickard* principle is probably that of *Katzenbach* v. *McClung*. Ollie's Barbecue, a Birmingham, Alabama, restaurant, was accused of violating Title II of the 1964 Civil Rights Act forbidding racial discrimination in accommodations in interstate commerce. The Court accepted as true the proprietor's contention that the restaurant did not serve out-of-state customers. Nevertheless, despite the fact that interstate travelers were not at issue, the Supreme Court reasoned that Ollie's Barbecue came within the jurisdiction of the civil rights law because a substantial portion of the food served by the restaurant came from outside the state.[9]

A Governmental Revolution

The governmental revolution consisted in the accretion of new functions (as listed in Table 2) that marked the end of federalism as a limit on the national government's reach. The Supreme Court yearly recognized and sanctioned the *fait accompli*. This did not put an end to the role of the state, whose governments continued to do what they had done traditionally. In fact they expanded. The national government was an add-on; it did not grow at the expense of the states.

The New Deal regulatory programs could reach down to the farmer growing a mere 23 acres of wheat. The New Deal redistributive programs laid the foundations of the welfare state. Although over

[8]Forty years later, in 1976, the Burger Court by a 5-4 margin held unconstitutional the 1974 amendments to the Fair Labor Standards Act, which applied federal minimum wage and maximum hours requirements to virtually all employees of state (and local) governments. The Court relied most heavily upon the Tenth Amendment, which the majority of the Court argued gave the states sovereignty over their own employees [*National League of Cities* v. *Usery*, 426 U.S. 833 (1976)]. Eight years later legal experts were still waiting for the Burger Court to carry out a counterrevolution by declaring more Congressional enactments unconstitutional, but that has happened only once, with the Court's invalidation of the legislative veto in *Immigration and Naturalization Service* v. *Chadha*, 103 S.Ct. 2767 (1983), and this case in no way directly affects Congress's power over the economy.
[9]*Katzenbach* v. *McClung*, 379 U.S. 294 (1964).

thirty years were to pass before people would begin to refer to their social security benefits as rights and entitlements, the welfare state was already a contractual reality—a new social contract—by the end of the New Deal. This contract was confirmed in the Employment Act of 1946. The act actually established no new programs. (It did set up a new agency, the Council of Economic Advisers, but the CEA has no function to perform other than that which is implied by its name.) However, the Employment Act is a milestone in the history of American government because it made explicit and official for the first time that the national government claimed for itself a responsibility to provide employment to people seeking it or to provide other support if employment was not available. This meant ultimately the national government would be responsible for every injurious act sustained by any individual citizen, and also for providing the conditions for every individual citizen's well-being. No matter that government has fallen short on both fronts. The establishment of those obligations solemnized the new social contract by putting the national government at the very center of American society.

From the programs of the 1930s to the normalization of the new social contract in 1946, the national government also embedded itself in the expectations of the American people. Psychologists would probably call this process an important aspect of political socialization, wherein the government actually became part of citizens' perspectives and their calculation of life chances. Giving the national government an important role is exhilarating and highly democratizing. But it is also risky, inasmuch as the fate of government becomes tied to the relative success of its activities. Note well the difference from the traditional system. Traditionally, the test of legitimate government was representation: Was "due process" observed in the adoption of important policies? When the rebels of '76 cried "no taxation without representation," the tax was less important than the process of its adoption. Since the New Deal, or at least since 1946, part of the test of good government has been productivity—service delivery, of what, to whom. Representation continues to be important, but the test of service delivery now outweighs it.

This change is of fundamental importance to the continuing legitimacy and stability of modern government. And its importance has intensified as it comes more and more narrowly to focus on the presidency. Thus, if by 1946 the test of legitimacy had shifted from repre-

51

sentation to the national government's capacity to govern (that is, to deliver services), it had, by the early 1960s, shifted to the president's capacity to govern. The system of government had become an inverted pyramid, with everything coming to rest on a presidential pinpoint.

An Institutional Revolution: The End of
Congress-Centered Government

Since the most prominent institutional feature of the traditional system was the centricity of Congress with its committees and parties, that arrangement's relatively sudden termination must be recognized as, in the American government context, a veritable revolution. In order to meet the demands of the Depression, Congress authorized the executive branch to undertake the great variety of activities already identified, and it appropriated the funds more or less adequately for each task. But more. Congress accompanied each program and each appropriation with a grant of authority and jurisdiction that left each agency pretty much to its own judgment as to what to do and how to do it. In effect, Congress said, "Here's the problem; go deal with it."[10]

Technically, this practice is called the delegation of power. In the beginning, members of Congress and prominent jurists attempted to rationalize or apologize for the delegation of power by arguing, first, that the emergency required it and, second, that administrative agencies were staffed by experts who were merely "filling in the details" of programs that Congress had constitutionally legislated. Recognizing that the agencies, epecially the regulatory agencies, were making policy decisions that Congress ought to be making, they attempted to soften the reality of delegated power by calling it "quasi-legislation" and "quasi-adjudication." Try as they might to gloss over the fact, however, they could not change it. One administrative agency after another was given power to make important public policy decisions that had hitherto been reserved to legislatures or, in fact, not made at all. The Supreme Court in 1935 ruled that such broad delegations of

[10]For a critical treatment of this approach, see Lowi, *The End of Liberalism*, 2d ed. (New York: Norton, 1979), p. 303, and passim; for an informative but less critical view, see Kenneth C. Davis, *Discretionary Justice* (Baton Rouge: Louisiana State University Press, 1969).

power violated the Separation of Powers. In *Schechter Poultry Corporation* v. *United States*, the Court declared the National Industrial Recovery Act (NIRA) unconstitutional on the grounds that among other things, Congress had failed to perform its legislative function by giving to the president and the executive branch a blanket power to enact into law whatever they preferred. Chief Justice Hughes asserted that such broad delegation "is unknown to our law and is utterly inconsistent with the constitutional prerogatives and duties of Congress."[11] As I noted earlier, however, the rule of the *Schechter* case was essentially extinguished by neglect. Except for wartime cases, in which very broad delegations of power from Congress to agencies were accepted, no further review of congressional enactments came before the Court on constitutional grounds. Delegations from Congress to executive agencies are as broad today as the NIRA's, and some are broader, despite the fact that there is no emergency to help justify lax practices on Congress's part. We are now so accustomed to broad delegations of power that no one any longer bothers to try to soften reality with a "quasi."

The new functions implemented by broad delegations of power from Congress to the bureaucracy introduced double contradictions in the prevailing theory of government. If the government were going to continue on the course set for it in the 1930s, then the theory about it would have to change with it—and little help could come from the Supreme Court because it had capitulated without the kind of argument on which new rationalizations of state are built.

First there would have to be a change in theory about what constitutes a good administrator. Second there would have to be a change in our concept of the presidency itself.

Support for a larger national state had always been coupled with theories and doctrines about the neutral administrator—trained, specialized, and capable of serving any master. Efficient, expert, and neutral bureaucracy was favored by pro-statists and by anti-party reformers who looked to bureaucracy as an alternative to party.[12] Part

[11]*Schechter Poultry Corporation* v. *United States*, 295 U.S. 495 (1935), pp. 489-91, 512, and 555.

[12]On this latter point, the most interesting analysis will be found in Martin Shefter, "Party, Bureaucracy and Political Change in the United States," in Louis Maisel and Joseph Cooper, eds., *Political Parties: Development and Decay* (Beverly Hills: Sage, 1978), ch. 7. The best analysis of civil service reform in relation to the history of government will be found in Frederick C. Mosher, *Democracy and the Public Service* (New York: Oxford University Press, 1968).

and parcel of this doctrine was the doctrine of the separation of politics from administration. As a young political scientist, Woodrow Wilson was one of the first to speak for the anti-party reformers, and it was in these very terms:

> The field of administration is a field of business. It is removed from the hurry and strife of politics. . . . It is a part of political life only as the methods of the counting-house are a part of the life of society; only as machinery is part of the manufactured product. . . . [There is] but one rule of good administration for all governments alike; . . . if I see a monarchist dyed in the wool, I can learn his business methods without changing one of my republican spots.[13]

This principle guided the original Civil Service Act of 1883, giving tenure to clerical and administrative employees in order to protect them from political interference. Twenty years later, in 1903, rules of the Civil Service Commission provided that civil servants take no active part in political campaigns or any related activities. The Hatch Act of 1938 extended the earlier rules to include all offices and employees of the executive branch.

This emphasis on the neutral administrator and the separation of politics from administration gained acceptance and moderate success only as long as "most of government's activities . . . concerned the provision of pretty well established services . . . [with] government a passive and reactive agent." Once government "became itself an initiator of programs and change . . . initiative, imagination, and energy in the pursuit of public purposes . . . [were] more important than efficiency. . . . Those purposes were political . . . herein lay a new dimension."[14] In other words, it was no longer possible to pretend that politics stopped at a certain point where administration began. The theory of the neutral administrator had to be supplemented in a way consonant with the realities of the 1930s and beyond.

One of the ways the theory was revised to meet the realities of agencies being given so much policy discretion was the adoption of the Administrative Procedure Act. Although the measure was not

[13]Woodrow Wilson, "The Study of Administration," *Political Science Quarterly*, 2 (June 1887), pp. 197 and 220. A good discussion of Wilson's theory of administration will be found in Vincent Ostrom, *The Intellectual Crisis in American Public Administration* (University, Ala.: University of Alabama Press, 1973), ch. 2.

[14]Mosher, *Democracy and the Public Service*, pp. 79-80.

passed by Congress until 1946, there was a serious move in favor of it as early as 1939. The major formal purposes of the APA were (1) to separate policy-making from adjudication, and to separate both from the routine implementation of agency policies; and (2) to establish a decision-making process that was very much like that of the judicial branch, with requirements for hearings, notice, and adversary proceedings that permit affected citizens some chance of input and redress before the implementation of administrative rules. Underlying these aims was the theory that if politics could no longer be separated from administration, then administration ought to be made more representative by means of appropriate procedural arrangements.

Another adjustment to the problem of delegation of power and its politicization of administration was the emergence of *management* as the key to administration. This concern for management, which harks back to the President's Committee on Administrative Management of 1937, provides a direct link to the revision of the concept of the presidency itself. The committee's acceptance of the proposition that politics could not be separated from administration had led it to the proposal that the Civil Service Commission should be replaced by a single administrator responsible directly to the president (see Chapter 1). This idea in its turn led to the development of the "institutional presidency" even before there was a head-on effort to revise the concept of the presidency itself. In other words, the formalization of the presidency as the center of *management* preceded the explicit theory of presidential power and presidential centricity that came to be recognized in the 1950s. Frederick Mosher has put this formalization best. To Mosher, the central theme of the President's Committee on Administrative Management was the

centralization of power and responsibility in the President. . . . In order effectively to exercise these powers certain fundamental changes were necessary, and these now read almost as the traditional *commandments* of public (and private) administration:

There should be clean, uninterrupted lines of direction from top to bottom, and of responsibility from bottom to top;

the President's span of control should be reduced to a manageable number by the consolidation of all administrative agencies into a limited number of departments;

independent agencies (principally the regulatory commissions)

should be brought within the framework of appropriate departments for all purposes except those purely judicial in nature;
the President's competence with respect to his administrative responsibilities should be greatly strengthened ("The President needs
help") by providing him an immediate White House Staff with a
"passion for anonymity"; and by giving him complete authority over
the key staff functions of the fiscal management, personnel, and
planning.[15]

What followed from this kind of general philosophy were reorgani-
zations aimed at making the president a more capable manager. The
Budget Bureau (later OMB) has already been identified as an instrument created to increase administrative responsibility to the White
House. Its powers included "legislative clearance," which was aimed
to prevent administrative personnel from going directly to Congress
to lobby for changes in their authority or powers. Even the delegation
to the president of "reorganization powers," limited only by the new
device of the "legislative veto," was inspired by the feeling of need to
permit administrative agencies to be political so long as the lines of
authority ran clearly to the chief executive redefined as chief manager.

This brings us to the second of the major adjustments to the
politicization of the administrative agencies: the change in the concept of the presidency and the new theory of president-centered national government. One should note that the new theory of the presidency emerges to a very great extent out of the effort to redefine the
theory of administration in order to cope with the politicization of
agencies resulting from the delegation of broad policy-making powers to them. It would seem that the managerial or institutional presidency emerged first, and the full-fledged presidency as the center of
government afterward. Whichever is the chicken and which the egg,
the fact is that these various currents of thought resolved themselves
in what we now take to be the inevitable and relatively good system
where government and democracy rest upon the presidency.
Richard Neustadt was able to put it this way by the late 1950s:

A president may retain liberty in Woodrow Wilson's phrase, "to be as
big a man as he can." But nowadays he cannot be as small as he might

---

[15]Ibid., p. 80; emphasis in original.

like. . . . In instance after instance the exceptional behavior of our earlier "strong" presidents has now been set by statute as a regular requirement. Theodore Roosevelt once assumed the "steward's" role in the emergency created by the great coal strike of 1902; [legislative Acts of the 1930s and '40s] now make such interventions mandatory upon presidents. The other Roosevelt once asserted personal responsibility for gauging and for guiding the American economy; the Employment Act [of 1946] binds his successors to that task. . . . Everybody now expects the man inside the White House to do something about everything. Laws and customs now reflect acceptance of him as the Great Initiator.[16]

Notice how theory and practice were developing together. As the theory of a democracy based upon a president's capacity to govern was evolving, it provided a logic and guidance for the kinds of reforms that would meet that requirement. The new system involving, nay, requiring strong presidents did not follow Topsy and merely grow, nor did it merely emerge as a result of Roosevelt's leadership or the guidance of his staff and successors. The presidency grew because it had become the center of a new governmental theory, and it became the center of a governmental theory by virtue of a whole variety of analyses and writings that were attempting to build some kind of consonance between the new, positive state and American democratic values. Eventually the theory and the practice were both accepted, to such an exent that political realism and academic political science require that both be treated as established facts. President-centered government is now embedded in the laws and routines of the national government. And the theory of presidential government is so strong that it becomes a criterion of good politics as well as the requisite of good government. The personal president is the result. Note the theme of Neustadt's book: "My theme is personal power and its politics: What it is, how to get it, how to keep it, how to use it. . . . how to be on top in fact as well as name."[17] This is not intended as a criticism but as an effort to place the modern presidency in history, to see where it came from and what combination of causes and principles created it. The new governmental functions, coupled with the very broad delegations of power to administrative agencies that Congress used to set them up, led to a fundamental revision of our govern-

[16]Richard E. Neustadt, *Presidential Power* (New York: Wiley, 1960), pp. 5-6.
[17]Ibid, p. vii.

mental practices, of our Constitution, and of our theory about good national government. It is the combination of these changes that makes the Roosevelt administration so important.

Out of these years of institutional change came the new sense that the president is the government and ought to have the capacity to govern. Making such governing possible also required a political revolution, so that the entire engine of American democracy could be harnessed to the presidential institution.

A Political Revolution

Reasonable observers can disagree over whether the governmental and insitutional changes brought on by the New Deal were historically inevitable. But it would be difficult to dispute the proposition that once those changes came to pass, political adjustments to them were certain to follow.

One of the most important political changes attributable to the New Deal is the change in president-Congress relations, which was a repetition in the political sphere of the institutional changes already mentioned. By creating the large bureaucracy and delegating broad powers of discretion to each of the agencies, Congress had forever altered the terms of discourse. Congress did not commit complete and irreversible legiscide. Many important case-studies since the New Deal show it actually holding the upper hand. Nevertheless, the traditional system of Congress-centered government has been replaced. A new book entitled *Congressional Government* would either be about the internal processes of Congress or would not be written at all.

Another important political change attributable to the New Deal actually antedates Roosevelt's administration but was brought to maturity during the 1930s. It is that multiplex of developments grouped under the concept of corporate or interest-group liberalism—the legitimation of organized groups and their formal as well as informal inclusion in the policy-making process. The National Recovery Administration (NRA) was an extreme example of corporatist politics, so extreme as to be declared unconstitutional by the Supreme Court. Nevertheless, the practices most clearly formalized in it can be seen in any number of other pieces of New Deal legislation, which in turn can be seen as a culmination of principles of government and politics already beginning to be practiced during World War I. Herbert Hoover, as secretary of commerce and as president, contributed to the theory as well as the practice of interest-group liberalism. However, the key was Roosevelt, whose hospitality to these ideas and practices, as well as the success of his administration in having them adopted into law, makes him the most important source of the new interest-group liberalism. Roosevelt was not a thinker; as such, Hoover was much more effective. Roosevelt was a broker, an eclectic, a pragmatist, an improviser, one who lived comfortably with great inconsistencies. Nevertheless, when there were conflicts among organized interests over what to do and how to do it, Roosevelt displayed a consistent preference for writing the conflicts into the legislation and providing for the group interactions to continue within the administrative process itself.

Important as these first two changes have been, however, two others are of much greater significance for this particular analysis. These are (1) the pushing of political parties toward the periphery of national politics; and (2) its correlative, the establishment of a direct and unmediated relationship between the president and the people.

The President and His Party

Just as the patronage state was hospitable to patronage parties, so the positive, programmatic state would be inhospitable. The presidential election of 1932 has been widely recognized as a rare "critical election," one that produces or arises out of a realignment of voter affiliations which do not return to the status quo ante. But what is more significant is the fact that *there has not been a critical election since 1932*. In other words, at some point following 1932, party *lines* became so weak that *realignments* became virtually impossible, probably irrelevant.

For many years before FDR, although there had been a declining trend in measures of legislative party discipline and of voter turnout and loyalty, the evidence of party viability was fairly strong. Parties were still relatively cohesive in the Congress of 1933, and it appears to have been Roosevelt's intention to reconstitute the Democratic party as a truly programmatic national party, operating as an instrument of the president. Roosevelt had been a product of traditional Democratic party politics, was at home in such an environment, and was

59

so lacking in hostility that he made his peace not only with the machines of New York but with those of other cities as well.[18] Moreover, he proved able to work through the Democratic leaders in Congress despite the fact that when he was elected president the party was still very much a southern one. After the long honeymoon of the "first New Deal," as enlargement of the New Deal began to bog down, Roosevelt committed himself to the remaking of the Democratic party in his image. The 1936 presidential election was his springboard.

No election ever came closer than 1936 to being a mandate—not only in the margin of victory but in the validation of a program. And, although corporatist politics remained prominent throughout the New Deal, Roosevelt publicly rejected the large corporate interests. He broke with the Liberty League and, by name, with conservatives and Wall Streeters, including Wall Street Democrats ("economic royalists" and "malefactors of great wealth"). Roosevelt had dominated in the 1936 nominating convention and the campaign as no candidate had ever done before. Through James Farley, he used thousands of relief jobs and millions of dollars in federal funds, before and after 1936, in an attempt to forge the Democratic parties of the several states into a national party with the president as party chief as well as chief executive. No wonder the Hatch Acts were passed in Congress amid expressions of denunciation of Jim Farley and fear of a dictatorial president. But that did not impede Roosevelt's effort to mobilize the congressional Democrats along with the Democratic constituencies. As the pressures of mobilization were mounting, Senator Burton Wheeler (D., Mont.) confronted a White House aide and asked, "Who does Roosevelt think he is? He used to be just one of the barons. I was baron of the Northwest. Huey Long was baron of the South. [Other leaders were also mentioned.] He is like a king trying to reduce the barons."[19]

The effort to reconstitute the Democratic party reached its climax

---

[18]For the history of parties in Congress during this period, see Julius Turner and Edward Schneier, *Party and Constituency: Pressures on Congress*, rev. ed. (Baltimore: Johns Hopkins University Press, 1970). On critical elections and their failure to occur in the last three decades, see Walter Dean Burnham, *The Current Crisis in American Politics* (New York: Oxford University Press, 1982). For a brief but enlightening treatment of Roosevelt and the Democratic party, see Shefter, "Party, Bureaucracy, and Political Change," pp. 240-43.

[19]Quoted in James MacGregor Burns, *Roosevelt: The Lion and the Fox* (New York: Harcourt Brace, 1956), pp. 341-42.

in 1938, when FDR carried out a plan brewing for many months to purge it of conservative members of Congress whose safe seats and committee seniority had indeed made them barons. Although he singled out only a few by name, he covered the country from coast to coast during the 1938 primary season in a whistle-stop campaign endorsing the new Democratic candidates against the old, snubbing the old for the new, and frontally assaulting a few others. This struggle all took place *within* the Democratic party; Roosevelt was making himself and his program the litmus test of party loyalty—indeed, of party membership:

> As the head of the Democratic Party . . . charged with the responsibility of the definitely liberal declaration of principles set forth in the 1936 Democratic platform, I feel that I have every right to speak in those few instances where there may be a clear issue between candidates for a Democratic nomination involving these principles, or involving a clear misuse of my own name.
>
> Do not misunderstand me. I certainly would not indicate a preference in a State primary merely because a candidate, otherwise liberal in outlook, had conscientiously differed with me on any single issue. I should be far more concerned with the general attitude of . . . those who say "yes" to a progressive objective, but who always find some reason to oppose any specific proposal to gain that objective. I call that type of candidate a "yes, but" fellow.[20]

Roosevelt even permitted Harry Hopkins, then administrator of the WPA, to oppose publicly the renomination of Senator Guy Gillette of Iowa—implying that WPA money would be used as patronage to support the Gillette opposition.

History records that Roosevelt's efforts backfired. But the lesson Roosevelt carried away from the campaign is one of his important legacies. This lesson was that *the president cannot depend upon locally organized patronage parties for an electoral or popular base sufficiently supportive of the needs of the presidency.* All presidents have needed a popular base. As the national government grew and as presidents became more central to it, the need for such a base grew. But until Roosevelt, the popular base was a party base—or an electoral base mediated by party. Roosevelt tried to leave as a legacy a more

---

[20]Quoted in William Riker, *Democracy in the United States* (New York: Macmillan, 1953) pp. 288-89.

relevant, programmatic party base for future presidents. In his failure, he left another kind of legacy. He left the beginnings of what was to become the plebiscitary presidency.

The President and the People

At least two dimensions of mass, anti-party politics reach back directly to FDR. One of these is the use of polling, and the other is the use of mass communications technology—the input side and the output side of communications in mass society.

The polling of public opinions by random-sample survey techniques has been technologically feasible at least since the late nineteenth century. Yet polling did not establish itself in politics until after 1936. It had been tried by the Republicans in the 1896 presidential election but was widely disapproved of as an intrusion into the democratic electoral process. As an entertainment, the magazine *Literary Digest* began taking and publishing the results of a presidential poll in 1916; it issued fairly accurate predictions of the presidential elections between 1924 and 1932, on the basis of an informal "straw poll" of millions of people reached through telephone directories and automobile registration lists. Although these do not appear to have been taken very seriously by presidential candidates, the *Literary Digest* was embarrassed virtually out of existence by its prediction of victory for Republican candidate Alf Landon in 1936. However, this exhibition of inaccuracy did not prevent Roosevelt himself from making use of surveys. Roosevelt commissioned his own public opinion polls on a number of occasions and by 1939 was carefully analyzing the results of the regular polls being conducted by the Gallup and Roper organizations and by many important publications, such as *Fortune* and the *New York Times.* The New Deal had nothing to do with the creation of the polling industry, the primary concern of which was commercial and consumer information, with an occasional "piggyback" question relevant to politics. But Roosevelt contributed significantly to the integration of polling into politics as he sought his own mass popular constituency. By 1960, polling had become so important to presidents that a pollster became a regular part of the inner core of each White House and presidential candidate organization. All these practices lead directly back to Roosevelt and his orientation toward the acquisition of knowledge about mass opinions.

The Roosevelt name is even more strongly connected to the "output" side of mass communications. So-called mass media, if the concept is broadly defined, existed before radio and television: Inexpensive, mass-circulation newspapers were politically important during the nineteenth century. However, mass-circulation newspapers, then and now, differ from radio and television in at least five ways that are particularly relevant to the establishment of direct relations between the president and the masses.

First of all, the electronic media have and newspapers lack *directness*. The first large newspapers were run by or closely associated with political parties. President Jackson, for example, relied upon the partisan newspaper *United States Telegraph*, which had a circulation of forty thousand. Even in the late nineteenth century, when the important newspapers were owned by independent companies unaffiliated with the major political parties, communications from political leaders, including the president, were *mediated* through writers of the articles and, more important, through the tight editorial control of the publishers. This is not to say that news stories coming out of the White House on Congress or the political parties lacked veracity. It means that the symbols and the general allusions were cooled off somewhere between the speaker and the reader. The newspapers were a mediating channel between politics and the masses. Radio and television are mediating forces when controlled by broadcast journalists. But they have the unique capacity to operate as a direct conduit rather than a mediating channel.

A second attribute differentiating newspapers from radio and television is *resistibility*. Newspapers are resistible because they must be purchased. Every conceivable sensational device has been used from time to time to entice consumers to purchase them, but even in their golden age newspapers were bought by a minority of citizens. Moreover, competition between newspapers within a single city permitted substitutability, and that alone performed as an extremely effective filter between the top political leaders and individual readers. A third differentiating characteristic is *passivity*, which radio and television permit and newspapers definitely do not. The newspaper requires the reader to meet it halfway, even with home delivery. The newspaper has to be actively read. In contrast, communications via radio and television can be received with no apparent effort. An effort is required to turn them off. Since so many political and commercial communications on radio and television are carefully planted between the episodes of entertainment, the recipient must make some very special and active effort to cut off the communication before it has been received.

Still another difference between newspapers and radio-television is *repeat-ability*. Both types of media provide for repeatability, but in vastly different ways. For printed communications, repeatability means the reader's option to go back over a communication, read it two or three times, and reflect upon what has been said. In contrast, repeatability in the broadcast media means the option of the *sender*, not the recipient, to keep repeating the same communication, over and over again, to a passive listener. (It has been suggested that the advent of inexpensive video cassette players may alter this situation, but it is difficult to imagine the average individual taping news shows and political commercials for later reflection.) Communications through the broadcast media, especially the famous thirty-second spots that originated in the early 1960s, are not only almost impossible to avoid but deliberately provide nothing worthy of careful analysis. In fact, since the brief commercials are built on impressions rather than logic, "instant replay" benefits the sender, not the receiver.

Fifth and finally, there is the differentiating characteristic of *ubiquity*—a capacity, lacking in newspapers, to be in all places at the same time. With the telegraph, and still later with the spread of news services such as Associated Press, newspapers could and did receive the same news stories more or less simultaneously. And frequently, hard-pressed editors print the news service stories just as they come off the wire. Nevertheless, especially in the days before radio and television, the dictates of competition in multiple newspaper communities led to product differentiation just as the dictates of competition in the age of mass communications have produced product uniformity. And even now, after the decline unto disappearance of the multiple newspaper communities, several national newspapers and news magazines compete with each other and also prevent the single local newspaper from being a monoply in the strictest sense. On the other hand, although there are now three networks and many independent stations, all in vigorous competition with one another, the tendency toward product uniformity is very strong where national news is concerned. Local coverage by local stations may indeed be differentiated because of competition. But national news, particularly any communication regarding the presidency, is aimed at a national audience and is shaped by national distributions of opinion. As with any oligopolistic competition, the smaller the number of competitors the greater the tendency toward the mode. What else can explain the struggles for ratings in the news category and the payment of enormous salaries for "anchor persons" whose main responsibility is to be charming as they read the news script?

Thus, at the very time when a president was seeking a direct relationship with the masses, an appropriate technology became available. Roosevelt did not invent the radio nor did the radio in any sense cause Roosevelt to seek this direct relationship. Let me emphasize once again that the increasing responsibility of the presidency and the severe difficulty of reaching the masses on his terms through his own political party were largely responsible for Roosevelt's resort to mass communications. From the very beginning of his administration, through his Fireside Chats and other means, Roosevelt masterminded the mass communications available to him. The technology plus his own ingenuity gave to his messages the directness, the *irre*sistibility, the passivity, the repeatability and, especially, the ubiquity that are the essence of mass communications. That other great contemporary leaders, such as Churchill and Hitler, discovered the same technology and used similar techniques only underscores and confirms the massifying of American presidential politics beginning with Roosevelt.

Roosevelt was the first personal president in peacetime, and his legacy can be summed up in a single concept, the *plebiscitary presidency.* He set its foundations and determined its initial directions. Roosevelt had pushed ahead politically on all fronts, and he was not backward in his efforts to be an effective national party leader. His failure in that area was so significant that it almost destabilized his entire administration. If at the same time he succeeded in achieving the same goals through direct mass political methods—over the heads of Congress and the party leaders—it became inevitable that these tactics would be repeated. Every success in that direction pushed the traditional political parties more to the periphery of national politics.

Is it possible that political parties would have stayed closer to the center of national politics if mass politics had not worked so well?

The question itself suggests that the two political approaches are probably contradictory: the more of one the less of the other. It also suggests the possibility of historical inevitability—the inevitable decline of national parties and the concomitant rise of mass national politics. My own opinion is that we are confronting a case of conditional necessity. That is to say, modern, programmatic government is an inhospitable environment for the old patronage-type parties and a patronage system of two parties. With the replacement of the patronage state, the patronage parties declined precisely because they did not make the kind of adjustment sought by Roosevelt. The vacuum created by their inadequacy was filled by a mass politics made possible by available appropriate technology. *Until another basis for political parties could be found*, party politics would not be a dependable weapon for the kind of presidential power that Congress and traditional parties had helped build and that the state they built depended upon. In building such a state, Congress and the traditional parties have undermined their own positions. At the same time it is quite possible that *reconstituted* parties could have made a comeback after the 1930s, and could even make a comeback in the 1980s. This kind of conditional necessity can be confronted once again after the actual conditions of the modern period have been more fully explored.

4

Presidents without Parties:
The Making of a New Constituency

The close association of partisanship with corruption
. . . is the result of circumstances, not of affinity. They
are really antagonistic principles. Partisanship tends to
establish a connection based upon an avowed public
obligation, while corruption consults private and individual interests which secrete themselves from view
and avoid accountability of any kind. The weakness of
party organization is the opportunity of corruption.

—Henry Jones Ford, 1898

FDR was dead. The war was over. The armed forces were
demobilizing. It was 1946, however, not 1918 or 1865. Big government
was not demobilized. New Deal programs were left untouched. The
president was getting more help. The Employment Act of 1946
amounted to a solemn pledge that the national government would
consider itself responsible for getting a job for anyone and everyone
seeking work. The number of personnel in the national government
dropped from its 1945 peak of 3.7 million to 2 million in 1948; but the
figure was still more than double that for the last prewar year, and it
was going to remain in the 2 million bracket. National security was
added to economic security as justification for governmental growth,
although it would be a mistake to conclude that national security
needs alone explain the American choice to keep big government after World War II. And it was an American choice. Fear of the Roosevelt legacies was drowned out in storms of criticism; opposition to

67

big government was denounced as reactionary and disregarded as Neanderthal McKinleyism—and may have been. The Old Guard was relegated to a small minority niche in the Republican party.

Fears of another kind, for a moment, got more attention than the fears of the Old Guard. These were expressed through the Committee on Political Parties of the American Political Science Association, appointed in 1946 to inquire into "the condition and improvement of *national* party organization." Three years later, the committee surfaced with its report, "Toward a More Responsible Two-Party System," which rates second only to the 1937 President's Committee on Administrative Management as a contribution by academics to public discourse on the fundamentals of American democracy.[1]

The committee opened its report with a recognition of several basic facts that was remarkable for the late 1940s, when the dust had hardly settled over FDR. Its starting premise was that something was wrong with the American party system. Its weakness

> . . . is a very serious matter, for it affects the very heartbeat of American democracy. It also poses grave problems of domestic and foreign policy in an era when it is no longer safe for the nation to deal piecemeal with issues that can be disposed of only on the basis of coherent programs. [P. v]

The following are, in my opinion, the committee's major conclusions in regard to the political parties and the party system:

> (1) Party organization remains substantially what it was before the Civil War. Under these circumstances the main trends of American politics have tended to outflank the party system.
> (2) The internal federalism of the two parties is greatly overbalanced toward the state and local level. No central figure or organ can claim authority to take up party problems or policies.
> (3) Party membership is beginning to mean nothing at all.
> (4) Changes in the social and economic structure of the United States, reflected especially in the decline of sectionalism, require a focus on national issues that the parties are unable to provide.

---

[1]"Toward a More Responsible Two-Party System," published as a special *Supplement* to the *American Political Science Review*, 44, no. 3, part 2 (September 1950). Emphasis in original. Excerpts from this publication are followed by page references in parentheses.

(5) The same economic and social factors that have nationalized issues have also produced more national interest groups that operate more independently than in the past even when in association with one or the other party. [Pp. 3-4, paraphrase]

In sum, although the political parties by 1950 still resembled those of the traditional system, everything else had changed to such an extent that the condition of the parties had become a serious problem. The committee recognized that although the presidency was not the only agency of change in this context, it was one of the most important:

> The presidency is the greatest political office in this country. There is no other republic, in fact, that entrusts to its President as much constitutional responsibility as Americans have entrusted to the President of the United States. [P. 93]

They reasoned that since the presidency had come to be defined as the only politically responsible organ of government with the whole nation as its constituency, Americans' natural tendency was to look to the president as responsible for formulating and implementing programs. The Committee went on, however, to observe that for these responsibilities to be discharged effectively, there must be

> *dependable political support . . . for the governmental program* as finally adopted. *When there is no other place to get that done, when the political parties fail to do it, it is tempting* once more *to turn to the President.* [P. 94; emphasis in original]

A system that vests such responsibility in the president can work well enough as long as the program has been democratically formulated within the president's party. However, when there is no party support for a broad program, the president has no choice but to work up a program of his own and then go out and build the necessary popular support for it. Here, according to the committee, are the implications of that way of operating:

> *When the President's program actually is the sole program . . . either his party becomes a flock of sheep or the party falls apart. In effect this concept of the presidency disposes of the party system by making the Presi-*

69

dent reach directly for the support of a majority of the voters. It favors a president who exploits skillfully the arts of demagoguery, who uses the whole country as his political back yard, and who does not mind turning into the embodiment of personal government.

A generation ago one might have dismissed this prospect as fantastic. At the midway mark of the 20th century the American people has [sic] reason to know better, from recent and current examples abroad, what it does not want. Because Americans are so sure on that score, they cannot afford to be casual about overextending the presidency to the point where it might very well ring in the wrong ending. . . .

Present conditions are a great incentive for the voters to dispose of the parties as intermediaries between themselves and the government. . . . [This] is an ominous tendency. [Pp. 94-95; emphasis in original]

Yet only a few intimations of this "ominous tendency" could have been caught in 1949-50. To other than the most discerning eyes, they were masked by the 1948 presidential election, thought by many to be a classic example of an election fought out between parties over programs and issues.

The continuing decline of political parties became more widely recognized as time went on, however. For example, V. O. Key, probably the leading political scientist of the 1950s, put the case very clearly in the last edition of his classic text *Politics, Parties, and Pressure Groups*, published in 1964:

The party organization is . . . accurately described as a system of layers of organization. Each successive layer—county or city, state, national—has an independent concern about elections in its geographical jurisdiction. Each higher level of organization, to accomplish its ends, must obtain the collaboration of the lower layer or layers of organization.

. . . When it is said that national party is a coalition, the reference may be to the coalition or combination of social interests for which the party speaks. . . . It is well to emphasize the fundamental importance to national party organization of the underlying coalition of social blocs and interests. Yet it remains for the politicians to work out the details in terms of the coalition. That process starkly reveals the nonhierarchical structure of national party organization. The party nationally tends to be an alliance of state and city leaders who work together most faithfully during a presidential campaign. The national committee is a gathering of sovereigns (or their emissaries) to negotiate and treat with each other rather than a staff conclave of subordinates of the national chairman. The basic coalition-forming process occurs in the national convention which nominates the candidate who succeeds in lining up a command-ing bloc of state organizations. The nominee symbolizes the terms of the coalition at the moment; the platform may make them explicit.[2]

This passage is worth quoting at length because it is representative of the early 1960s understanding of the situation throughout political science and political journalism. By that time, however, no one was attempting to appreciate the place of that traditional party system within the context of the new system of government. In little more than a decade, the theory of the governing presidency—what came to be called the "institutional presidency"—had become so widely accepted that the fears expressed by the APSA Committee about a strong presidency without a political party came to appear rather quaint. In 1961, with the return of the Democrats and the politics of joy, all concerns had moved away from the problem of how to head off the governing presidency to the problem of how to make it a reality.

Even in states where the traditional major parties have been able to keep their grip on local affairs, they have lost their moorings where the new presidency is concerned. This chapter will explore the par-ties' continual drift toward the periphery of national politics and will attempt to locate the new constituency of that new presidency.

Intimations of the Future: From CFE to CREEP

Dwight D. Eisenhower was not the first great hero to be elected president, nor was he the first to be bigger than his own party. But he made at least two precedent-setting contributions to the personal presidency.

General Eisenhower had lived at such a distance from domestic politics that as a postwar hero he was claimed by both parties. Presi-dent Truman had recruited him to be the next nominee of the Demo-cratic party, and he did not publicly declare himself a Republican until early during the 1952 presidential year. Ike literally took the 1952 presidential nomination from "Mr. Republican," Senator Robert Taft of Ohio. In the process he made the two fundamental contribu-

---

[2]V. O. Key, *Politics, Parties, and Pressure Groups*, 5th ed. (New York: Crowell, 1964), pp. 16 and 330.

71

tions to the new presidency without intending to and without appreciating their significance. The first was the delivery of a telling blow against the legitimacy of party leader control of delegates to the nominating convention. The second was the precedent he set with his commitment to run a presidential campaign separate from the national committee of his party.

Undermining Party Leader Control of Delegates

In 1952, selection of delegates by election through primaries was still relatively unimportant, and even less so was selection of delegates legally or morally pledged to a specific presidential candidate. In any case, Eisenhower stayed a considerable distance away from the primaries. Although he won several state primaries and trailed Taft only 27 percent to 36 percent in total primary vote, he did little campaigning in those states, concentrating on states where party leaders chose the delegates and had them validated in state conventions and caucuses. As the Republican convention approached in the summer of 1952, Eisenhower had fewer firm delegates than Taft. As was traditional, a large proportion of delegates were unpledged, a situation that produced a great deal of uncertainty.

Thus, at the very outset of the convention, the Eisenhower managers were forced to make a bold move: They officially questioned the credentials of several state delegations whose members, pledged to Taft, had been selected by the traditional method of virtual appointment by professional party leaders who imposed their choices on the district and state conventions and caucuses. The Eisenhower forces went before the credentials committee of the Republican National Convention and argued that Taft leaders had acted autocratically in those states in order to obtain their delegations, over the protests of the local Eisenhower Republicans. Since the credentials committee, under Taft control, was less than sympathetic, the Eisenhower group took their objections to the convention floor in the form of a "fair-play" motion. This motion not only opposed the seating of these Taft delegations; it went further by providing that delegates whose credentials were in question would not be permitted to vote on any motion until their own right to sit had been settled. Since it is always difficult to vote against something called "fair play," the Eisenhower

72

motion managed to sway enough neutral delegates to gain the majority vote and thereby unseat the Taft delegations.

The Eisenhower victory on this motion did a great deal more than adding Eisenhower delegates—more, even, than impressing the convention with an Eisenhower show of force in advance of the balloting. Those were merely the immediate gains. The long-range consequence of this veritable coup d'etat was to weaken the foundations of the traditional system itself. Eisenhower's victory in that nomination sounded the death knell for the system of selection so eloquently described by former Tammany leader Edward Costikyan:

> The first thing a candidate who wants a nomination from a convention should realize is that the delegates themselves are not free agents, nor are they individuals subject to persuasion . . . [i]n short, the delegate is the property of his leader.[3]

From that time onward, delegates increasingly became factors in their own right. The spread of the practice of selecting delegates by primaries and, especially, the spread of the practice of having them pledge themselves to an announced presidential candidate contributed fundamentally to the establishment of the separate identity and right-of-choice of each delegate independent of the state party leadership. But the legitimacy of party leader control of delegates, the legitimacy of the delegate being the "property of his leader," *was already seriously undermined even before the significant spread of selection of pledged delegates by primary elections.* And once such undermining had taken place, of course, the role of the presidential nominating convention itself was almost completely changed. That part of the story remains for Chapter 5.

CFE: The Direct Strategy

The second precedent established by Eisenhower in 1952 was the commitment to run a presidential campaign separate from the Republican National Committee. Presidential candidates before Eisenhower had made some use of "citizen politics." For example, there

[3]Edward N. Costikyan, *Behind Closed Doors: Politics in the Public Interest* (New York: Harcourt, Brace & World, 1966), pp. 166 and 167.

had been hundreds of Willkie clubs during the 1940 campaign. But not until Eisenhower had there been an effort to form these citizen groups into a national organization for the purpose of running a campaign independent of the political party. Out of this effort came Citizens for Eisenhower (CFE), which was composed of many thousands of volunteers. Some of them were probably ordinary Republicans; but most were Independents leaning Republican and "Democrats for Eisenhower."

This approach was very consonant with Eisenhower's personality and his attitude toward party politics. His separateness from his party extended even to resentment and neglect of decisions about job patronage. Eisenhower appears to have recognized that his own popularity was so much greater than his party's that he could only damage his position by too strong an association with it. Eventually, the Republican party in Congress became such a frustration to him that during his third year of office he actually contemplated starting a third party of his own.[4] In an excellent summation all the more impressive because it was made in 1956, very close to the actual situation, Samuel Lubell observed: "Eisenhower might be termed a substitute for a reshuffling of both parties. At present neither party seems quite capable of commanding the trust of an effective majority of the country. . . . So tangled are the lines of partisan cross-conflict that it appeared easier and quicker to achieve national unity by rallying around a personal leader than by waiting for the parties to reshuffle themselves."[5]

It was natural, in terms of the immediate situation, that if such an outside strategy were to be adopted, the Republicans would be the party to adopt it. In 1952, after twenty years of Democrats and all the patronage that had been available to them, the GOP was very much a minority party that could not hope to win without massive defection of Democrats as well as the mobilization of first-time voters. But what is historically significant is that the Eisenhower strategy outlived Eisenhower and became common to the Democratic party as well as the Republican. Another decade was required before Eisenhower's first precedent—the breaking of party leader control over dele-

[4]David Broder, *The Party's Over* (New York: Harper & Row, 1971), pp. 7-8. See also Robert J. Donovan, *Eisenhower: The Inside Story* (New York: Harper & Row, 1956).

[5]Samuel Lubell, *The Future of American Politics* (New York: Doubleday Anchor edition, 1956), p. 251.

gates—became established. But his second precedent—the independence of presidential campaigns from the party—was established almost immediately.

Adlai Stevenson in 1952 maintained his personal headquarters in his home in Springfield, Illinois, primarily to dissociate himself from the Truman administration and from the Democratic National Committee operating in Washington. If this was the cause of many complaints in 1952, professionals were even more irritated by the 1956 decision to follow Eisenhower with a Volunteers for Stevenson-Kefauver.

By 1960 the pattern was fairly well established. John Kennedy boosted the practice several notches by making elaborate use of volunteers outside the state party organizations to run his state primary races. As David Broder describes the 1960 Kennedy approach, it sounds astonishingly similar to, albeit more elaborate and vigorous than, the Eisenhower approach:

> The organizational secret of Kennedy politics was so simple that it was often overlooked: It was a politics of personal involvement, on a massive scale. . . . [W]hat gave him his critical advantage, I believe, was his distinctive ability to make his supporters become his workers, and to utilize their efforts effectively. . . . What he had shown was a talent for going outside the normal political channels and enlisting, in large numbers, the energies of enthusiastic political amateurs. . . . While Kennedy always thought of himself and was considered a partisan Democrat, he held back from ever being an "organization man." . . . On the basis of their Massachusetts experience, John Kennedy and his brothers developed a healthy contempt for most old-line organization Democratic leaders. . . . The point is, that despite his Democratic heritage, despite his personal and family links to some of the established powers in the party, Kennedy won the nomination essentially by going outside the organization, using "political amateurs," to round up votes in the primaries and thus forcing the professionals . . . to accept him as the nominee.[6]

Although different in some respects because the Democratic party was the majority party, the Kennedy post-convention approach to electoral organization was in many ways very like Eisenhower's. Kennedy did appoint his key political adviser, Lawrence O'Brien, to the position of director of organization for the Democratic National Committee—indicating that he intended to maintain his control of

[6]Broder, *The Party's Over*, pp. 18-25.

the party and to use it as his own instrument. But he also created a Kennedy-Johnson Volunteers Organization and appointed Byron White its national director. This organization drew thousands upon thousands of amateurs to the campaign. Many of them had already been active in the state primary campaigns for Kennedy. The Democratic National Committee in 1960 was headed by Senator Henry M. Jackson, but he was in every respect a figurehead. The entire Kennedy campaign organization, including the national committee and all the other volunteer committees, was under the management of Robert F. Kennedy.[7]

Kennedy's use of volunteers, and their distant relationship to the local and state political organizations, were rich in implications for what was to come. As Theodore White put it, the Kennedys borrowed, unknowingly, from the ancient Mandarin Chinese practice of never appointing any individuals to a government position in their native province. Kennedy volunteers were assigned to service outside their home states. Many of them in fact looked with suspicion upon organized political parties, and they were in turn suspected by the local party leaders because their loyalties extended directly to the national ticket. Friction between the regular organization and the volunteers led Lawrence O'Brien to send "coordinators" to each state to arbitrate their disputes. Eventually, O'Brien had 43 such out-of-state coordinators trying to contain the friction between Kennedy's personal organization and the established local and state party organizations.[8]

If Oscar Wilde was right and nothing succeeds like excess, nothing could have been a more successful expression of the tendency of presidents to build their own personal organizations than Nixon's CREEP in 1972. Although truly a loyal Republican partisan who had worked long and hard throughout the country for party candidates and fundraising efforts, especially during the dry years of the 1960s, Nixon nevertheless followed the practice of having his own campaign committee and his own staff for the control of his presidential campaigns. As the candidate of the minority party and an Eisenhower associate, he was all the more mindful of the need to differentiate him-

[7]Key, *Politics, Parties,* p. 457 and sources cited pp. 457-62.
[8]Theodore H. White, *The Making of the President, 1960* (New York: Atheneum, 1961), p. 272.

self from state and local Republican candidates to draw conservative Democrats, especially unhappy 1968 Wallace supporters, to his cause. What started moderately in 1968 culminated in 1972 in the Committee to Reelect the President (CREEP). The successes and failures of that important organization are too well known to repeat here. Suffice it to say that it was a logical extension of strategies employed by all Republican and most Democratic candidates since 1952. Jimmy Carter, the most outside of all presidential outsiders, was hell-bent to create a separate campaign organization. To emphasize his point, he set up his operation in Atlanta, encouraged little relationship between the Atlanta organization and the Democratic National Committee headquarters in Washington, and gave the Democratic National Committee very little access to him. This brings to mind the report by Senator Robert Dole, who, after serving as Republican national chairman during the 1972 Nixon campaign, confessed that he had had virtually no communication with the president during the election year.[9]

A few original twists added by Ronald Reagan do not obscure the similarity of his practices to the established pattern. His 1980 campaign was run from two headquarters, neither of which reported to the Republican National Committee. One of them, which White called "Base Camp," was in Arlington, Virginia, and was run by Edwin Meese and William Casey. The other, which was composed virtually entirely of Californians, was constantly on the plane traveling with Candidate Reagan. White called it the "Damage Control Squad."[10]

Getting ready for 1984, President Reagan varied the established pattern once again by appointing Paul Laxalt general chairman of the Republican party, a new position superior to that of chairman of the Republican National Committee, a post he filled with Frank Fahrenkopf, who had served as chairman of the Nevada Republican party while Laxalt was governor of that state. As a trusted aide and close friend of President Reagan, Laxalt was charged with coordinating all

[9]Reported in Joseph Parker and Edward Kearny, "The President and Political Parties," in Edward Kearny, ed., *Dimensions of the Modern Presidency* (St. Louis: Forum Press, 1981), p. 93

[10]Theodore H. White, *America in Search of Itself* (New York: Harper & Row, 1982), p. 386.

campaign activities, including those of the national committeee, those of the Republican congressional committees, and Reagan's own reelection efforts.[11]

The Reagan-Bush '84 campaign added spice to the pattern set with CRE and running through CREEP. Although Reagan is the most partisan president at least since Richard Nixon, like Nixon, he kept his presidential campaign independent of the rest of the party, including the Republican National Committee and the Republican Congressional Committee. The campaign was run out of the White House, with Reagan making most of his field forays within a radius that permitted him to sleep each night in his own bed. His partisanship came through clearly in the total control of the Republican convention by the Reagan Right, in the favor he gave to radical right-wing groups, and even in the conservative, religious/moral approach he took to the traditional Democrats he reached out to. Walter Dean Burham has observed, correctly, that the Republicans in 1984 hoped for a true partisan realignment comparable to that in 1932.[12] But the Republican approach was *partisan* without being *party*. Reagan did attempt to help certain GOP candidates for the House and Senate, but his efforts were very partial, seldom hands-on. In response to criticisms that Reagan had not tried to use his coattails, Edward J. Rollins, chairman of Reagan-Bush '84, responded in a manner that tends to confirm the very independence he was attempting to deny. "No president is modern times has done more for his party than Reagan," he said. "He set up a political office in the White House to help congressional candidates. He cut hundreds of [television and radio] spots for them. He did fundraisers."[13] Reagan conducted his independent campaign in full awareness of the polls, which showed that many voters, especially Democrats, favored Mondale's policy positions but were willing to vote for Reagan on the basis of personal popularity. That sort of thing is not transferable.

Nixon's CREEP can no longer be considered in any respect exceptional. Excesses of campaign behavior and the criminal efforts to cover up that behavior in the ensuing two years are matters quite in-

[11]Roger G. Brown, "The Presidency and the Political Parties," in Michael Nelson, ed. *The Presidency and the Political System* (Washington: Congressional Quarterly Press, 1984), p. 321.

[12]Walter Dean Burnham, personal correspondence with the author.

[13]Quotation from Lou Cannon, "The GOP Is Sizing up Reagan's Coattails for a Ride to Victory," *Washington Post National Weekly Edition*, September 24, 1984, p. 11.

dependent of the campaign organization itself. CREEP was normal and, in fact, was validated by imitation by both parties after 1972. More important, the pattern and practice of separate campaign organizations for president are but a reflection of the larger pattern that has become institutionalized: the plebiscitary presidency. Formation of the pattern had begun with the receding of the traditional national parties to the periphery. It continued as local and state parties weakened to such an extent that they were unable to oppose reforms that imposed mass participation on the presidential nominating process. The requirements of getting the nomination in such a wide-open process forced each candidate to develop a rough and ready national organization. That organization and its independence from political parties are validated when one of the candidates is nominated. And it does not end there. The continuation of the pattern is summarized nicely by Richard Pious, who wrote: "The election [campaign] continues the separation of the presidential nominee from the national and state party organization. Once nominated, the candidate does not disband his personal following and rely on the National Committee to run his campaign."[14] Nor does the process end there. The so-called transition period is also carried on independent of the party of the president-elect. It is only natural for the administration to be structured the same way. But that belongs to a later part of the story. Other features of the politics of the modern period must be introduced first.

Confirmations of the Future: The Revolution in Participation

The rise of the president's personal, mass constituency and the decline of party as an organized intermediary will be projected in four important dimensions of participation: (1) split-ticket voting; (2) split electoral outcomes; (3) the rise of the Independent; and (4) the spread of insurgency. Since each is a relatively dramatic development, questions of causation will inevitably arise. It is to me compelling to draw the arrows of causation from the modern state through the presidency to the decline of party and thence to the changes in

[14]Richard Pious, *The American Presidency* (New York: Basic Books, 1979), p. 100.

participation patterns to be described here. Others will draw arrows from technological change (especially in mass communications) to changes in political participation to changes in government. And there are still other possible explanations. But causation need not detain us. The issue of concern is first to describe the phenomenon and then to assess its consequences, not search for its causes. These four dimensions of participation, whether they are causes or effects, will help make plain the problem of particular concern here, the constituency of the plebiscitary presidency.

Ticket Splitting

The phenomenon of split-ticket voting, which has been expanding for many years, can really be said to have begun with the adoption of the Australian ballot in the late nineteenth century. Until then, each party printed its own ballot listing only its own candidates for each office, a practice that made secrecy in voting almost impossible, and ticket splitting almost equally difficult. To split a ticket, a voter had physically to superimpose with paper and paste on his party-provided ballot the name of the candidate of the other party for whom he wished to vote. The Australian ballot, a government-printed ballot listing all candidates of all parties, provided for secrecy; it also made ticket splitting a lot easier.[15]

The first visible signs of ticket splitting appeared at the beginning of the Progressive period, with the election of Theodore Roosevelt in 1904 and the presence of important third parties. The practice spread through the 1920s, contracted during the 1930s, and turned on its modern upward trend after 1948: In other words, it emerged as parties weakened and spread as parties grew weaker. After 1960 ticket splitting achieved a "breakaway pace," and scholars who study split-ticket voting are the ones most likely to speak with alarm about "party decomposition" in the United States.[16] The pattern can be

[15]A good treatment of the Australian ballot and its consequences will be found in Benjamin Ginsberg, *The Consequences of Consent: Elections, Citizen Control and Popular Acquiescence* (Reading, Mass.: Addison-Wesley, 1982), pp. 93-96.

[16]See, for example, Walter Dean Burnham, "American Politics in the 1970s: Beyond Party?," in W. N. Chambers and W. D. Burnham, eds., *The American Party Systems* (New York: Oxford University Press, 1975), p. 317; and Burnham, *Critical Elections and the Mainsprings of American Politics* (New York: Norton, 1970), ch. 5.

seen clearly and consistently in two kinds of data. One of those is the spread of percentages of split outcomes, with one party winning at the top of the ticket and the other winning on the lower levels. The other is data from post-election surveys, showing that the proportion of the electorate reporting straight-ticket voting dropped from 62 percent in 1948 to 38 in 1972, rising slowly to 41 percent in 1976 and dropping back again in 1980 to 37 percent. This tendency is consistent throughout the nation, region by region.[17]

Ticket splitting was so prevalent by the time of the 1972 election that the Michigan Survey Research Center (SRC) had to report that party identification was no longer as significant a determinant of presidential voting as was ideology. Now if one understands ideology, as defined by behavioral researchers, to mean simply a set of responses to questions regarding positions that major candidates took on important public policies, we are actually finding ourselves in the presence of a *propensity of voters since the late 1970s to take the person, the personality, and the behavior of the head of the ticket into account.* The converse is the tendency of voters to take less and less into account the habits and traditions of the parties and party organizations. David Broder's popular book *The Party's Over* was written with this pattern very much in mind. But Broder was neither first nor alone in his concern for what the academicians have referred to as destabilization and decomposition. And the important aspect of this destabilization is the splitting off of voters from parties whenever presidential candidates are at issue, a point that leads directly to the next section. Let it be noted here that ticket splitting had to account for Ronald Reagan's decisive victory in 1980, because identified Republicans made up only 29 percent of the electorate. As Burnham put it, "At the end of the day, Reagan had won 28 percent of the self-identified Democrats and Carter only 12 percent of self-identified Re-

---

[17]Walter Dean Burnham, "American Politics in the 1970s: Beyond Party?" in W. N. Chambers and W. D. Burnham, eds., *The American Party Systems*, 2d ed. (New York: Oxford University Press, 1975), p. 317; and Burnham, *Critical Elections and the Mainsprings of American Politics* (New York: Norton, 1971), pp. 106–11; Everett C. Ladd, *Transformations of the American Party System* (New York: Norton, 1975), pp. 296–97; also George H. Gallup, *The Gallup Poll: Public Opinion 1980* (Bloomington, Del.: Scholarly Resources Inc., 1981), pp. 260–61. Strong confirmation of the pattern is found in a Michigan Survey Research Center study comparing gubernatorial electoral outcomes to state and local outcomes, reported in Ladd, pp. 297–99.

publicans."[18] But note well: This means that *at least 40 percent of those who identified themselves as affiliates of a party voted opposite their party in the presidential race.* And not counted here are those party affiliates who also split their tickets for Senate and House elections. No doubt, there is a destabilization in general, of which a large proportion surrounds the presidency. Burnham refers to the pattern as having a "very marked institutional division-of-labor character." He continues:

> The bulk of recent analytical work on presidential elections has made crystal clear that this office . . . has become the vortex of all the combined passions, intensities and multiple cleavages . . . now at work in the electorate. . . . [And] this pattern cannot be readily extended to other levels of election as a matter of course. On the contrary: the emerging shape of congressional elections, with its growing support for incumbents of both parties, bespeaks quite directly the lack of any ideological polarization at all similar to those operating at the presidential level.[19]

This specialization of the electorate's focus on the presidency is still more strongly confirmed by the three other dimensions to be considered.

Split Results

The practice of split-ticket voting will tend to produce split results, unless in a two-candidate race there is equal splitting in both directions. A review of the relationship between the presidential elections and virtually all other elections produces at least one clear and unmistakable impression: The presidential electorate is independent. For many years, elections for state legislatures and the House of Representatives have been a picture of stability. Throughout the country, electoral outcomes have been consistent with party identifications. Democrats have enjoyed roughly 47 percent of the electorate, with Republicans enjoying about 25 percent. Including those who call themselves Independent but also report that they lean consistently

[18]Walter Dean Burnham, "The 1980 Earthquake: Realignment, Reaction, or What?" in Thomas Ferguson and Joel Rogers, eds., *The Hidden Election* (New York: Pantheon, 1981), p. 104.
[19]Burnham, "American Politics in the 1970s," p. 344.

Table 4. Split results, 1940–72. Proportion of districts giving plurality to congressional candidate of one party and presidential candidate of the other party

Year	Number of districts analyzed	% Split results
1940	362	14.6
1944	367	11.2
1948	422	22.5
1952	435	19.3
1956	435	29.9
1960	437	26.1
1964	435	33.3
1968	435	31.7
1972	435	44.1

Source: Walter Dean Burnham, "American Politics in the 1970s: Beyond Party?" in Chambers and Burnham, *The American Party Systems*, p. 321.

toward one party or the other, one gets an average of roughly 57 percent for the Democrats and 32 for the Republicans. Either way, that comes roughly to a margin of 60-40, and if 1946 and 1952, which Eisenhower made an exceptional year in a number of respects, are excluded, the typical distribution of House seats from 1930 on has been close to 60 percent Democratic and 40 percent Republican. There was a slight drop in that ratio thanks to President Reagan's coattail influence in 1980, but party affiliation and electoral results have otherwise been consistent with each other in the House of Representatives; and exactly the same holds true for the lower houses of state legislatures. Yet, during the 28-year period between 1952 and 1980, there were seven presidential elections, of which four—1956, 1968, 1972, and 1980—had outcomes dramatically at odds with congressional and state legislative results.

Burnham provides confirmation with a different kind of analysis. In 1940, the outcomes of voting for Congress and the president were analyzed in 362 congressional districts. In 14.6 percent of these the vote was split, in such a way that the plurality went to the candidate for Congress of one party and to the presidential candidate of the other party. This percentage dropped to a low of 11.2 in 1944, but then the proportion of districts with split results began an upward trend, which culminated with 44.1 percent of 435 districts analyzed in 1972 (see Table 4).

Split results of this consistency and degree suggest that what presidential coattails remain are rather short and hard to grasp. Although

Figure 3. The relationship between voting in the 1974 election and the 1976 election.

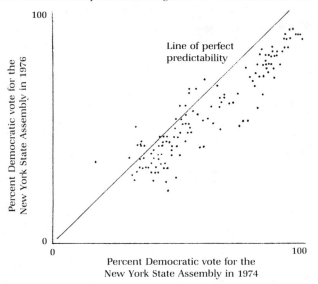

Percent Democratic vote for the
New York State Assembly in 1974

Using actual data from the New York State Assembly elections in 1974 and 1976, the relationship between the percentage of the Democratic vote for each assembly district from the two elections was aggregated and produced a product-moment correlation coefficient of 1.86.

Source: Data from *The New York Red Book* (Albany, N.Y.: Williams Press, 1975, 1977). Used by permission.

that is true, the situation is still variable. In each presidential election, members of the House and Senate make their own individual decisions as to how closely they wish to associate themselves with the presidential candidate of their party—that is, how tightly they wish to grasp the coattails. There have been some famous instances of candidates systematically avoiding the presidential candidate, no matter what the latter's inclinations were. In 1956, Democrats stayed away from Stevenson in droves. All over lower Manhattan were signs saying "Vote Dan Fink for municipal judge, and anybody you want for president." Many Democrats were very tentative, to say the least, about their association with the Mondale candidacy in 1984. In contrast, most Republicans were very eager to associate themselves with President Reagan's candidacy, even if they were not entirely in favor of the specifics of his program. But even though the coattails effect is itself variable from candidate to candidate and from one

84

Figure 4. The relationship between socioeconomic status and voting.

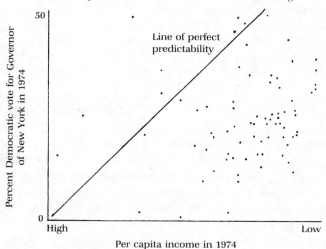

The relationship between the percent Democratic vote for governor in 1974 and the per capita income aggregated for all counties produced a correlation coefficient of 0.07, which is statistically insignificant.

Sources: Data for the vote are from *The New York Red Book* (Albany: Williams Press, 1977). Used by permission. Income data are from U.S. Department of Commerce, Bureau of the Census, *City and County Databook* (Washington, D.C.: Government Printing Office, 1977).

quadrennium to the next, one thing remains constant from election to election, and all the data confirm it: *The presidency has its own independent constituency.*

Partisanship remains a significant force in many local elections, a fact dramatically portrayed in Figures 3 and 4. Note in Figure 3 how closely the dots hover near the line of perfect predictability, indicating that, in the aggregate, voters in each county were so consistent across time that a very accurate prediction of the next election could be made on the basis of the aggregate voting pattern from the previous election for the same office. That partisanship is a much better predictor than socioeconomic status is indicated by the fact that the dots are distributed much further away from the line of predictability on Figure 4. Here we see the strength of partisanship. But since partisanship is not organized within parties, it does not extend reliably to all levels of election. The higher up one goes toward governorship and presidency, the less stable and consistent partisanship proves to be. And among all elections, the presidency is an office apart. The presidency is taken into account for itself. The president and all candidates for president are taken into account for themselves personally. The picture of a specialized presidential constituency ought to be emerging increasingly clearly.

The Rise of the Independent

Another trend, equally dramatic and equally noted with alarm by students of political participation, is the growth of the Independent sector. By 1952, those who called themselves Independents already made up 22 percent of the electorate—compared to 47 percent Democrats and 27 percent Republicans. Twelve years later, the proportion of those identifying themselves as Independents was still about the same. After 1964, however, the preference for Independent status began to grow. By 1976, Independents accounted for 36 percent of the electorate; they outnumbered Republicans 36 percent to 23, with Democrats comprising 40 percent. In 1980, despite the intensified partisanship attributed to Reagan's candidacy, Independents still outnumbered the Republicans 37 percent to 23, with Democrats holding at about 40 percent. The added intensity of the 1980 presidential race had simply wiped out the "don't knows," pushing most of them into the ranks of the Independent voters.

A closer look puts the rise of the Independents in a somewhat more sober perspective. Surveys follow up questions about party affiliation with questions asking all self-professed Independents whether they are "leaning toward" the Democratic or Republican party. This type of question reduces the category of pure Independent by more than half, to 5-6 percent in 1952 and 14-15 percent in 1980 (depending on which survey the data are drawn from). And this distinction between the Independent and the "Independent leaning toward" is important, since recent research has shown that the "Independent leaners" actually vote more consistently with the party they are leaning toward than those who identify themselves as weak but actual affiliates of the party.[20]

[20]Raymond E. Wolfinger and Steven J. Rosenstone, *Who Votes?* (New Haven: Yale University Press, 1980).

On the one hand, this means that an obituary for political parties would be premature. On the other hand, it reinforces the main point of the present analysis: Independents, whether they are pure Independents or only Independent leaners or "rhetorical Independents," make it a habit and a matter of pride to concentrate on the personalities and positions of individual candidates. To call oneself an Independent is to indicate publicly an anti-party, personalized relationship to elections or offices. Even where Independents resolve the choice regularly in favor of one party or the other, their orientation is nevertheless a much more personalized one. And, since voters have a great deal more personal information about the president and other ticket leaders than about other candidates, a personalized relationship is most likely to be established there. Whatever their actual behavior may be, Independent voters are making anti-party values a civic virtue.

The Spread of Insurgency

To say that partisanship has remained stable at the local level is only to state the minimal case. The situation with the two major parties at local and state levels is stable in no sense except that many voters continue to use party references to guide their voting choices. Organizationally, the parties are declining. Party leaders at state as well as local levels are losing control of their own party organizations and processes; party organization itself has become peripheral to political life, even where there is lively partisanship. *The so-called two-party system has become little more than two mounds of partisanship which cannot be directly observed but only measured by sample survey research.*

Since there are so many state, local, and county parties, no simple generalizations can be made. However, among many experienced activists and observers there is probably a consensus that party organizations are weak in most states, close to nonexistent in others, and declining in virtually all. Political scientists disagree over causes and consequences: Most lament the decline, and some applaud it. But they all tend to agree on the decline itself. They also tend to agree on the litmus test of party organization vitality: control of nominations. Operationally, the two essential tests of party leadership in an organization are (a) minimizing contested nominations—that is, insurgency; and (b) defeating insurgents with regular designees wherever insurgency cannot be prevented. Note in this context these remarks by Austin Ranney, one of the leading analysts of party organization during the past three decades:

> There are today no officers or committees in the national parties and very few in the state and local parties who can regularly give nominations to some aspirants and withhold them from others. To be sure, in many states party committees and leaders often publicly endorse particular primary candidates, and my impression is that those endorsed win more often than they lose. Yet it is equally common for party organizations to make no endorsements or other visible efforts to support particular aspirants; and even when they do it is not unusual for a well-known and well-financed "outsider" to beat them.[21]

Ranney's general impressions can be confirmed at least in one extremely important case study, that of New York City over a period of thirty-five years (see Figure 5). During this period, the five counties that make up the City of New York included three of the best organized political parties in the United States: the New York County Democratic organization (otherwise known as Tammany Hall), the Kings County (Brooklyn) Democratic organization, and the Bronx Democratic organization. The parties in the other counties, Queens and Richmond (Staten Island), were well organized also, though probably did not qualify as machines. As Figure 5 shows, there has been a spectacular increase in the number of contested nominations since the 1940s. (Actually it began in the 1930s.) The unevenness of the trend lines is attributable to the fact that odd-numbered years are strictly local election years, whereas even-numbered years involve either gubernatorial or presidential elections. But the overall direction is very clear, and by the 1970s party leader control of nominations was the exception, not the rule. Meanwhile, at the state level (not included in Figure 5) the Democratic organization had weakened to such an extent that it was unable after 1958 to withstand the reform efforts to convert the New York state nominating procedures from conventions to primaries. Since nomination by primaries is so much more difficult to control than nomination by conventions, the failure

---

[21]Austin Ranney, *Curing the Mischiefs of Faction: Party Reform in America* (Berkeley: University of California Press, 1975), pp. 129-30.

Figure 5. Democratic nominations contested in New York City primaries

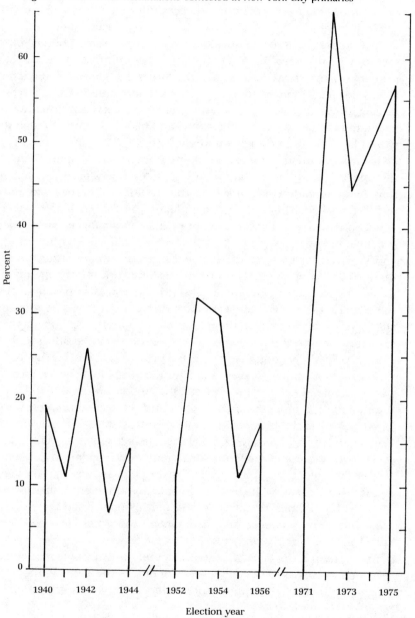

of party leaders to prevent the adoption of primary laws for state nominations after years of having successfully fought them off is in itself indicative of a significantly weakened party organization.

This points again to the question of causation. Many political observers would agree with V. O. Key that "the adoption of the direct primary opened the road for disruptive forces that gradually fractionalized the party organization. . . . [T]he primary system freed forces driving toward the disintegration of party organizations and facilitated the construction of factions and cliques."[22] But although it would be difficult to disagree entirely with Key, it seems to me that he is correct only up to a certain point. Primaries were immediately disruptive of party organization only in states where party organizations were already weak or where the tradition of parties was not well established. This was, for example, true in the weak-party state of Wisconsin, the first state to adopt primaries as a formal statewide practice. But many state party organizations adjusted to primaries and survived for quite a while after the reform was imposed upon them. Take Tammany Hall and the other New York county organizations. The system of nomination by primaries was imposed upon them in 1911. Yet, even 30 years later the party organizations were still able to control most of the nominations, both by minimizing the number of contested primaries (as shown on Figure 5) and also by working effectively enough in contested primaries to win for the "regular" designee. Indeed it was only after the 1950s that the New York party organizations became so weak that they were unable to keep the nominating process under control and the leadership began to avoid making endorsements in primary contests. Most younger political scientists and journalists, let alone citizens, will not even be familiar with the use of the terms "insurgent" and "regular" in the context of the nominating process. The main point here is that though primaries have always been a democratizing, therefore a disruptive force, within political organizations, *as long as parties had a solid grip on government, the leadership had enough resources to maintain a relatively strong grip on its most important decisions, nominations.*

Rather than a single causal direction, there is probably an interactive effect here. As parties became peripheral to government, they no longer could effectively oppose such democratizing reforms as nomi-

[22]Key, *Politics, Parties,* p. 342.

90

nation by primaries, and once primaries were adopted, parties found it increasingly difficult to adapt to them. Then as parties lost their grip on the nominating process, it became more and more difficult for them to maintain a significant place at the center of government, and they were pushed further toward the periphery. In some states this spiraling effect was immediate. In others, as in New York, it took a fairly long time. But it has happened to different degrees everywhere, and to the extent that it has happened, there is a looser and more fluid relation between citizens and the government. Democratization of the parties has also opened them up to many citizens whose attachments to them are weak or even nonexistent. For instance, in many states with "open primaries," voters who are neither enrolled in a party nor have any particular affinity for it can decide to vote in the primary at the last minute, if there is an exciting contest or if they have an opportunity to vote for the weaker candidate in order to ensure victory for the candidate of the opposing party. Finally, and ironically, as Nelson Polsby and others have shown, voters who participate in primaries are of higher average income, have far higher average education, and are much younger, much whiter, and in general more in the mainstream than those who on the average participate in general elections.[23] But for our purposes here, the important image to convey is fluidity—increasing fluidity.[24]

The moorings of the voters are now so loose that, regardless of any partisan consistency displayed in local elections (which is lessening too), their relationship to the presidency is highly personal. This helps to account for the fact that, although there is a substantial majority of Democratic voters, this majority is almost never reflected in the votes for president. In six of the ten presidential elections since 1948, the fall-off has been enough to elect Republicans. Fluidity also helps to account for the fact that in the August following each convention there has been a very wide opinion spread between the Dem-

[23]Nelson Polsby, "Reform of the Party System and the Conduct of the Presidency," in James Sterling Young, ed., *Problems and Prospects of Presidential Leadership in the 1980s* (Lanham, Md.: University Press of America, 1982), pp. 103-21, esp. p. 109.

[24]"The decline of partisan strength affects all conclusions reached by [the major voting studies]. Even if party identification still served as an important 'perceptual screen,' fewer voters would have strong screening mechanisms . . . [and] the reduced proportion of strong partisans . . . would mean that a larger proportion of the electorate would be susceptible to short-term political forces. . . . [W]e must now conclude that the prospects for instability have increased": Paul R. Abramson, *Political Attitudes in America* (San Francisco: W. H. Freeman, 1983), p. 75.

ocratic and Republican nominee that in all but one case (McGovern) has very significantly narrowed by election time. When the spread has favored the Republican, the Republican has won, and vice versa. But all this suggests that the personal appeals of the presidential candidates make a great deal of difference in the vote.[25] Fluidity also partly explains why presidential candidates gain or lose nationally without regard to the amount of money or campaigning devoted to voters in a particular state: as one researcher into political behavior put it, "National culture overwhelms local considerations in a presidential election. . . . The relative level of spending in a state between two [presidential] candidates doesn't matter."[26] Fluidity. National fluidity.

Confirmation of the Future: The Revolution in Expectations

During the 1960s, another kind of behavioral pattern began to emerge from the surveys of the commercial and the academic polling organizations. Up until that time, when a pollster asked a sample of respondents such a question as "How much of the time do you think you can trust the government in Washington to do what is right?" about 75 percent responded positively, that the government in Washington could be trusted to do what is right "just about always" or "most of the time." Roughly the same response patterns appeared up through 1964.[27] Since then, however, positive responses to that type of question have been dropping. One researcher, using a more sophisticated four-item "index of political trust" demonstrated that, with some variations depending on which party holds the White House, there has been a steady decline of political trust from those earlier highs of over 70 percent downward sharply toward 45 percent in 1974. By 1978 the average level of trust for Democrats was slightly over 40 percent and that of Republicans around 35. By 1980 both had dropped to 35 percent or below, with "strong Republicans" giving a 19 percent response to the political-trust index.[28]

[25]"Opinion Roundup," *Public Opinion* (New York: American Enterprise Institute, June/July 1984), pp. 40-41.

[26]Gary Jacobsen, quoted in Ronald Brownstein, "Public Seeing Campaign through Eyes of the TV Cameras," *National Journal*, September 22, 1984, p. 1757.

[27]Abramson, *Political Attitudes in America*, p. 193.

[28]Ibid, pp. 198-99.

These studies eventually reached the attention of President Jimmy Carter. Carter had obviously instinctively sensed this decline in trust; in 1976, he had taken as one of his major campaign themes his effort to restore trust in government and to make it "as good as the American people." In a famous speech of July 15, 1979, he confronted his own failure to reverse the trend, and cited a "crisis of confidence [that] strikes at the very heart and soul of our national will." He recognized "widespread public perception that our institutions are not performing well," stressing "an increase in cynicism," the "distrust of young adult voters," and an "American malaise."

Since dramatic trends of this sort are rarely found in statistical studies, these were bound to attract a great deal of attention and controversy. In their book *The Confidence Gap*, the ubiquitous Seymour Martin Lipset and coauthor William Schneider attempt a synthesis. They reexamined virtually every major poll as far back as polls go and even tried to pierce the attitudinal fog of the era before the 1930s by reviewing relevant impressionistic studies. In what is as close to a definitive work on the subject as we are likely to get, they confirmed what they called the decline of confidence, showing not only that the decline began in the mid 1960s but that there were no signs of its bottoming out. This is the "confidence gap," which is a result of distrust coupled with a weak sense of personal political efficacy—that is to say, distrust plus loss of *self*-confidence. And the confidence gap divides not only the people and big government but also the people and big business, big labor, the professions, the churches, and educational institutions. The gap is deep as well as wide, and its presence is felt in all walks of life, all occupational groupings, age groupings, and educational levels. There have been some signs of an upward turn in 1983-84, but not enough as yet to ease the concern Lipset and Schneider expressed at the conclusion of their book: "The United States enters the 1980s . . . with a lower reserve of confidence in the ability of its institutional leaders . . . than at any time in this century. . . . Although the evidence on the surface seems reassuring, there are disturbing signs of deep and serious discontent."[29]

Nonetheless, despite so clear and consistent a story given by all the major polls during the past twenty years, the findings can be misin-

[29]Seymour Martin Lipset and William Schneider, *The Confidence Gap* (New York: Free Press, 1983), pp. 411-12.

terpreted. Lipset and Schneider give one case of such misinterpretation, in a fascinating reanalysis of attitudes in the context of California's Proposition 13 of 1978, the first great popular movement against taxation in our epoch. Lipset and Schneider argue that the success of the referendum was seen by Carterites and Reaganites as a rejection of government. They show, however, that a closer look will reveal that those who favored drastic reduction in government's taxing power *tended all the same to favor most of the programs of government.* Still further probing suggested that many of the respondents to the polls assume that financing for the programs could come from greater efficiency. Thus, it was performance, not government itself, that was deemed the failure.[30]

Insightful as *The Confidence Gap* is, however, the authors themselves have provided only one interpretation of the data and, in my opinion, far from the best one, because they continue to accept the phenomenon being studied as indicative of lack of trust or confidence in *government.* Two insights that flow directly from their book and from the studies on which it is based suggest a different approach. The first insight is that government, business, and labor—all big institutions—are tied together in the public mind. Many political scientists and historians would call this corporatism, or corporate capitalism, to convey the idea that each major institution supports the other under broad government sponsorship. Large-scale surveys suggest that ordinary people are beginning to get the same idea. In other words, the ordinary citizen, who is fairly rational and knowledgeable, has begun to see as "public" all institutions holding great power.

The second insight is that all big institutions are judged in the public mind in terms of the services they render rather than the power that they hold. For example, in one of the most important studies cited by Lipset and Schneider, over 50 percent of the respondents polled rated the top three obligations of business as: serving the public interest, producing, and providing jobs.[31] Obligations to make a profit and to serve the stockholders were far down the list. Thus, firmly embedded in the public mind is the relatively new idea that institutions, including government, are to be trusted and ac-

---

[30]Ibid., pp. 342-46. Their interpretation is confirmed by occasional reports in *Public Opinion,* a bimonthly journal published by the pro-Reagan, anti-national government American Enterprise Institute .

[31]Lipset and Schneider, *Confidence Gap,* p. 174.

corded legitimacy not in terms of the effort they make or in terms of the amount and character of the representation they provide but in terms of service delivery. The same kinds of attitudes are held in regard to big business and big labor—not antagonism toward the institutions themselves but toward their performance: What have they done for us *lately?*

Therefore, an interpretation perfectly in accord with the data but very much at odds with the "confidence gap" is a *sense of vigilance toward public objects* and a *rational evaluation of public agencies in terms of the actual promises made by those agencies.* Mainstream ideology, once deeply anti-statist, has been revised over the past three or four decades to redefine the state as virtuous and to reorient expectations of government agencies in terms of the government's own assertion of responsibility for all aspects of society's welfare. This is the new social contract alluded to earlier. If the contract is to be based on service delivery, rather than arrangements for or degrees of representation, then it is only natural and rational for the typical citizen to reduce the level of trust in government to a point where each government service can be judged rationally in terms of its adequacy and timeliness, the distribution of costs and other burdens it entails, and the service's distribution in terms of overall social needs, social classes, and so on. It is very probable that such a democracy —let us call it a "services democracy"—would have as one of its standard characteristics a low level of trust in general within which the evaluation of particular services would vary according to the distribution of specific approval and disapproval ratios.

This seems to be precisely what is happening. Ronald Reagan entered national government at a time when about 75 percent of the American people expressed *dis*trust in it. But those same respondents were highly variable in their views of each of the specific policies associated with President Reagan. First of all, 67 percent of a 1984 Harris Survey sample responded that it was "fair to judge Reagan [and presumably any other president] on the basis of the success of his specific policies." At that time, 68 percent of the sample judged his policy of sending Marines to Lebanon a failure, 66 percent judged his efforts to get nuclear arms reduction a failure, and 59 percent judged his efforts to help those hit hardest by recession a failure. Overall, they tended to like President Reagan, and 53 percent believed that he had had more successes than failures. About the same percentage approved generally of the way he was doing his job as

95

president. But they went on judging *specific* policies and actions rather severely.

How these attitudes add up at election and reelection time is not at issue here. The main point here is that the new regime—this Republic of Service Delivery—has developed a relatively discerning citizen who looks rationally, skeptically, and distrustfully on the services being rendered by its institutions. And it is important for present purposes to add that citizens look directly at government and government services, no longer through the prismatic representational lenses of a political party.

This is no "malaise." And it will not go away with good PR. It will not go away even with improved government services, although some of the indicators turned upward in response to the upturned economy of 1983-84. It is the new relationship, a rational relationship directly between government and citizen that is a reflection of and an adjustment to the new social contract.

A few summary observations will point the analysis directly toward the plebiscitary presidency. First, the four dimensions involved in changed participation indicate a specialized and separate presidential constituency. This is what the president inherits by becoming the center and the embodiment of the modern positive state. Second, political parties are at the periphery, sometimes successful at maintaining a connection with voters for local offices but in general unable to maintain any regular, policy-relevant relationship among its own candidates and between them and the voters. Third, citizens have learned to look directly at government and to evaluate the government and shape their votes in terms of service delivery. In the Second Republic, the government has become its own politics. Agencies are its parties. We grow accustomed to speaking of agencies developing their constituencies. It is perfectly normal for government to print the electoral and primary ballots. It is no longer newsworthy for government to subsidize the presidential elections and the campaigns for presidential nominations. Finally, since the president has become the embodiment of government, it seems perfectly normal for millions upon millions of Americans to concentrate their hopes and fears directly and personally upon him. It is no wonder that United States has developed such a tremendous stake in the "personal president" and his personal capacity to govern.

5

The Future Is Here:
The Plebiscitary Presidency

**The larger a community becomes the less does it seem
to respect an assembly, the more is it attracted by an individual man. A bold President who knew himself to
be supported by a majority in the country, might be
tempted to override the law, and deprive the minority of
the protection which the law affords it. He might be a ty-
rant, not against the masses, but with the masses. But
nothing in the present state of American politics gives
weight to such apprehensions.**

—James Lord Bryce, 1889

The displacement of parliamentarianism by executive
government is surely one of the most significant world political developments of the twentieth century. Democracies as well as authori-
tarian regimes have become executive governments. In this light, the
Second Republic of the United States may be seen as an inevitable
product of history—Congress tardily responding because of the Depression with broad delegations of power to the executive branch
and continuing to do so after the emergency had passed.

Putting the American Second Republic alongside other parliamentary democracies, such as Britain or France, may at first seem reassuring in its consonance with historical development: Government
has everywhere come to be centered in the executive; executives can
be as democratic as legislatures, if not more so. However, direct comparison to the parliamentary democracies falls down rather quickly.

97

Although all have centered more and more on the executive, and although their legislatures have relegated themselves to secondary positions as institutions of consensus rather than as creative bodies, the United States is distinctive in one special and problematic respect: *The United States is the one major democracy without some kind of system of collective responsibility.*

As early as 1889, Lord Bryce was remarking upon the distinction between the British "government" and the American "administration" as the collective label for the head of government and his ministers. When the British refer to the "government" they have in mind a collective reality. In the United States, the "administration" is a collection, not a collectivity. Its accumulation of executive powers came at the expense of collective responsibility.

The American Constitution does not recognize a cabinet. Article II makes mention of "Heads of Departments" and provides that these are to be appointed by the president with the consent of the Senate. But that is about as far as it goes. These Heads of Department have no collective identity nor were they ever given any collective function. Recent presidents have made public efforts to utilize their cabinets as collective bodies; but these attempts are usually made early in an administration and quickly abandoned. The only collective aspect of the top political appointments in Washington is that attributed by outside observers attempting to read into the pattern of appointments the character or nature of the president's political coalition and the extent to which it has any class, ethnic, religious or, for that matter, ideological orientation. There is so little collectivity among the top appointees that few of them know the president well before their appointment, almost none of them have had any dealings, political or otherwise, or extensive acquaintance with each other, and there is nothing on record to suggest that many of them become well acquainted during their actual service in office. To appropriate a powerful concept from Hugh Heclo, we truly have a "government of strangers." According to Heclo, "most political appointees come and go quickly and they are engaged much of the time in trying to get some leverage over the behavior of their nominal subordinates."[1]

---

[1]Hugh Heclo, *A Government of Strangers: Executive Politics in Washington* (Washington: Brookings, 1977). This particular passage is a paraphrase of Heclo's impressions by Randall Ripley and Grace Franklin, *Bureaucracy and Policy Implementation* (Homewood, Ill.: Dorsey, 1982), p. 55.

They must take up their very heavy administrative responsibilities immediately, and thus they have neither basis nor opportunity for discovering or developing a collectivity once they have been appointed.

The Second Republic of the United States has gone a step beyond the distinction made by Lord Bryce. The center of responsibility is neither "the government" nor "the administration," but the presidency—or what we have come to call the institutional presidency. The lines of responsibility run direct to the White House, where the president is personally responsible and accountable for the performance of the government. It might be worth saying that there is also no compensating source of collective responsibility in the American political parties, but in parliamentary democracies cabinet and party responsibility are inextricably intertwined. In any practical sense, it is difficult to imagine the one without the other.

There is no need to idealize the British system or the American past. Since World War II, the British have come close to the ideal of collective responsibility but have little to be proud of as far as governmental effectiveness is concerned. Under our own traditional system, there was little need to have or develop a collective cabinet or a responsible party because the national government had so little to be collective or responsible about. But none of this weakens the case for collective responsibility. In this and succeeding chapters we will witness the mischievous consequences of its absence.

Presidential government began as an effort to solve the problem of effectiveness. Because of the president's ability to bring national power into focus and to implement national policy energetically, presidential government offered a means of confronting and even counterbalancing large institutions in the private sector. But as with most complex situations, today's solution is likely to be tomorrow's problem, and in fact, at least five problems of presidential government have already been identified. The first is the concentration of government in the presidency. Associated with this is the refocusing of mass expectations upon the presidency, indeed the person of the president. A third but related problem is the redefinition of democracy as delivery. A fourth is the weakening of the one type of group that stood between the government and the masses, the political parties.

With the pushing of parties toward the periphery of politics, the fifth problem can be seen: The vacuum left by the parties has been filled by what have come to be called the "special-issue groups" and by the masses.

There probably are no more interest groups today than in the past; and most of those in the past were special-issue groups as are those of the present. The difference today is, and the reason why people speak of them as a new problem, is because interest groups now enjoy direct and unmediated access to the president and the administrative agencies. Traditionally, interest groups went to Congress and competed with each other for access. This process is called lobbying. Today, more and more such politics is played directly in the executive branch, for the attention of the President and the agencies. It is now so commonplace it needs a label. I propose to call it *corridoring*.

Related to this problem of direct access for special-issue groups is the more general phenomenon of direct participation by groups and by masses of individuals. In the late 1960s there were frequent and strident demands for what was then called participatory democracy. These came from the political right as well as the left. Although fewer of these demands are being made today, at least in the United States, the phenomenon persists: Without effective political parties and with direct group access now common and legitimized, there was naturally a clamor on the part of many thousands of individuals to gain for themselves individually what organized groups seem to have gained. Some direct access for individuals is provided by the requirement of hearings and other public decision-making processes. Some is also provided by government use of public opinion polls. The polls have themselves become a vital aspect of direct representation in government. All the methods of accommodating group demands and mass opinions are democratizing. But they also tend toward fragmentation, not responsibility.

The problems thus far identified are either problems inherent in presidential government, or those imposed on presidential government by people who were concerned about its possible excesses. But all of them are part of a newly emergent institution; they are not discrete phenomena. What remains is to see how they interact, shaping the structure of the institution and the conduct of each president. The most dynamic manifestation of this complex interaction is the presidential selection process.

As presidential candidates participate in the selection process, they contribute something socially and politically important that goes well beyond their own goal of being nominated and elected. Being elected is the immediate and intended outcome of the process, that which motivates all the candidates. But social scientists are quick to distinguish between intended and unintended consequences, between the manifest functions and the latent functions of any repeated actions.

One of the broader, unintended consequences of the selection process during most of the traditional period was that it contributed to—virtually created—the national party system and consistently reinforced the national two-party system. For roughly three out of every four years, political parties were entirely localized phenomena; national parties drifted in the shadows of the undead. During the fourth year of each quadrennium, the requirements of presidential selection brought the local parties and state political elites together, and the result was usually some fairly meaningful continuity within each of the two parties across the entire nation. This seems to have been true even in the 1896–1932 period, when most of the states were one-party systems. Thanks to the presidential selection process, these local and state parties melded into a workable national two-party system—even though the reality was in fact two competing one-party systems. The United States owed its effective two-party system almost entirely to the unplanned integrative influence of the presidential selection process.

With the advent of big government, the nature of the presidential selection process's consequences for the political system began to shift. The shift is reflected in the vocabulary change, from "party rebuilding," to "coalition building." The most notable result was the "Roosevelt coalition." Though it is true that Roosevelt was also a party builder who attempted to transform the Democrats into a modern programmatic party, his political failures are associated with his efforts at party building and his political successes with his role as a broker among interests. It is also true that the Roosevelt coalition was formed and maintained largely within the Democratic party. But the units of interest mattered more than the party bosses. That is to say, the Democratic party became more a broad umbrella under which a collection of interests centered around the presidency, and less an organization comprised of geographically separate units pulled together for the presidential election every four years.

101

That Roosevelt's coalition within the Democratic party was a transitional phenomenon rather than a new political system can now be seen in light of additional years of perspective. The weaker the party structures became, the more difficult it was to join interest units in a stable coalition within the parties. Presidential candidates went on through the 1950s and 1960s trying to "rebuild" the Roosevelt coalition or to form new coalitions around middle class and corporate interests, or around the sun belt versus the frost belt, and so on. There continued throughout that period to be talk of critical elections and party realignments, as though the shifting of interests was continuing to take place within a party framework.

Journalist Samuel Lubell offered some of the most brilliant on-the-scene analyses of the consequences for parties and elections of the Roosevelt revolution and the Roosevelt coalition. It is all the more remarkable in that he was writing in 1952, before Eisenhower's election, trying to anticipate a political world in which the Roosevelt coalition was a new principle of organization that would be adapted to the changing realities of a post-Roosevelt world. Lubell didn't bother interviewing the party bosses, who traditionally built the local and state organization into a presidential party every fourth year. Instead he concentrated on interests and issues, and saw the main conflicts being fought out among interest leaders within the majority party. As some interests won out, others that were frustrated would be chipped off into the minority party, contributing to its rise as the new majority coalition. There could, within his "new theory of political parties," be a combination of organized interests operating within parties giving us political change and adaptation within a party system.[2] Many analysts continued until after 1972 to expect another critical realignment of the political parties. But subsequently most of them came to the conclusion that we had entered a new era in which there might no longer be a critical election with a critical realignment. Note the reasons for this turn of history as provided by the most important of the analysts:

> The American electorate . . . is undergoing a critical realignment of a radically different kind from any in American electoral history. This critical realignment, instead of being channeled through political parties as in

[2]Samuel Lubell, *The Future of American Politics*, 2d ed. (New York: Doubleday Anchor, 1956), ch. 10.

the past, is cutting across older partisan linkages. . . . [It is] a critical realignment to end all critical realignments . . . a realignment whose essence is the end of two-party politics . . . a point in time at which we close a very old volume of history and open a brand new one.[3]

Burnham gives a less satisfactory picture of political life beyond party. That picture can be best provided by going back and taking a closer look at the presidential selection process, since it is both a cause and a reflection of the broader politics of which it is a part. The question is: If the selection process once contributed to the construction and maintenance of parties and the two-party system; and if somewhat later the presidential selection process contributed to the construction of interest-group coalitions within a party framework; then what does the selection process contribute to now?

The New Selection Process

Within less than twenty years of the Founding, government and politics had so changed that the selection process had to be altered. The Twelfth Amendment was an effort to make such an adjustment. Within twenty years of that, government had again changed to such an extent that the selection process was once more readjusted, this time from King Caucus to the convention system of nomination. Within twenty years of the Roosevelt Revolution, government and politics had again changed so much that the selection process had once again to be altered. No one had a particular new shape for it in mind. A succession of adjustments by degree accumulated to result in a fundamental change in principle.

From the advantage of hindsight it is possible to appreciate now that adjustments were already beginning in the 1940s and 1950s as state laws and party rules began to provide for the selection of increasing proportions of delegates through primaries. Nonetheless, a delegate by and large remained, in the words of Tammany leader Ed Costikyan, "the property of his leader." State party leaders continued to have the power; sometimes the presidential nominees were not

---

[3]Walter Dean Burnham, "American Politics in the 1970s: Beyond Party?" in W. N. Chambers and W. D. Burnham, *The American Party Systems*, 2d ed. (New York: Oxford University Press, 1975), pp. 308–9.

mentioned at all during the period when the delegates were chosen. In those instances where there was a general state-wide "preference primary," the choice of candidate was usually a separate item on the ballot, in no way legally binding on the delegates who were elected at the same time. Preference primaries were indeed often referred to as beauty contests because of their lack of bearing on party leader control of the state delegations to the nominating conventions. In 1952, fewer than 15 percent of the delegates to the Democratic and Republican conventions were elected in primaries in which they were pledged to vote for a particular candidate at the conventions. The remaining roughly 85 percent of the delegates were chosen in various ways, including primaries, but were tied to their delegations and did not function individually. By 1968, however, 17 states provided for pledged delegates, who comprised over 30 percent of the respective Democratic and Republican nominating conventions. By 1972, 53 percent were delegates pledged to a candidate (from 23 states); in 1976, 68 percent of the delegates were so pledged (from 29 states); and in 1980, just under 74 percent (from 31 states) were elected according to pledges they made to their electorates. After 1976, the Democratic party went the ultimate distance by adopting its Rule F(3)c, which bound all convention delegates "to vote for the presidential candidate whom they were elected to support for at least the first convention ballot, unless released in writing by the presidential candidate." Following the 1980 elections, the Democratic party not only rescinded that rule but explicitly released all delegates from any formal obligation to follow their pledge. Therefore, the present interpretation of the rules in both parties is that delegates may run on a pledge to support a specific candidate and may be morally obligated to implement that pledge at the conventions but not legally or formally bound. But even with the formal changes toward permissiveness in the rules of the Democratic party prior to 1984, fewer than 25 delegates (of a total of nearly 4000) revoked their pledge on the first ballot—until Mondale had reached his majority and the opposing candidates stood at the podium and asked that the nomination be made unanimous.

Thus, rules to the contrary notwithstanding, the traditional system of delegates going as state units to be built upon by their state delegation leaders has been completely broken. Two experts on the nominating process put it this way: "By 1972, the linkage between candidate preference and delegate selection had been tightened so much that the free agents of past primaries—'favorite sons,' 'bosses,' and 'uncommitted' delegates—had almost disappeared."[4] This means that the presidential selection process has been permanently altered, and this alteration is equal in historic importance to the celebrated alterations following the crises of 1800 and 1824.

The new process of selection and its implications can be made clear in one general and composite picture, a picture that applies to either party when it does not control the White House. Like the traditional nominating process the new one begins toward the end of the third year of the presidential cycle, with leading politicians testing out the possibilities of becoming presidential candidates. In recent years the typical candidate has been a senator, but the governorship remains an important source of candidacies. The candidacy is announced, and then there follows the scramble for early endorsements and media attention. The campaign begins in earnest as the earliest states approach the day for making delegate choices—usually starting in February of the presidential election year, most often in Iowa and New Hampshire.

In the early "straw polls," caucuses, and primaries, the important goal for any aspirant is to do better than predicted by the major polling agencies and the most prominent journalists. More vital than winning over other candidates is winning over "expectations." On the basis of these early victories over expectations, the more successful candidates attract some of the smart money, and this enables them to finance the campaign in the next set of primaries. The number of candidates may begin to decline after the first or second round of primaries, but the goal remains the same for those who stay in—to attract enough of the smart money to keep the volunteers at work and to impress a few more state and local political activists, in order to bootstrap the campaign toward additional delegates. Federal laws enacted in the wake of Watergate attempted to relieve nomination candidates of some of the burdens of dependency on rich political opportunists, the source of the so-called smart money. Federal formulas provide public funds to match individual contributions of up to $250 for presidential candidates in the pre-convention campaigns.

[4]James Lengle and Byron Shafer, quoted in Nelson Polsby and Aaron Wildavsky, *Presidential Elections: Strategies of American Electoral Politics*, 5th ed. (New York: Scribner, 1980), p. 84.

105

But even if one takes into account only the legally and formally reported funds, federal subsidies provided for only 27.8 percent of the pre-convention expenditures in 1980, and about 30.5 percent in 1976. Some of the remaining money comes from PACs and the rest from borrowing. The latter is usually a subterfuge for donations outside the wording of the law, because drawing accounts are set up for candidates with no expectation that the amount spent will ever be entirely repaid.[5] Thus, despite the federal efforts, each campaign in each state is a struggle for electoral success to get money and a struggle for money to meet the next electoral challenge.

During the early primaries in particular, positioning is also of great importance. Although candidates are not free to vary their policy positions at will, the extreme decentralization of the selection process permits them to adjust their approaches and styles, and these adjustments have policy implications. The successful candidate is usually the one who is sufficiently apart from the others on the left-right spectrum, without being on the fringe, where there are few voters. Luck is a factor, but a great deal of conscious maneuver is involved. Carter in 1976 had the center-right to himself in the all-important New Hampshire primary, partly because of Senator Henry Jackson's late entry into the presidential race and partly because Carter deliberately distanced himself from the liberals Morris Udall and Birch Bayh. In largest part because of this split, Udall came in second in six primaries, three of them very close losses to Carter. Carter was already being marked a winner by the time Jackson intruded into the space on center-right. In 1980, Ronald Reagan's position on the right of the Republican party, distant from all his adversaries except the nonentity, Representative Philip Crane, was of fundamental importance to his success. Attacks by the liberals on Reagan's policies, such as George Bush's criticism of Reagan's "voodoo economics," did not help the liberals against each other.

Candidates move thusly from one state primary to the next, accumulating delegates and money and delegates while at the same time trying to impress the major journalists that they are doing better

[5]Good treatments with figures will be found in Michael J. Malbin, ed., *Money and Politics in the United States: Financing Elections in the 1980s* (Chatham, N.J.: Chatham House, 1984); an excellent evaluation of the easy ways available to avoid the letter and spirit of the campaign finance laws will be found in Brooks Jackson, "Loopholes Allow Flood of Campaign Giving by Business, Fat Cats," *The Wall Street Journal*, July 5, 1984, pp. 1 and 16.

than expected. All of this routine is now so commonplace that it tends to mask a very significant pattern, central to the new nominating process. Gerald Pomper provides an opening to a fresh look beneath the surface with an observation made following the 1980 campaign: "Aspirants to the White House no longer needed to win the favor of party leaders; they could take their case directly to the voters in these primaries. . . ."[6]

It is extremely important to emphasize here that presidential candidates can lay claim to very few acquaintances in the typical state as they enter to campaign for its delegates. They may line up a few in-state residents at the start of the campaign, but they all bring with them a number of energetic volunteers, often students, from outside the state to help and to attract residents who will become delegates and campaigners themselves. To the extent that they succeed, they not only impress the smart money and the journalists who keep them in the race; from state to state, the more successful candidates also actually amass delegates. But I must stress here again that while each candidate is building an acquaintance directly with the voters —unmediated by parties or party leaders—*the candidates rarely get to know the delegates they've won.* And, because of the great pressure to move on to the next state, the opportunity to get acquainted with the delegates after the primary takes place is just as limited as the opportunity beforehand. Even candidates with long periods of service in the Senate—who presumably can spread patronage as well as acquaintances throughout the country as soon as they are bitten by the presidential bug—even they may lack close or dependable acquaintances in many of the primary states.[7]

Another factor makes acquaintanceship still more superficial. As the party leadership has been pushed more to the periphery of the nominating process, more and more of the candidates for delegate

---

[6]Gerald Pomper, ed., *The Election of 1980* (Chatham, N.J.: Chatham House, 1981), p. 2.

[7]This situation has become even more serious in the past eight to twelve years, especially among Democratic candidates, due to a drastic decrease in the number of senators who participate as delegates in the nominating conventions. Howard Reiter reports that the number of Democratic U.S. senators participating as delegates dropped from a typical 70 percent in the 1950s and 1960s to a lowly 18 percent in 1976 and 13.8 percent in 1980. The rate of participation in conventions by Republican senators held up during that period, but of course until 1984 there were far fewer Republican senators to go around. Howard Reiter, "The New Age of Presidential Nominations," unpublished manuscript, University of Connecticut, 1984, Tables 4.4 and 4.5.

have been people entirely new to politics, especially presidential politics. For example, in 1948, 64 percent of the Democratic delegates and 63.9 percent of the Republican were attending a nominating convention for the first time. In 1952, 61 percent of the delegates of each convention were first-timers. This means that nearly 40 percent were repeaters with some experience and acquaintanceships in presidential politics—at a time when it did not matter much anyway, since the leadership in both parties was still very much in control. But during the very two decades when party leaders began to lose their control of the delegates, the number of first-timer delegates took a tremendous jump. In 1968 the number of first-timers was still about 65 percent in the two parties. In 1972 this figure had jumped to 83 percent among Democratic delegates and 78 percent among Republican delegates. In 1980 the percentages of first-timers were 87 and 84 respectively.[8]

After more than seven months, more than thirty primaries, and campaigns in a number of other states where selection by convention or caucus is no less demanding and the people no better acquainted, the surviving presidential candidates approach the convention with a collection—indeed a congeries—of delegates more or less pledged to themselves. The candidates have literally amassed their delegates. These delegates have almost nothing in common with the presidential candidate except their pledge. They have almost nothing in common with each other except their pledge. Delegates from the same state pledged to the same candidate hardly know each other, and few of them even have a common background of political party activity outside the presidential year. (How else to interpret the data reported by a succession of polls in 1984 that a very substantial proportion of the Hart delegates would not support Mondale if he were nominated, and a substantial proportion of Mondale delegates said the same in the case Hart were nominated?) Moreover,

---

[8]The figures for previous service as delegate are based upon careful estimates, by several scholars, of the delegate rolls provided by the two national committees. There are some discrepancies between sources as a consequence. However, the discrepancies in no way change the main point of the story, which is the absence of acquaintanceship and familiarity among participants. Sources include: Paul T. David, et al., *The Politics of National Party Conventions* (Washington: Brookings, 1960), pp. 349-50; James W. Davis, *National Conventions in an Age of Party Reform* (Westport, Conn.: Greenwood Press, 1983), p. 71; and Loch K. Johnson and Harlan Hahn, "Delegate Turnover at National Party Conventions," in Donald Matthews, ed., *Perspectives on Presidential Selection* (Washington: Brookings, 1973), p. 148.

if the delegates from the same state pledged to the same candidate have little connection with each other, even less do they have any connection or acquaintance with delegates pledged to the same candidate selected from other states. When the primary season is all over, the nominating conventions are little more than an accumulation, an amassing of the delegates chosen in separate campaigns by separate strategies and separate understandings, gathered together to cast their vote more or less slavishly for their candidate. They are no longer the property of the state delegation leader. Although they now have an identity, they are largely reflections of the voters.

There are many fascinating stories about the struggle for the presidential nomination at traditional conventions. The most familiar is the 1920 Republican nomination story immortalized (and probably greatly embellished) by journalist Mark Sullivan. There are different versions of what was actually said by Harry Daugherty, the campaign manager for Warren Harding, but following is a fair representation of the prediction he made and then brought about:

> Well, there will be no nomination on the early ballots. After the other candidates have failed . . . the leaders, worn out and wishing to do the very best thing, will get together [about 2 o'clock in the morning around a table in a smoke-filled room]. . . . I will be with them and will present the name of Senator Harding. When the time comes, Harding will be selected, because he fits in perfectly. . . . He is the logical choice, and the leaders will determine to throw their support to him.[9]

The same sort of story can be told of one of our more scrupulous politicians:

Honorable Samuel Galloway   Chicago, March 24, 1860

My dear Sir:

I am here attending a trial in court. Before leaving home I received your kind letter of the 15th. Of course I am gratified to know I have friends in Ohio who are disposed to give me the highest evidence of their friendship and confidence. . . . My name is new in the field; and I suppose I am not the *first* choice of a very great many. Our policy, then, is to give no of-

---

[9]Most of the quote comes from Mark Sullivan, *Our Times* (New York: Scribner, 1935), VI, p. 37; the bracketed insert comes from a version preferred by the editors of John Bartlett, *Familiar Quotations*, 14th ed. (Boston: Little, Brown, 1968), p. 859a.

fense to others—leaving them in a mood to come to us, if they shall be compelled to give up their first love. This, too, is dealing justly with all, and leaving us in a mood to support heartily whoever shall be nominated. . . . Whatever you may do for me, consistently with these suggestions, will be appreciated, and gratefully remembered. Please write me again.

Yours very truly,
A. Lincoln[10]

The moral in these stories and many others like them is that party leaders were managers of the campaigns of presidential candidates, that they were able to control blocs of delegate votes, and that the votes of lesser candidates and "dark horses" could be combined so as to deprive a leading candidate of a majority, after which deals could be made leading to the victory on a later ballot of one of the lesser candidates. To paraphrase Lincoln, the goal was to be the *most widely shared second choice*. Most conventions went beyond one ballot, and those that did so were usually lost by the candidate who got the most first-ballot votes.

But stories about leaders bargaining with one another, about being the most widely shared second choice, and about second and third and fourth ballots all belong to the distant past. Such accounts of leadership strategy sound rather quaint today. The last Republican convention that went beyond the first ballot was the 1948 one, which Thomas Dewey took on the third ballot. The last Democratic convention that went beyond one ballot was in 1952, when Adlai Stevenson was nominated on the third. Stevenson is also the last candidate of either party who won the presidential nomination without entering most of the primaries and winning more pre-convention delegates than anyone else. Since 1952 there have been instances of uncertainty prior to the first day of a presidential nominating convention; nevertheless, the wit who said we could now hold our conventions by mail is no longer very far from the truth. Conventions are still worth the trouble and expense, but no longer because they settle the question of the presidential and vice presidential nominees. They are valuable as the first step in the presidential election campaign; they

[10]Quoted in James MacGregor Burns, "The Case for the Smoke-Filled Room," *New York Times Magazine*, June 15, 1952, p. 9; emphasis in original.

110

are worth millions in nation-wide publicity. And they are all the more valuable to the presidential candidates because a very large proportion of the millions of dollars needed to hold a convention is paid by the federal government. Immediately following the 1984 Democratic convention, and even before he had left San Francisco, New York's Senator (and former academic political scientist) Daniel Patrick Moynihan observed that "the convention does not decide and it does not debate. . . . [T]he nomination is settled before the convention begins. . . . We have to make up our arguments to have on the floor so that television has something to cover." He and his colleague Joseph F. Crangle, chairman of the Erie County Democratic Organization (Buffalo), observed that not only were convention results predetermined; the delegates "merely serve as scenery for the television cameras. Delegates cannot even introduce resolutions at the convention." They remarked further that the staffs of the major candidates have largely replaced the old-fashioned political bosses in keeping the delegates informed and telling them where, when, and how to vote. Many of the delegates, they reported, had not even been qualified for the ballot lot at the time of their selection, and had to make arrangements for that afterward. The fact that many were not even residents of the districts they represented suggested to these two professional politicians how superficial the whole process had become.[11]

However, Moynihan and Crangle put too much blame on the spread of the primaries and the post-1968 party reforms. There is no question that the post-1968 reforms contributed to the weakening of parties and their conventions, but these reforms contributed to and accelerated a decline *that was already in train*.[12] As I argued before, the introduction of reforms that severely weakened the parties was very much a reflection of the fact that political parties were already too weak to resist the reforms. Moreover, the Democratic party has already set up another reform commission for 1985 that will contribute still further to the weakening of the parties and of the major party

[11]Interview with Daniel Patrick Moynihan and Joseph Crangle by Frank Lynn, "Two New York Democrats Reflect on Importance of Conventions Past," *New York Times*, July 20, 1984, p. A10.

[12]Cf. Reiter, "The New Age of Presidential Nominations," passim. For an assessment of the degree and nature of the influence of the post-68 reforms, see Nelson Polsby, "Reform of the Party System and the Conduct of the Presidency," in James Sterling Young, ed., *Problems and Prospects of Presidential Leadership in the 1980s* (Lanham, Md.: University Press of America, 1982), pp. 103-21.

organ that has already become vestigial, the presidential nominating convention.

Because of the absence of party leaders, state party units, and an institution in which meaningful bargains can take place, the ultimate nominee of the so-called party does not possess a coalition, does not represent a coalition, and does not contribute in the quest for the nomination to the formation of a coalition. The very notion of a coalition is violated by the popular base of the presidential nominee. A coalition is a fusion of unlike parts, an association formed by compromising conflicts into an interdependent organization, with something of a common history, a common sense of purpose, and even a set of common goals. Such coalitions have been so difficult to put together that they have tended to last eight to twelve years. The popular base that results in the present selection process is not a coalition but an accumulation or an agglutination. The appropriate image is conveyed by the idea of candidates amassing delegates. We need a new term for the result, and I propose to call it a *flux*, a word drawn from physics that is intended to convey the picture of individual particles revolving around a center of gravity or flowing across a given point—independent particles with nothing in common but a temporary center of focus. This is the beginning point of the construction of the presidential constituency—this congeries or flux of delegates and other political activists who have almost nothing in common except the nominee and will last in any meaningful way only if the nominee is elected president.

The Campaign: The Making of the Plebiscitary President

The presidential campaign is a continuation of the personal relationship between the candidates and their popular base—only more so because the organization and strategies of each nominee have been validated by the nomination itself. Without uncertainty about the nomination, with full command of a veritable army of volunteers and services, and with a sense of presidential greatness already made palpable in the form of Secret Service protection for the candidates, the campaign is the time the true nature of the plebiscitary presidency—scale, celebrity, centricity, and isolation—can first be appreciated. Part of what stamps the office with its special character has already been seen: the separate campaign organization, the fourfold revolution in participation, and the directness of the relationship between the president and the people. These factors all come together during the campaign. At that time we can begin to see how they will affect the behavior and perspective of presidents.

Although the organization of a presidential campaign is an extension of the campaign organization of the primary season, there is a difference in that the apparatus of the national committee becomes the property of the nominee, as titular head of the party. The national committee, with its headquarters in Washington, is no resource to sneeze at. However, presidential candidates can find its apparatus as much a problem as an opportunity. Even when they name their own chairman, which is typical, candidates maintain their distance from the national committee. Although different personal reasons are offered for this strategy of separation, most candidates probably share a desire to stay as far away as possible from a body associated with the most recent president of their party. Most of them want to encourage Independents and affiliates of the opposite party to split their tickets for president, and this requires a soft-pedaling of the candidate's own association with the party. But whatever rational reasons exist, there is also the presidential mystique itself. A candidate for president must be above party. A candidate for president must, in the language of the theater, be a "single."

Being a single sets such a limit on personal appearances that every one has to be a media event. Richard Nixon made a terrible mistake in 1960 vowing to make an appearance in every state of the United States. No one is likely to follow him in that, but all candidates follow Nixon in another strategy, which was to speak "over the heads" of the press by using television. It is precisely because local stations and networks are media, not mediators, that candidates turn to television in their need to reach the people directly. At least half of all presidential campaign budgets is directed to mass communications, especially television. Expenditures for activities in the precincts including knocking on doors and passing out bumper stickers and buttons have been shrinking. So has the budget for local staff and for newspaper ads. In 1976, of just under $22 million officially spent by the Ford campaign, $10 million of it went to "media."[13] Almost an additional

[13]Stephen J. Wayne, *The Road to the White House: Politics of Presidential Elections* (New York: St. Martin's, 1980), pp. 171-72.

million dollars went to the conduct of polls, the input side of the mass communications loop. The 1980 Reagan campaign spent $14.5 million on TV and radio. (The figure for polling expenditures was not available.) The Carter campaign spent $20.5 million. In both instances the expenditures amounted to well over half of the money the two national campaigns officially controlled.[14]

Marshall McLuhan may have been exaggerating with his famous observation "the medium is the message," but it is undeniable that television has an effect on presidential candidates. Many traditional political tactics just do not work. Ted Kennedy found that his finger-jabbing histrionics were not as well suited for a television campaign for president as for a Massachusetts rally. As it turns out, what is required for good television is the same as what is required for a good plebiscitary presidency. This is not accidental.

Most presidential candidates have achieved a certain amount of presidential presence before their nomination. Virtually all of them have had long political careers, usually in the Senate or the governor's mansion, and have constantly been in the public eye. Although their announcement of their presidential candidacy some fifteen months before the election can come as a surprise to millions of Americans, it does not come as a surprise to them. They have had an opportunity to prepare themselves and their demeanor for the special status presidential candidacy confers. So we almost never have a chance to assess its impact upon their demeanor. However, 1976 did offer an opportunity, because no person could have been found anywhere in politics who was more modest and unprepossessing—less presidential—than Jimmy Carter. And the distance he traveled toward presidential demeanor must be attributed to the selection process or the presidency itself.

Carter's initial persona was one of complete modesty. This quality showed in everything from his self-deprecating sojourns as a modest guest in modest homes, carrying his garment bag over his shoulder, to his antagonism to Washington, to his antagonism to politics and politicians, to his antagonism to making promises. But once he did begin to approach the possibility of actually winning the Democratic presidential nomination, he began to be a great deal more presiden-

[14]Herbert E. Alexander, "Making Sense about Dollars in the 1980 Presidential Campaigns," in Malbin, *Money and Politics in the United States*, pp. 24-27.

tial, making the success or failure of government itself dependent upon his election, his own *personal* election. Carter began enlarging himself, in the promises he made and the rhetoric with which he made them. His vocabulary became more and more inflated and his references more and more personal. One study identified 111 promises Carter made during the primaries and the election campaign. As Theodore H. White put it, these promises "were fair and decent promises; they embodied of every hope of every group and institution that good-will people had created in reaving the old system. . . . No hope any liberal had expressed anywhere at any time would be ignored."[15]

Although Carter was not the first candidate to make unrealistic promises in highflown language, he was distinctly modern in making them immensely large and intensely personal. But nothing had prepared him for such an inflated and arrogant view of himself. Nothing had prepared him to state that the income tax was "a disgrace to the human race" and would be reorganized forthwith. Nothing had prepared him to state that he would put all agencies on a "zero base." Nothing had prepared him to say that he would reorganize welfare, reach all the poor and mistreated, clean up the environment forthwith, and also balance the budget within three years. The job and the process were doing it to him. It was happening before the inauguration in anticipation of the job. With his cardigan sweater and the silencing of the band playing "Hail to the Chief," Carter tried to maintain the aura of modesty after he took office. But there was a new factor, substantially and palpably, and that was *personality*. This is something he shared with his predecessors and his successor. The plebiscitary presidency is a personal presidency and that fact can already be seen in the campaign. The personality of the president— perhaps we should call it the personhood of the presidency, regardless of the character of the incumbent—is a combination of Jesus Christ and the Statue of Liberty: Bring *me* your burdens. Bring *me* your hopes and fears. Bring *me* your search for salvation.

The isolated, personal presidency can already be seen during the campaign in the practice of polling as well, and in the place of the pollster within the campaign organization. Although polling was important before the 1970s, pollsters were then either independent

[15]Theodore H. White, *America in Search of Itself* (New York: Harper & Row, 1982), pp. 196-97.

outsiders or technicians on the staff of the candidate. Pollster Louis Harris was probably the first to work as a close adviser to a candidate, John F. Kennedy in 1960. Patrick Caddell may have been the first pollster to occupy an official place as a policy and strategy adviser to a candidate. Caddell, who started as a pollster with George McGovern in 1972, joined Carter in 1975 and quickly became a strategist as well as a sampler. In 1976 and 1980, Caddell was in the inner circle that planned Carter's campaign, and he remained a close adviser while Carter was president.

Despite Ronald Reagan's greater experience in public relations and his greater confidence as a communicator to the masses, he employed a pollster in the same way. Richard Wirthlin became such an important adviser in 1980 that Reagan fired his chief strategist early in the nomination campaign and gave Wirthlin all the duties of chief strategist, theme developer, advertising targeter, and information processor. On the morning after election day in 1980, Wirthlin was one of the first Reagan leaders to be interviewed by the journalists of the networks and the large newspapers.

Some day we will probably look back to September 1980 as the moment when polling truly came of age: It was then that everyone in every party agreed to let John Anderson's participation in the presidential debates depend upon whether he got 15 percent support in the public opinion polls immediately prior to the staging of the first debate on national television. This probably marked the first public recognition that polling holds a major place in the decision-making process.

Polling did not create the direct and unmediated relationship between the president and the mass public. Like TV, polling is only a reflection of the new scheme of government already established under the Second Republic. It is merely the correlative of mass communications. But without polling, television would be insufficient, and television, once established, became the central nervous system of the modern plebiscitary presidency. An observation made toward the end of the 1976 presidential campaign by TV journalist Sander Vanocur deserves a great deal of reflection:

> This campaign *was* television. . . . If you look for the buttons, the bumper stickers, the billboards and other forms of political graffiti . . . you could not find them. Too expensive. Save the money for the media.

116

. . . I think this is a burden that television is not equipped to bear. The political process is too complicated . . . for a medium that is designed, perhaps unwittingly, to make brief claims on our attention span.

We have heard from the pundits in the press and on television that it has been a lackluster campaign, devoid of issues. But who is responsible? It is not the candidates. They would be fools if they tried to explore issues in a medium that measures out the world in 30-second takes . . . mocking any attempts at reasonable political discourse.[16]

Presidential Transition: Gestation Period of the Institutional Presidency

Just as the nomination validates the pre-convention machinery and the flux around it, the election validates that of the campaign. In fact, the independence from the political party and the absence of long-term political acquaintances and long-term coalitions can perhaps be seen better during the post-election period than at any other time.

The Transition period is now official, having been recognized by Congress with a $2 million plus appropriation. This is truly an expansion of the establishment of the new selection process. Where once the rotation of political appointments was considered an intrinsic part of party government—the spoils system at the top, where it has always been accepted as legitimate—this process now has official designation and government sponsorship. Significantly, the change began after 1960, at President Kennedy's urging. The Second Republic was deliberately developing a politics all its own.[17]

Official designation and a government subsidy do not change the fact that the president-elect has just under three months after the general election to make the appointments and related decisions that will give shape to his administration. The timing has become an important problem because the Transition Period is truly the gestation period; in the Second Republic, without the resources of a strong party, each president-elect must begin literally from scratch. Prior to 1952, before ratification of the Twentieth ("Lame Duck") Amendment, the four-month period between the November election

---

[16]Sander Vanocur, quoted in White, *America in Search of Itself*, pp. 193-94.

[17]Good coverage will be found in Richard Neustadt, *Presidential Power: The Politics of Leadership from FDR to Carter* (New York: Wiley, 1980), ch. 11.

117

and the March 4 inauguration seemed like a dangerously long time. As Neustadt put it in his 1980 reflections, "That timing looks marvelous today,"[18] when the entire administration, so many times larger, has to be put together in eleven weeks. Presidents-elect have tried their best to make a virtue of this necessity; and they may well be sincere about it. In the early Kennedy administration, the reference was to "the best and the brightest." With Jimmy Carter it was "nothing but the best." No doubt, each president-elect values the flexibility that comes with freedom from obligations to party leaders, members of Congress, and old hangers-on. Kennedy, being closer to the traditional period, actually tried some recruitment through party channels but very quickly replaced them with his own recruitment methods, which enabled him "mainly to go out and try to find people outside the normal political channels."[19]

The appointments made during the Transition are, therefore, in a direct line of continuity with the presidential politics of the pre-convention and the campaign periods. The most important part of this process is, of course, the cabinet-level appointments. At this level, very few appointees have any close working relationship at all with the president prior to appointment. Few cabinet-level appointees have had any business or personal connection with the president; and even fewer have had any ideological or programmatic relationship with him linking them together in factional struggles within their political party. Moreover, most cabinet-level appointees have been outsiders to Washington as well. Despite John Kennedy's fifteen years of service in Washington prior to his election, only two of his top appointees had significant national administrative experience, and few had any direct association with him. For example, he knew little about Secretary of State Dean Rusk beyond the fact that the appointment would enable Kennedy to be his own secretary of state. His secretary of the treasury, Douglas Dillon, was a Republican with no connection to the president-elect. The secretary of defense, Robert McNamara, was the chief executive officer of the Ford Motor Company and a total enigma as far as party politics was concerned. And so it went through most of Kennedy's top appointees, with the special exception of his attorney general (his brother). Even his budget director, David Bell, was brought to his attention by an academic

[18]Ibid., p. 219.
[19]Quotation from a Kennedy aide in Heclo, *A Government of Strangers*, p. 93.

adviser. As for sub-cabinet political appointments, Kennedy was if possible still less oriented toward party and acquaintanceship. Heclo reports that Kennedy cut the pattern for most of his successors by setting up a small network of evaluators around the country to send names to the transition team, along with confidential evaluations of those so nominated. Many of them were people with connections to the Democratic party, but that was simply one item of information rather than a reflection of a central party recruiting process. Since 1964, Kennedy's evaluation process has been systemized by his successors.[20]

Few of Nixon's cabinet appointees were insiders to national administration, and few were personally close acquaintances of Richard Nixon. For the large number of sub-cabinet political appointments Nixon seems to have been no more loyal to his party than were his two Democratic predecessors to theirs. Looking back on those three presidents from the post-Watergate perspective of 1976, Richard Neustadt observed that at least until the 1960s, political parties and the well-established political figures in Congress provided "fairly clear reference points to help reduce the uncertainties" of staffing in the cabinet and among the top political executives. He went on to observe that "what makes the instability of presidential staffing seem so stark today is that this stable context now has all but vanished, part of it declining with our party organizations, all the rest suspended by persistent ticket-splitting."[21]

President Carter, apparently to compensate for his own lack of experience, appointed eight cabinet members (of thirteen) who had had some federal administrative experience. But at the same time, Carter had almost no prior acquaintance with these appointees, and *almost none of them knew each other.* Neustadt reports that Carter put far more funds into personnel and "transition planning" than had any of his predecessors.[22] But this in no way changed the pattern. He had little to do with the outgoing president, Gerald Ford, and he remained steadfastly in Plains while a number of his top recruiters were in Washington. Part of the transition time was of course spent on programs and administrative decisions, but Carter was also

---

[20]Ibid., p. 90.

[21]Quoted in ibid., p. 92.

[22]Neustadt, *Presidential Power* (1980), p. 218. The Carter transition staff was six times the size of Kennedy's.

extremely careful about personnel recruitment. Nevertheless, his was a "government of strangers" even more than those of his immediate predecessors.

President Reagan had a slightly, but only slightly, greater than average degree of acquaintance with his top appointees. He made sixteen cabinet-level appointments, defining cabinet to include the major traditional heads of departments plus the UN representative, Special Trade Representative (STR) and the directors of the Office of Management and Budget and CIA. Of these, only five had by any measure been close to Ronald Reagan before 1980, and only three—Caspar Weinberger, William French Smith, and William Casey—go back with Reagan more than ten years. Two others—Richard Schweiker and Drew Lewis—grew close to Reagan during and after the 1976 abortive effort to win the nomination. Only one—Special Trade Representative William Brock—had a relationship to Reagan through the Republican party. At least five other top appointees were brought in to integrate the opposing factions of the Republican party, and none of these had had any prior relationship with President Reagan. At least two and possibly three of the remaining were truly nonpolitical, having neither personal nor party connection with Reagan, but displaying some ideological affinity through their writing or civic activity. These include UN Representative Jeane Kirkpatrick, Interior Secretary James G. Watt and Agriculture Secretary John R. Block.

Of equal if not greater importance is the fact that very few of these people knew each other prior to their appointments. And those who did have some acquaintance with each other had gained almost none of this through experience in Washington dealing mutually with questions of national and international management or policy. These top political executives are not unlike the delegates to the nominating conventions: They are generally newcomers and outsiders; they have little if any party experience; and they have almost nothing in common except their loyalty to or dependence upon the president. Thus, the "flux" of discrete particles around the center of gravity also seems to symbolize the political context as the president-elect assumes office. Neustadt quotes with approval an observation by Canadian/British political scientist Anthony King that the way to characterize government of the Carter period is "atomization."[23]

[23]Ibid., p. 212.

Though this term is a bit extreme, Neustadt suggests, in that it implies "undifferentiated dust," he nevertheless agrees that "it is useful shorthand for a number of developments in recent years."[24] Moreover, lest King or Neustadt convey the impression that atomization is particular to the Carter administration, let me beg to differ. Modern presidents vary only in the degree of atomization. None of them has shown an ability or inclination to avoid it.

Much the same thing could be said of the pattern of top appointments during the latter days of the traditional period. However, two important distinctions can be made. First, as late as 1951 it was still possible to see that appointments reflected the "bargaining necessities of the presidential nominating process or personal friendship."[25] Second, as the national government grew and modernized, the pattern of top appointments became more atomized, not less. The more the need for central management, the less of it there seemed to be. Today, Heclo notes, political executives "will have played little part in the election responsible for their presence in Washington. . . . The President's traditional handshake and photograph will be his way of saying both hello and goodbye."[26]

Plebiscites Plutocratized: The PACs

Election is the only relationship between the president and the public provided for by the Constitution and the laws. Political parties changed this by providing not only another relationship between the president and the public but also the means for it—in manpower as well as money. With the decline of parties, the president finally approached an unmediated relationship with the masses, but institutionalized means for dealing with it had to be developed.

A president has ample means of maintaining the mass relationship. The presidential press secretary is, of course, the most concrete representation of it; but he is only "the apex of a huge public relations apparatus in the Executive Branch which devotes an extraordinary amount of staff, resources, and time to generating a positive image of the president."[27] Estimates of the precise amount of staff and money

[24]Ibid.

[25]Leonard D. White, *Introduction to the Study of Public Administration*, 4th ed. (New York: Macmillan, 1954), p. 46.

[26]Heclo, *A Government of Strangers*, pp. 87-88.

[27]Reported in Raymond Tatalovich and Byron W. Daynes, *Presidential Power in the United States* (Monterey, Cal.: Brooks/Cole, 1984), p. 117.

121

spent on the president's relation with the masses are difficult to come by. One high-ranking official in the Ford administration estimated that more than 60 percent of the political staff's time was spent on one or another kind of presidential public relations. During the Carter administration, it was estimated that more than 30 percent of the 49 White House assistants making more than $40 thousand a year in 1977 were dedicated to media relationships.[28] And the expenditure of staff time is not the only calculation that would go into a proper estimate. White House space would have to be included as well as facilities and technology for radio and television and an internal staff concerned with coordinating the media activities of all of the executive agencies, especially the big media-oriented agencies like the Pentagon, NASA, the FBI, and the USIA.

However, these resources are not available until after the president is elected. Presidential candidates still have to find much of their own means, even though the cost of being plebiscitary is now borne in part by the national government. The principle of public funding of presidential elections was legally established in 1971 and was substantially expanded by the Federal Elections Campaign Act of 1974, in the wake of the campaign finance abuses of 1972, culminating in the Watergate scandal. Herbert Alexander, America's foremost expert on campaign money, estimates that of the $275 million spent in the 1980 presidential elections, about 37 percent—$100.6 million—was supplied by the federal government.[29] Alexander's estimates include $27.9 million in federal matching funds provided the Republican and Democratic candidates seeking the nomination and about $8.1 million subsidizing the two conventions. But we also know that (1) public funds are providing a decreasing proportion of the total amount spent on elections; and (2) the known and reported expenditures are a decreasing proportion of the total amount actually spent.

The burdens of being plebiscitary are all the heavier because of the severe limits on the ability of state and local political parties to participate in presidential elections at any phase. Evidence has already been presented to suggest that political parties have grown weaker at state and local levels. But even in states where parties still have some traditional muscle, they are constrained in the pre-convention

[28]Ibid.; see also Michael Grossman and Martha Kumar, *Portraying the President: The White House and the News Media* (Baltimore: Johns Hopkins University Press, 1981).
[29]Alexander, "Making Sense about Dollars," pp. 11-12.

period by internal factional division and tend to make a virtue of avoiding commitments among presidential candidates. After the convention and during the campaign itself, state and local parties are still severely limited in the amount of help they can offer. Federal Elections Campaign Act provisions include elaborate reporting requirements that discourage many parties from directly involving themselves in the national election. David Adamany reports that of almost 4000 jurisdictions in which local parties might organize, only 124 Democratic committees in 26 states and 186 Republican committees in 27 states actually registered in 1980 to spend money in presidential election campaigns. Since 1979, party committees have been exempted from reporting contributions under $1,000 and expenditures of more than $5,000 in behalf of presidential candidates for activities such as furnishing sample ballots and circulating bumper stickers and other materials.[30] Still, the local parties, even with the help of state parties and the Republican and Democratic national committees, simply do not have the manpower or the access to political money that can make them a significant and dependable force in plebiscitary presidential elections.

The only alternative for candidates was the private sector—in a word, the PACs. The same federal election campaign laws of 1971, 1974, and 1979 that liberalized government subsidies for elections also liberated the private sector, albeit in ways not wholly anticipated. For our purposes here, the most important feature of the new laws was the freeing of the labor unions and corporations to form "non-party committees." Thus, although the overall purpose of these laws was to weaken the political influence of special interests, the laws ended up making the situation worse.[31] Although a Supreme Court decision invalidated the provisions that sought to restrict individual contributions, contributions by individuals direct to campaigns did decline in favor of contributions to PACs.[32] The name

[30]David Adamany, "Political Parties in the 1980s," in Malbin, ed., *Money and Politics*, pp. 93–106.
[31]Michael Malbin, "Looking Back at the Future of Campaign Finance Reform," in Malbin, ed., *Money and Politics in the United States*, pp. 233-34.
[32]*Buckley* v. *Valeo*, 424 U.S. 1 (1976); Bruce F. Freed, "Political Money and Campaign Finance Reform, 1971-1976," in Jeff Fishel, ed., *Parties and Elections in an Anti-Party Age* (Bloomington: Indiana University Press, 1978), pp. 241–55; and John Green, "Federal Campaign Finance: Money, Representation, and Congressional Behavior," Ph.D. diss., Cornell University, 1980.

123

given to the basic unit of this new money-raising/spending industry was the Political Action Committee. Within a year of the 1971 legislation, there were 480 active PACs. By 1976 there were 1,146. By 1980 this number had grown to 2,010 and although the figures for 1984 were not known at this writing, that for early 1983 of 3,371 indicates that the growth trend has not yet leveled off.[33]

PACs now contribute a good deal more to national candidates than political parties do. For example, in 1980, PACs contributed $74.4 million to support and oppose candidates in federal elections while party committees gave only $6.2 million in contributions and $17.4 million in expenditures aimed directly at helping candidates—a difference of better than 3 to 1.[34] And, as I suggested earlier, this actually understates the case, because PACs as well as private individuals can extend further assistance to candidates and parties in ways that escape reporting requirements and therefore depress the totals offered here. First, a substantial proportion of gifts to national party committees are from top PAC donors cementing alliances between the PAC and the party. In 1981–82, one Dallas oilman gave $8,650 to Republican committees and $19,100 to major conservative PACs. Another was a Republican Eagle (a $10,000-a-year donor) and a $5,000 donor to the National Conservative PAC (NCPAC). Second, as reported earlier, candidates can be given loans in the form of drawing accounts at banks, where interest may in fact be charged, but where there is little if any expectation that the loans will eventually be paid back. (Even if they are paid back, the successful or unsuccessful candidates can take their own good time after the electoral necessities have passed.) Another method is what is now called "bundling." As an enterprising *Wall Street Journal* reporter put it, rather than gathering individuals' voluntary donations into its own bank account and writing PAC checks directly to candidates, sometimes a PAC urges its supporters to make out personal checks directly to a candidate's campaign. Legally, the donations can then be counted as coming from the individuals, and the $5,000 limit on PAC contributions to a particular candidate thus evaded. But the checks can then be gathered together—bundled—for delivery to the candi-

---

[33]Federal Election Commission, "Report on Financial Activity, 1977-78, Party and Non-Party Political Committees" (Washington, D.C.: Government Printing Office, 1979); and Adamany, "Political Parties," pp. 101-2.
[34]Adamany, "Political Parties," p. 102.

124

date, so that the PAC gets the credit though it does not have the legal reporting liability.[35] So that the impression be not left that all this activity is carried on by the new radical right PACs, it should be noted that the Council for a Livable World, a pro-freeze group, used the bundling technique to provide nearly $300,000 to nine of its high-priority Senate candidates in 1984.[36]

Another impressive fact is that PACs can provide funds at times and places where no other sources of political money are available. Candidates are most vulnerable at early points during the nominating process when party organizations are reluctant to make endorsements and every victory over "expectations" is critical. As Herbert Alexander has observed, candidate organizations focus "a disproportionate amount of time, energy, and money planning on making a showing that would trigger new financial and related support and would create a psychological impact that could be built upon to sustain the candidate through the remaining season of delegate selection."[37] This problem is exacerbated by the legal limits for spending in each state, a limit pegged to the state's voting-age population. These spending limits have forced presidential candidates not only to depend upon PACs but to conspire with them to evade the spirit of campaign regulations by encouraging or permitting PACs to make "independent expenditures." To take one case, according to the *National Journal*, the Fund for a Conservative Majority spent over $60,000 in New Hampshire for Ronald Reagan in 1980 when his campaign expenses were dangerously close to New Hampshire's $294,000 legal spending limit. The same PAC spent over $80,000 for Reagan at the same critical juncture in the 1980 Texas primary. This $140,000 at sensitive moments is more important than the total of $600,000 the Fund spent to help Reagan throughout the country in 1980.[38]

PACs, now a vital new political force in American politics, are all the more important because of their independence of political parties. There have always been interest groups in America, and most of them have in fact been "special-issue" groups. But they pose a special problem in our era, first because with the decline of political parties

---

[35]Brooks Jackson, "Loopholes Allow Flood of Campaign Giving by Business, Fat Cats," *Wall Street Journal*, July 5, 1984, pp. 1 and 16.

[36]Ibid., p. 16. Note also that this amount was gathered by July 5, with four months of campaigning, and need, still left.

[37]Alexander, "Making Sense about Dollars," p. 15.

[38]Case cited in ibid., p. 16.

125

the groups now enjoy more direct access to Congress and to administrative agencies responsible to the president, unmediated by the old traditional party leaders, and second, because of their more direct involvement in the electoral process. The traditional distinction between interest groups and political parties, established as historical verity in the textbooks, is that parties are concerned with controlling government through control of personnel while interest groups seek to control government by more or less accepting the personnel and trying to influence their policies. This distinction has broken down not only because of the long-range decline of political parties but more directly because of the collaboration of party leaders in the so-called reform of campaign laws that permitted private interests to organize for purposes of direct involvement in elections. The 1971 and 1974 federal election campaign laws really gave birth to the PAC phenomenon.

As to the significance of that phenomenon, it has been said by many observers that PACs are a nationalizing force, in the sense that they are organized nationally and funnel campaign money from private individuals to candidates around the country according to a "single-issue" or a unified ideological or programmatic commitment. But at the same time, PACs are also an *atomizing* force because individual candidates reach PACs, or are reached by PACs, on an entirely individual basis. Whatever dependency or influence relationship is developed (and one can argue how strong the influence is), it is an accumulation of isolated cases. In this sense, therefore, the PACs reinforce the pattern of the disappearance of real coalitions and the emergence of a flux of individual and group particles around a presidential, and occasionally congressional, center of gravity.

This is not by any means a world of chaos. Bills get drafted. Parliamentary rules are observed. Parties by name still exist, and majority parties have enough continuity to permit members to elect leaders in the House and Senate who can provide enough leadership to develop and maintain an agenda, or calendar. Votes are taken, and bills are passed. As always. Moreover, members of the same party vote together more often than they vote with members of the opposite party. Take, for example, the "party unity scores," which measure the percentage of times each member of Congress votes with the majority of his/her party when the majority of the other party is on the opposite side. Party unity scores were never high when compared to true party government, as in the British House of Commons. And party unity scores have been generally on the decline during this century. But still, the average of all party unity scores of all members of both parties show that things are not very different now from what they were twenty-five years ago, and at times there is a bit more party unity than in the past. For example, in 1960, average party unity among Democrats was 64 percent and among Republicans 68 percent. In 1968, party unity among Democrats had dropped to 57 percent and among Republicans to 63. By 1976, however, both were back up to 65 and 66 percent, respectively. In 1981, the first year of Ronald Reagan's administration, party unity among Democrats was 69 percent but among Republicans it had jumped to 76 percent. By 1983, Democratic unity had jumped to 76 percent, with Republican unity at 74 percent.[39] (See Table 5.)

However, this moderately positive amount of party *regularity* in the House and Senate is not to be confused with effective party organization and party *discipline*, of which there is little. As in the electorate, partisanship still counts for a great deal in Congress; but, as in the electorate, two mounds of partisanship can produce most of the observed regularity without any particular effort on the part of party leaders. Party leaders no longer have anything much more than partisanship to appeal to when they go to individual members to ask for their vote on a controversial roll call. In the second place, the "party unity" score reviewed above is a very permissive measurement of party affiliation. If we slightly raised the threshold of partisanship, counting only those votes on which 60 percent (rather than 51 percent) of the two parties opposed each other, there would be far fewer votes to tabulate and also a much lower party unity score. One indication of the decline of real party discipline (as distinct from mere partisanship and regularity) is the history of what analysts have called "party votes," where 90 percent of one party votes in opposition to 90 percent of the other. These votes are so named because at the 90 percent level of solidarity the behavior of members of the legislature begins to resemble behavior in a real party organization con-

---

[39]*Congressional Quarterly Almanac* (Washington, D.C.: Congressional Quarterly Inc., various years, 1960-84). Scores given here are for members of the House and Senate combined. Party unity in the House tends to run a bit higher on the average than party unity in the Senate, but not enough for our purposes to require reporting separate averages for the two chambers.

Table 5. Party Unity

Composite party unity scores showing the percentage of the time the average Democrat and Republican voted with his party majority in partisan votes in recent years.

Year	Democrats	Republicans
1983	76%	74%
1982	72	71
1981	69	76
1980	68	70
1979	69	72
1978	64	67
1977	67	70
1976	65	66
1975	69	70
1974	63	62
1973	68	68
1972	57	64
1971	62	66
1970	57	59
1969	62	62
1968	57	63
1967	66	71
1966	61	67
1965	69	70
1964	67	69
1963	71	72
1962	69	68
1961	76	71
1960	64	68

Source: Congressional Quarterly Almanac, various years, 1960–84.

text, such as the British House of Commons. In the several sessions of Congress around the turn of the century, better than half of all roll call votes were party votes. By the beginning of the New Deal, 23 percent of the roll call votes qualified. During the Truman administration, which many consider the last period in which there were still vestiges of party discipline, around 15 percent of the roll call votes were party votes. During the epoch of liberal congresses, 1958–64, 8 percent of the roll call votes qualified as party votes. As we approached the 1980s, less than 1 percent of all the roll call votes pitted 90 percent of the Democrats against 90 percent of the Republicans.[40]

[40]Julius Turner and Edward Schneier, Party and Constituency: Pressures on Congress, rev. ed. (Baltimore: Johns Hopkins University Press, 1970), pp. 17, 37; Congressional Quarterly Almanac, 1973, pp. 2H-99H; and Congressional Quarterly Almanac, 1979, pp. 2H-237H.

At the same time, the percentage of roll call votes that were *bipartisan*—where the majority of both parties voted on the *same side* of the issue—went from around 35 percent during the New Deal to 45 percent during the late 1950s, to over 60 percent in the 1960s and 70 percent in the 1970s. Nowadays, as many as 10 percent of the members of the House of Representatives vote more often with the other party than with their own!

In our day and age, the only time political parties in Congress show any organizational vitality at all is when the president's own position is known and the president's commitment is strong. Randall Ripley offers a fascinating test case of this phenomenon by comparing the votes of the president's own party on a given bill when it came up for final passage with the votes of that same party later on when the president had vetoed the bill and Congress was attempting to override the veto. In one case, passage of the Vocational Rehabilitation Act of 1973, only 2 of the 37 Republican senators voted in accord with President Nixon's announced opposition to the bill. In contrast, on the Senate vote to override the veto, 31 of 41 Republicans present voted to sustain President Nixon. This means that Republican unity jumped from 5 percent to 76 percent after the presidential factor was introduced. Ripley reports three other case studies under Republican presidents during the 1970s, where party unity following the presidential veto jumped from 31 percent to 87, 44 percent to 68 and 65 percent to 84, respectively. Two such cases are reported for the Carter administration. On one, party unity jumped from 26 percent to 69 following the injection of the presidential veto, and in the second, from 18 percent to 46.[41]

Here again, the preponderance of the evidence suggests that it is the presidency that introduces the greater orderliness into party behavior and constitutes about the only sign of party discipline. What we have—as in the national electorate—is two mounds of partisanship, given most of their direction by the president or taking direction from presidential cues. This is not to suggest that every president in every instance is exerting strong leadership. It is a well-established fact that President Carter was ineffective as a legislative leader, whereas Ronald Reagan should be credited for greater effort and greater effectiveness in this role. But either way, party regularity

[41]Randall Ripley, *Congress: Process and Policy* (New York: Norton, 1978), p. 202; and *Congressional Quarterly Almanac*, 1979, p. 29.

in Congress is primarily attributable to the presence of the president, especially in those instances where the president's position is well demarcated and his support is made unmistakably clear.

President Reagan's successes early in his administration gave the impression that the parties could be brought to a responsible programmatic role in national government. This was to be an important part of a Reagan legacy. In 1981, almost no Republicans defected in the Senate or the House whenever there were key roll call votes on important Reagan bills. In three all-important votes on tax cuts and spending cuts, Senate Republicans voted for the president's program 41–1, 50–2 and 51–2; in four parallel votes in the House, the Republican members voted, respectively, 190–1, 188–1, 189–0 and 190–1. Republican regularity remained high through 1981 and into 1982. But when Congress confronted the second round of cuts, plus an expanding deficit, a turndown in the economy, and a declining presidential performance rating, the appearance of new party organization and discipline turned out to be no more than an unusually long honeymoon. As one expert analyst put it, "Like legislative outbursts in the past, the Reagan juggernaut soon ran out of steam."[42]

Critical for Republican solidarity in 1981 was a parliamentary maneuver made possible by the 1974 congressional reforms whose aim had been to enable Congress to consider all appropriation bills together and within an overall spending ceiling adopted earlier in each session, with which all spending proposals would be "reconciled." The president's legislative leaders presented to Congress a Reconciliation Bill that incorporated *all* Reagan's spending cut proposals. This tactic shunted aside virtually all committee and subcommittee deliberations and effectively prevented individual members of the Senate or House from touching single agencies or items, however important to them the single issues were. Much like a trick play in football, the reconciliation approach was unlikely to work more than once a game (or season, or administration). Not only was it not repeated in 1982; Congress took back the initiative, Republican congressional solidarity settled down to slightly above average (as shown above), and the Reagan approach turned out to be tactical rather than structural.[43]

[42]Roger Davidson, "The Presidency and Congress," in Michael Nelson, ed., *The Presidency and the Political System* (Washington: Congressional Quarterly Press, 1984), p. 387.
[43]Allen Schick, "The Budget as an Instrument of Presidential Policy," in Lester Salamon, ed., *Governance: The Reagan Era and Beyond* (Washington: Urban Institute, 1985).

The Republican National Committee (RNC) has had extraordinary success since the late 1970s in attracting money. Still more impressive is the national Republican organization's centralization of its financial activities, from the expansion of its Republican Eagles to organized fund-raisers to mass direct mailings. The RNC has also succeeded to an unprecedented extent in centralizing the distribution of these national resources to state and county organizations and to individual candidates for House and Senate. So wise and well organized has the RNC been that it has managed to concentrate national funds on races involving new GOP candidates against Democratic incumbents (whereas, in the Democratic party, the big shares still go to those who least need help).[44]

I can, however, identify at least six reasons why this success has not been converted and probably cannot be converted into a reconstituted national party of the sort Roosevelt sought in 1938 and Reagan was perhaps seeking in 1981. First, although the RNC had to depend far less than the DNC on PAC donations, this is only a matter of degree. Second, a substantial portion of the direct RNC money came from individuals heavily involved in conservative PACs. Third, a large but indeterminate number of individual members of the House and Senate get PAC money and thereby maintain their independence from any effort the RNC or a Republican president might make to set conditions on contributions made to them by the RNC. Fourth, a substantial (though again indeterminate) part of RNC strength and GOP congressional solidarity is attributable to the close and relatively recent ties between the GOP and the resurgent conservative movement. This closeness was dramatically revealed at the 1984 Republican National Convention, where there was almost no dissent on any issue, including the most conservative principles in the platform. But unless there is a fundamental restructuring of the Republican base, this conservative solidarity will not become the party itself, and loosening of the GOP is close to inevitable. Fifth, there would also have to be a more fundamental restructuring of Congress before there could be real party organization, Republican or Democratic. Even when members of Congress get together, it is more likely in an informal, bipartisan voting bloc (or caucus) than through their party. Roger Davidson reports that before 1970 there were very few such caucuses,

---

[44] A very good comparative review through 1984 will be found in Thomas Edsall, "The GOP Money Machine," *Washington Post National Weekly Edition*, July 2, 1984, pp. 6-7.

and their existence was kept as quiet as possible. By the end of the 1970s there were about eighty. Examples include the Northeast-Midwest Coalition (also known as the "Frost Belt Caucus"); the Textile Caucus; the Senate Steel Caucus; the Black Caucus; the Arts Caucus; and, my favorite, the Mushroom Caucus.[45] Finally, the most important reform in recent years, the congressional budget process adopted in 1974, did nothing to integrate Congress as an institution. As Charles Jones puts it, "the bulk of the reforms were not integrative at all but more expressive or representative in nature. This greater fragmentation and participation can result in diverse policy innovation but very limited institutional response to presidential initiative." Despite the solidarity and partisanship of 1981, there has been a "gradual disintegration of the budget process and the emergence of scores of members in business for themselves."[46]

Reflecting upon this age of private financial armies and national television technology, James Reston, surely the dean of American journalism, made the following observation:

> To see what is happening to leadership in this town, you must go into the basement of the Capitol. The television studios and videotaping facilities there are part of a revolution. The Congress today is the most intelligent I've seen, but members have no party loyalties and no institutional loyalties and they are using those facilities to broadcast back home, to make proclamations on issues on which they have only been very quickly briefed. Now, each of them can—and does—act like a little President.[47]

PACs contributed to this state of affairs but did not create it. Congress created it. The decline of political parties threatened to leave the field of electoral politics to those of personal wealth, closing off lower income candidacies almost completely. Congress liberalized restrictions on organized private finance and in the process unintentionally erected an enormous barrier to the recomposition of political parties along lines consonant with the modern positive national state. The long-range result was further atomization of the leg-

[45]Davidson, "The Presidency and Congress," p. 376.
[46]Charles O. Jones, "A New President, a Different Congress, a Maturing Agenda," in Salamon, ed., *Governance*; quoted from typescript, pp. 33-34.
[47]Quoted in Richard Reeves, *American Journey* (New York: Simon & Schuster, 1982), pp. 350-51.

islature, despite the appearance of a moderate amount of continuing party regularity.

Congressional atomization has forced the president all the more to develop a mass popular base outside and beyond Congress. If the capacity to govern requires that presidents regularly succeed in being a strong enough center of gravity to overcome atomization and to impose a pattern on the flux of particles, extreme measures can all the better be justified. If this requires an occasional foreign policy fix, then a fix there'll be. In September 1983, when President Reagan's approval ratings had taken a turn for the better but were not necessarily going to continue to resist the downward tendency of all his predecessors, one of his White House advisers observed in a private interview, "We need a major victory somewhere to show that we can manage foreign policy." Another presidential aide added, "We need a win somewhere, whether it's in Central America, the Middle East or with the Russians."[48] We now know that he did not actually need a "win" but only a dramatic event; and we also know that he got several such events, spaced so well that his ratings remained buoyant. This pattern, by which the plebiscitary presidency was introduced in Chapter 1, can now be seen as an inherent part of that presidency's institutionalization in the Second Republic of the United States.

[48]Quoted in Hedrick Smith, "Reagan's Crucial Year," *New York Times Magazine*, October 16, 1983, pp. 44 and 52.

6

The Performance of Plebiscitary Presidents: A Cost-Benefit Analysis

> **No nation . . . should ever permit itself to be governed from a hallowed shrine where the meanest lust for power can be sanctified and the dullest wit greeted with reverential awe.**
>
> **—George Reedy**

As with a machine, so with a human institution, the ultimate test is performance, and the judgment of performance depends upon the weight of the cost against the benefits. Cost-benefit analysis nowadays implies hard data and established formulas culminating in a quantification of all variables in a numerical rendering of the ratio of cost to benefits. Unfortunately, the potential for quantification is almost inversely related to the seriousness of the problem. No one can quantify the relevant cost and benefits of the presidency; yet the seriousness that defies quantification cries out all the more for evaluation. So we must steadfastly follow Chesterton's advice: "If a thing is worth doing, it is worth doing badly."

The burden of evaluation is substantially lightened if there is a clear criterion to start with. None other than Alexander Hamilton provided such a criterion in his original essay proclaiming the virtues of the presidential institution as it was conceptualized by the Founders. In *Federalist* No. 68, after a detailed explanation of the selection process, Hamilton commended it with the following observation:

Though we cannot acquiesce in the political heresy of the poet who says:

"For forms of government let fools contest—
That which is best administered is best,"—
yet we may safely pronounce that the true test of a good government is
its aptitude and tendency to produce a good administration.

George Reedy was extending Hamilton's logic as he developed the
thought which was used to open this chapter. Observing that the factor absent in most of the works on the presidency "Is the impact of
the institution on individuals," he went on to affirm: "The question is
whether the structures have created an environment in which [presi-
dents] cannot function in any kind of a decent and humane relationship to the people whom they are supposed to lead. I am afraid—and
on this point I am a pessimist—that we have devised that kind of a
system."[1]

The only trouble with Reedy's insight is that he did not stick to it.
Both as a journalist covering the U.S. Senate for two decades and
then in the White House as a special assistant to Lyndon Johnson,
Reedy was struck by the force of personality as well as the influence
of the institutional environment. This led him to appreciate, too
much in my opinion, the difference between the two realms. He insisted: "In the White House, character and personality are extremely
important because there are no other limitations. . . . Restraint must
come from within the presidential soul and prudence from within
the presidential mind. The adversary forces which temper the actions of others do not come into play until it is too late to change
course."[2]

Many other professional president watchers agree with this last
point, most notably James David Barber. His celebrated book *The
Presidential Character* is an effort to analyze and predict presidential
performance on the basis of a psychological theory. Barber was not
the first political scientist to apply psychology to presidents; in fact
his Yale graduate school classmate Erwin Hargrove published before
him a theory of presidential leadership based upon personal insecu-
rity.[3] But Barber's was more comprehensive and attempted to be
more systematic. Barber began with a fourfold classification derived
from an assumption that presidential personalities exist in two di-

[1]George Reedy, *The Twilight of the Presidency* (New York: New American Library,
1970), p. x.
[2]Ibid., p. 30.
[3]Erwin Hargrove, *Presidential Leadership* (New York: Macmillan, 1966).

mensions. One dimension is whether they are active or passive in their approach to the job and the other is whether they are positive or negative in their attitude toward power politics in general. Thus, presidents can be active or passive as regards their commitment to the office, and they can be positive or negative as regards how much enjoyment or satisfaction they get from politics in general and the presidency in particular. Performance or conduct then can be predicted in terms of a mixture of these two dimensions.

To Barber, and to many others, the best president is an active-positive president, because presidents ought to be vigorous, and it is probably a good thing if they are happy in their work. But more to the point, active-positive presidents *behave* in a manner predictably different from, say, active-negative presidents or passive-negative presidents, etc. In the twentieth century, Barber's active-positive presidents are Franklin D. Roosevelt, Harry Truman and John Kennedy. His active-negative presidents are Herbert Hoover, Lyndon Johnson, and Richard Nixon.[4]

This is not the place to evaluate the psychology/character approach; it is my intention only to use it to help identify and justify its alternative, the institutionalist approach adopted in this book. The success of Barber's analysis was launched by his devastatingly accurate prediction of President Nixon's behavior. But Barber was probably as far off-base with Jimmy Carter (whom he called active-positive) as he was on with Richard Nixon. An institutionalist approach does not deny the relevance of individual psychology but treats it as marginal in the context of the tremendous historical forces lodged in the laws, traditions, and commitments of institution. Character—or the part of it that contributes to an individual's predispositions—is determined through experiences all during the successful candidate's life prior to the assumption of the presidency. Even if we could know the true psychological composition of the character of such complex politicians, there would be no way to know what part of their psychological makeup would be determinative. And the psychological assumptions inherent in character analysis do not allow for basic changes in psychology that might occur immediately before and dur-

[4]James David Barber, *The Presidential Character: Predicting Performance in the White House*, 2d ed. (Englewood Cliffs: Prentice-Hall, 1977) A very good analysis and critique of the Barber system will be found in Raymond Tatalovich and Byron W. Daynes, *Presidential Power in the United States* (Monterey, Cal.: Brooks/Cole, 1984), pp. 376-95.

ing the presidency itself. For example, Herbert Hoover and Jimmy Carter might very well have been deliriously happy with politics until bad news and political opposition turned a joyful game into a painful ordeal. We can either say that their psychological makeup changed, as a result, from positive to negative, or we could say, as I do, that their characters probably remained the same but they had to adjust themselves to the demands of the institution.

In contrast, the institutionalist approach does not require deep psychoanalysis of each president. It can be predictive by studying only the publicly available facts about institutions (no need for "inside dope"). And it is more optimistic: If we are truly locked into character and personality as they are shaped in important politicians throughout their childhoods and careers, we have little prospect of reforming the presidency except by perfecting psychological tests that are so sensitive to relevant personality traits that we can identify and weed out all the character types except the active-positives, which is presumably the type we must have in a governmental system to which a president's capacity to govern is central. Who is prepared to let the choice of presidential candidacies rest upon psychological profiles such as the ones the FBI does on potential terrorists? If, on the other hand, presidential performance can be understood and predicted in terms of the institutional environment, there is a chance that changing the institutional environment can improve performance, whatever the psychological profile of the next president.

Continuities in the Behavior of Plebiscitary Presidents

A main aim of any institution is to make the behavior of its members more predictable. Operationally, this means that a particular "model of behavior" is written into all institutions, especially an institution as publicly circumscribed as the presidency. Predictability is attained in largest part by the imposition of roles and obligations. Roles are learned and obligations are internalized over the long stretch of any politician's rise to power, and though in that sense they certainly become aspects of character, these roles and obligations are common to all politicians to varying degrees. Some roles and obligations are assumed unconsciously, and others are imposed, as a precondition for advancement. Still other roles are adopted rationally and self-consciously—that is, the top politicians perceive what the best roles and most effective obligations are. How presidents will in fact behave when they occupy that particular institution will be determined marginally by their psychologies or characters. But the amazing thing is the continuity and regularity of their behavior despite great differences in individual psychology/character. Ustinov's track on the Rock of Gibraltar was adopted precisely because of the image of determined behavior that it conveys.

In the institutionalized model there are three categories of presidential performance: (1) Keeping the initiative; (2) Keeping the initiative in the White House; and (3) Democratizing presidential power while enhancing it. Each will be taken in turn.

Keeping the Initiative

Presidents attempt to keep the initiative largely through *program*. The executive branch is the source of a never-ending flow of policy proposals. Moreover, there is a strong presumption that the proposals that go from the executive to Congress have been carefully filtered through the legislative clearance process of the Office of Management and Budget. The budget process and legislative clearance are no longer as important to the development of the president's program as they were through the 1950s and 1960s into the early 1970s, in large part because of the enormous growth of legislatively mandated entitlements and of off-budget commitments including actual expenditures and loans and loan guarantees. But the process of legislative clearance has a long tradition as the foundation of the development of the president's program and contributed fundamentally to the emergence of the administrative presidency and the theory that all presidents have to be strong presidents.[5]

Presidential proposals fill the congressional agenda and tend to dominate congressional hearings and floor debate, not to speak of the newspapers. And presidents try to maintain the initiative, or at

[5]For an outstanding treatment of the background and the more recent changes in the budget and the president's program, see Allen Schick, "The Budget as an Instrument of Presidential Policy," in Lester Salamon, ed., *Governance: The Reagan Era and Beyond* (Washington: Urban Institute, 1985).

least the appearance of initiative, by speeches, messages direct to Congress, off-the-record comments, on-the-record comments, press conferences, and strategic appearances around the country as well as in Washington. President Reagan even brought back the radio.

Need for the initiative has been as strong in our two most recent presidents as in their immediate predecessors, despite the fact that both campaigned against Washington, implying that the presidency itself could be wound down a turn or two. Carter fitted in with his Democratic predecessors as a legislative activist.[6] But Reagan, far from being the "laid-back" president many had expected, was also an activist, dominating Congress's agenda as few since FDR had. In his first year, President Reagan set the agenda which would determine executive-legislative discourse for the rest of his term.[7]

Why seek to gain and maintain the initiative? In the first place, there is a statistical reason: If the president is able to fill Congress's agenda, his chances of getting a lot of what he wants may be improved. The second and equally important reason for trying to maintain the initiative is the need to gain and maintain the *reputation* for power, in hopes that the reputation for power will produce power itself. Neustadt opens and closes his classic work with just such thoughts, for example: "In short, his power is the product of his vantage points in government, together with his reputation in the Washington community and his prestige outside."[8]

It is also the sort of thing George Reedy had in mind in the chapter of his book entitled "The Monopoly of Authoritative Answers."[9] Beyond that, in case power does not result from the reputation for it, the initiative is also sought because it may convey the illusion if not the reality of capacity for governing. If the public in the Second Republic has begun to judge the capacity to govern by service delivery rather than by adequate representation, a lot of programmatic activity, filled with new proposals for action, might, at least in the short run, contribute to public satisfaction.

Although all these reasons for seeking the initiative seem plausible and logical, certainly not irrational, the president confronts a pro-

---

[6]Richard Neustadt, *Presidential Power* (New York: Wiley, 1980), p. 215.

[7]Charles O. Jones, "A New President, a Different Congress, a Maturing Agenda," in Salamon, ed., *Governance*.

[8]Neustadt, *Presidential Power* (1980), p. 131.

[9]*Twilight of the Presidency*, chapter 4.

found dilemma. The data on public opinion approval and disapproval, as displayed in Chapter 1, suggest that the more the president courts his constituencies, the more he is likely to alienate them. Except in foreign policy, each and every initiative is divisive. And even in foreign policy the unifying effect is only temporary; once a foreign policy event is domesticated, it, too, tends to be become divisive. But the plebiscitary president seems to have no choice but to continue trying to maintain the initiative. The same people—the mass public and the Washington community and Congress—who are likely to be alienated with each initiative, are nevertheless watching for signs of the efficacy, capacity, and energy in government that democratic theory now tells them are essential.

Keeping the Initiative in the White House

Initiative is more than the program or the budget; it is more than the executive program or the executive budget; it is more than the request of the government or the thrust of the administration. The imperative is the *president's* program, the *president's* budget, the *president's* administrative initiative, and so on.

George Reedy vividly described the resulting footwork in his 1970 book:

> The concept of the president who works around the clock is deep in American mythology. . . . Even in the case of President Eisenhower, his assistants thought they had to keep up appearances regardless of their chief's disdain for dissimulation. Jim Haggerty, his press secretary, was notorious for "saving up" official papers and announcements to release while the president was on vacation—thus preserving the illusion that it was a combination of work-and-play holiday. . . .
>
> Another measurement of the "workload" can be found in the long-standing custom of the White House Press Office of scouring the executive agencies for items to release to the newspaper correspondents . . . [who] have found themselves bombarded on a daily basis with releases on waterfowl conservation, minor grants for pollution abatement, and education projects for Indian reservations. Such releases rarely make headlines but their sheer bulk creates the impression of unending activity on the part of the President.[10]

[10]*Twilight of the Presidency*, pp. 32-33.

140

The image of work extended through the Carter presidency, and with more than average substance, because Carter was, to a fault, a working president. Between 1982 and 1984, President Reagan appeared to be an exception in that he made little effort to create an impression of minute-by-minute hard work. Nonetheless, he kept the White House and the presidency at the epicenter of government at all times, albeit in his own way. His approach will be taken up in its turn.

All recent presidents have tried to make the cabinet a kind of board of directors. But those efforts start early and end quickly. Presidents downgrade their cabinets and upgrade the White House: "Strong presidents," wrote Richard Pious, "have reason to downgrade the cabinet and prevent its institutionalization. A collective cabinet with its own staff could become a competitor for 'The Executive Power' and come to function as a 'council of state.' . . . Because presidents reserve their prerogatives for themselves, they hold few meetings, permit no votes and deny the cabinet any staff resources."[11] Cabinet members are themselves aware of the shortcomings of the cabinet and the likelihood that no initiative of theirs will go anywhere unless it becomes presidential initiative. For this reason, cabinet members "prefer to 'boycott the agenda.' . . . Each participant operates on the premise that his or her department's interest will best be served if none of the other secretaries comments on its affairs."[12]

The downgrading of the cabinet in favor of the White House Staff has been almost institutionalized. It is not accidental that journalists popularize the staff of each administration as the "Irish Mafia," the "German Mafia," and the "Georgia Mafia." Each president in the Second Republic, in trying to create the functional equivalent of a political party and party government, has gathered around himself those people who fought most of the battles with him during the long struggle through the campaign and the election. These are his trusted political friends, and their value to him was proved time after time by the successes that brought them all to the White House.

From an informal group of fewer than a dozen people whose sole purpose was service and personal solace for the president, the White House Staff has become a large and relatively formalized organization that reached 550 by 1972 (not counting special personnel assigned

[11]Richard Pious, *The American Presidency* (New York: Basic Books, 1979), p. 241.
[12]Ibid., p. 240.

141

from other agencies but remaining on the original agency budget). The number dropped slightly under Ford and Carter, but rose even higher under Reagan (see Table 1). Organizationally separate from it, and even more numerous, are the personnel in the Executive Office of the President (EOP), which grew to its maximum size, around 5,000, in the mid 1970s. (There was disagreement even then over how many people EOP included, but even the minimum number claimed by John Ehrlichman at that time was 3,700.) The Executive Office of the President is made up primarily of specialists, organized in separate overhead units, such as OMB. The White House Staff is made up more of generalists. Although many of the top White House Staffers are "special assistant" for a particular task or sector, the types of judgments they are supposed to make and the kind of advice they are supposed to give are a good deal broader and more generally political than that which comes from the EOP or from the departments.

Generally speaking, the EOP represents what is called the "institutionalized presidency," while the White House Staff represents the presidency itself, or the alter-ego of the president. Together, the institutionalized presidency and the presidential alter-ego have diminished still further the power and status of the cabinet and the stature of the individual department heads. Differences of personality definitely help to explain the particular ways that each president in the Second Republic has met the requirement of maintaining initiative in the White House. But the interesting and significant thing is that each president has felt that requirement and has made an effort to meet it. For example, President Carter, who found so many of the requirements of presidential power distasteful, built probably the largest White House Staff of all. In 1981, at the time of transition from Carter to Reagan, the special assistant for national security affairs had a personal staff larger than that of the secretary of defense; the special assistant for international trade negotiations had a staff larger than that of the secretary of commerce; and the special assistant to the president on wage and price stability had a staff larger than that of the secretary of the treasury. Their personal staffs were, respectively, the National Security Council staff, the staff of the Office of the Special Representative for Trade Negotiations, and the staff of the Council on Wage and Price Stability. That these are all aspects of the institutionalization of the White House and the presidency should not mask the fact that the situation is almost monarchical; the people in this apparatus are personally loyal to the president and the president alone and are so lacking in political autonomy and independent resources that they truly qualify as "White House eunuchs."

Once again, the most interesting case is President Nixon. Too much of what has been written about his efforts to meet the requirements of presidential initiative has aimed to show him as a pathological personality when in fact a more dispassionate look will show that he was a rational person dealing very rationally with the requirements of the job as they have been constructed under the Second Republic. Nixon began rather typically with the appointment of cabinet officials strong enough in their own right to give promise of central and collective control of the far-flung administrative agencies. He announced very early that he did not want a cabinet of "yes-men," and he announced to his new administrators as a body that the sub-cabinet appointments would be their responsibility. Almost immediately he began to regret both commitments, and well before the end of his term he was on an entirely different track.[13] His new track, one for which he became quite well known, was to control everything, including the cabinet officials themselves, from the White House through a closely trusted staff with whom he consulted almost exclusively. By early 1972, people could joke about Nixon's "secret cabinet," referring to the lack of prominence or influence of the department heads. As humorist Russell Baker put it, "The Secretary of Transportation is named Volpe, and the Secretary of Agriculture, Butz. Both were photographed with the President when they were appointed and are seen in Washington from time to time. Rumors that there is a Secretary of Labor are unfounded."[14]

Despite Nixon's announcement soon after his inauguration that he would stick with the cabinet and even avoid having a chief of staff as his mentor Eisenhower had had, he built a White House Staff second to none. Nathan reports that by the end of the third year, the EOP staff had doubled in comparison to the Johnson years, and the White House Staff had grown so large that it not only filled the White House but occupied almost all of the space on the sixth floor of the Execu-

---

[13]Detailed recountings of each of Nixon's efforts to maintain control in the White House are provided in Richard P. Nathan, *The Plot that Failed: Nixon and the Administrative Presidency* (New York: Wiley, 1975), esp. chs. 3-5. Although I rely on Nathan's account, he would not necessarily agree with the analysis I have based on it.

[14]Quoted in ibid., p. 51.

tive Office Building next door.[15] Though, as I noted earlier, the exact numbers of personnel cannot be stated accurately because of borrowed staffers, it is quite clear that Nixon had built a bureaucracy to control the bureaucracy.

Although Nixon stuck with this pattern through his first term, he already had plans to change it as soon as reelection was accomplished. His goals in the 1973 changes, which Nathan refers to as "the plot that failed," are extremely meaningful for the plebiscitary presidency even though Nixon was prevented from carrying them out. The plan had two parts. First, he intended to remove several of the stronger and more outspoken members of his cabinet, replacing them with persons more dependent on the president, and to add—an especially significant point—one of his most trusted associates as an assistant or deputy secretary to be the direct line of communication between that department and the White House. This part of the plot he carried furthest, because it was strictly within his discretion. He kept his topmost people in the White House, but the second rank of extremely effective and well-trusted staffers he dispersed to the departments, as undersecretary of transportation, undersecretary of interior, assistant secretary of treasury, and undersecretary of the then HEW.

The second leg of the plan was even bolder and more important. He proposed to take four of the heads of domestic departments and give them joint appointments as "counsellors to the president." They would continue as heads of their respective departments but they would be unequal among equals. They came to be called "super secretaries" who were forming a "super cabinet." And there is truth in that. These four super secretaries were intended to be part of a Domestic Council (conceptualized as equivalent to the National Security Council), and to chair important White House policy committees. They were to be given authority in a chain of command between the president and the other members of the cabinet as well as the White House Staff people. Each was to be held responsible for an area of programmatic or policy activity defined by the three or four major departments within his area. The chief advantage to the president would have been the existence of a real cabinet of political stature but one in a direct chain of command to the operational agencies. A

[15]Ibid., p. 45.

144

second advantage would have been the super secretaries' stronger claim to executive privilege, as special assistants to the president, when they confronted antagonistic questions from Congress. With this sort of super cabinet plus the trusted White House Staff and the former staffers strategically located as assistant and deputy secretaries, President Nixon could perhaps have achieved the control and continuity in the White House that both Eisenhower's military staff concept and the Kennedy-Johnson combinations of White House Staff and programmatic control had failed to bring about.

Paradoxically, the plan was not only denounced as a pure power grab but was used as important evidence of President Nixon's personal paranoia. It confirmed the theory that he was a "negative-active" president and that he willfully isolated himself from the outside world. But given the added perspective of a decade, it seems more likely that what Nixon was trying to do was not only logical but active and positive. Since the cabinet is a great deal more exposed to the public and closer to the constitutional scheme of things than the White House Staff is, it appears to me that an approach to control via a two-tiered, super cabinet is more active-positive than many of the solutions sought by other chief executives. But this is a mere quibble. What is pathological, paranoid, and perverse about the plebiscitary presidency is not the human beings who occupy the office; it is the job and the demands it logically generates. Every recent presidency has been isolated and has seen the need for isolation. Toward the apex of a plebiscitary office with great power there is isolation, inevitably. It is no longer a matter of individual personality or idiosyncracy.

Ronald Reagan is a departure in style from Carter and Nixon, but in his own way he has met the demands of the plebiscitary presidency —and, ironically, his own way is both Nixonian and Rooseveltian. Much of the Nixon strategy followed from an assumption he and his closest advisers made that "operations is policy."[16] Reagan has in practice agreed with this while keeping the policy initiative as well. The Nixon administration was not lacking in policy achievements, but the policy innovations of that period were as much congressional as presidential. Nixon conceived of the control problem as one of controlling the bureaucracy by imposing his directions and his per-

[16]Ibid., p. 62.

sonality on it; that was his primary means of trying to keep the initiative and meet the demands of celebrity. With Reagan there was never any mistaking the source of the key proposals that made up the lion's share of Congress's agenda. In matters of program and policy initiative, Reagan has quite appropriately been compared to Roosevelt and to Lyndon Johnson. But at the same time he was like Nixon, putting himself in the vortex of policy implementation as well.

The move toward this sort of control began during the Transition; Reagan's Transition teams were far more numerous than those of Kennedy and Johnson, and the effort to tie all agencies politically to the White House was as extensive as that of any predecessor.[17] So many members of these Transition teams were appointed to positions in agencies they studied that "a new level of politicization . . . was achieved, reaching well . . . into subbureau levels across the government."[18] Few OMB directors were ever given budget and fiscal powers, and the power to speak for the White House, as David Stockman was given by Reagan. And central power spread far beyond budget matters to involvement in all the decisions made by regulatory agencies. White House regulatory control was maintained through the Office of Information and Regulatory Affairs of OMB, which claimed (and generally deserved) credit for displacing statutorily mandated agency authority. This office and these practices were not those of a president committed to deregulation in a truly smaller government with a smaller presidency. They were indications of precisely the reverse. If Reagan had wanted to reduce national government and the presidency, he would have sought real deregulation with statutes terminating whole agencies or regulatory programs. Instead he sought no termination at all. Carter had a better record of real deregulation. Reagan sought *hegemony* over all the agencies, sometimes to reduce them in size but at all times to get and keep the initiative over what was regulated, and how much.

In 1976, Jimmy Carter pledged to reduce nineteen hundred federal agencies to two hundred. As president he accomplished the opposite. President Reagan entered office in 1981 dedicated to a smaller government and a smaller presidency. Within three years he had accomplished the opposite. In terms of the deficit and the size of the

---

[17]Chester Newland, "Developing the Reagan Program," in Salamon, ed., *Governance.*
[18]Ibid., quoted from typescript, pp. 12-13.

national debt, he had given us the largest government we ever had. And, what is more interesting, instead of a smaller presidency, he gave us one of the most prominent we have ever had. No president's persona has ever been more prominent and more the property of the mass public. And despite his reputation for being "laid back," one glance at the White House table of organization will suggest that however little work Reagan intended to do as president, and however little he wished to remain informed of the decisions being made, his intention was nevertheless to maintain sole possession of the national government within the White House and nowhere else. (See Table 6.)

Centralization of responsibility toward the person of the president and the isolation associated with that are both now sewn into the fabric of the Second Republic. They are no longer matters of individual character or personal idiosyncracy. It was the active-positive Jimmy Carter who fired the most vigorous and outspoken members of his cabinet, and it was the passive-positive Reagan who forced the resignation of Alexander Haig because of his effort to be an active-positive secretary of state, and that of James Watt because Watt was so vigorously carrying out what appeared to be Reagan's own policy preferences at Interior. Why this virtual compulsion on the part of even the least paranoid of presidents to maintain such a tight control of initiative in the White House and to be so jealous of those who seem most vigorous in trying to help the president meet his tasks? I can think of at least three good reasons, and they have applied to all presidents in the Second Republic, regardless of psychological profile. The reasons are legal, institutional, and cultural. A word on each will be worthwhile.

The most compelling reason for keeping the initiative in the White House and not sharing it is that the legal responsibility for all but a very few functions in the national government rests with the president and the president alone. When Truman said "The buck stops here," he was stating more a legal reality than a personal preference. The delegation of power from Congress to president is a delegation of responsibility; it is a delegation from principal to agent. There are such exceptions as the independent commissions, including the Federal Reserve—but the public holds the president responsible for these too. In any case, for all the rest, the lines of legal responsibility run direct to the president, and there is nothing in the world he can

Table 6. The White House Office, 1983

Counsellor to the President
Chief of Staff and Assistant to the President
Deputy Chief of Staff and Assistant to the President
Assistant to the President and Press Secretary
Assistant to the President for National Security Affairs
Assistant to the President and Deputy to the Chief of Staff
Assistant to the President for Legislative Affairs
Counsel to the President
Assistant to the President for Cabinet Affairs
Assistant to the President for Communications
Assistant to the President for Policy Development
Assistant to the President for Presidential Personnel
Assistant to the President and Director of Special Support Services
Deputy Counsellor to the President
Assistant to the President and Deputy to the Deputy Chief of Staff
Assistant to the President for Management and Administration and Director of the Office of Administration
Assistant to the President for Political Affairs
Assistant to the President for Intergovernmental Affairs
Assistant to the President for Public Liaison
Deputy Assistant to the President for Political Affairs
Deputy Assistant to the President and Director of Speechwriting
Deputy Assistant to the President and Director of Public Affairs
Assistant Counsellor to the President
Deputy Assistant to the President for Presidential Personnel
Deputy Counsel to the President
Deputy Assistant to the President for National Security Affairs
Deputy Assistant to the President for Intergovernmental Affairs
Deputy Assistant to the President for Legislative Affairs (House)

Deputy Assistant to the President for Policy Development and Director of the Office of Policy Development
Deputy Assistant to the President
Deputy Assistant to the President and Deputy Press Secretary to the President
Deputy Assistant to the President and Director of Media Relations and Planning
Deputy Assistant to the President for Legislative Affairs (Senate)
Deputy Assistant to the President for National Security Affairs
Deputy Assistant to the President for Public Liaison
Deputy Press Secretary to the President
Special Assistant to the President for National Security Affairs
Special Assistant to the President and Deputy Director of Public Affairs
Special Assistant to the President for National Security Affairs
Special Assistant to the President for Communications
Special Assistant to the President for Public Liaison
Special Assistant to the President and Executive Secretary of the Cabinet Council on Management and Administration
Special Assistant to the President for Policy Development
Special Assistant to the President for Policy Development
Special Assistant to the President for Public Liaison
Special Assistant to the President for Policy Development
Special Assistant to the President and Special Assistant to the Chief of Staff
Associate Counsel to the President
Special Assistant to the President for Private Sector Initiatives
Special Assistant to the President for Legislative Affairs
Special Assistant to the President and Chief Speechwriter
Special Assistant to the President for Legislative Affairs
Personal Photographer to the President
Special Assistant to the President
Special Assistant to the President for National Security Affairs

Special Assistant to the President for Intergovernmental Affairs	*Special Assistant to the President for Public Liaison*
Associate Counsel to the President	*Senior Associate Counsel to the President*
Special Assistant to the President for Policy Development	*Associate Counsel to the President*
	Special Assisant to the President for Legislative Affairs
Special Assistant to the President for Intergovernmental Affairs	

Source: U.S. Government Manual, 1983–84 (Washington: Government Printing Office, 1984), pp. 81–83.

do about it without confronting Congress to change the legislation itself. I find it astonishing that presidents never veto legislation because too much responsibility is delegated, especially when the delegation is so vague that the responsibility is impossible to meet.[19] Intrepidly taking their oath of office, presidents thereby accept all the responsibilities delegated through the accumulated legislation of the previous half century and more, and they seem to be ignorant of the dirty little secret of their accumulated responsibilities until they actually enter the White House. It is almost like the naive newlyweds who are told nothing about sex, childrearing, or the economic struggle until well after the wedding. Once the secrets are discovered, both newlyweds and presidents try to meet the responsibilities with whatever means they can devise—and simultaneously to keep up appearances.

The second reason for maintaining the initiative in the White House is a reinforcement of the first. Quite brutally, there is no institutional basis for sharing responsibility. Having been made a star by the selection process and the structure of the office, the president personally must shine so brilliantly and generate so much gravity that the rest of the Washington universe will revolve in an orderly fashion around him. Unfortunately, stars find it difficult to share their light; to share the light risks creating a second center of gravity rather than a satellite. That there is no institutional basis upon which a president can truly entrust powers and responsibilities may be a very commonplace fact about the American system. But it is a commonplace whose significance is entirely missed. Nothing in our system of selection or government grooms top appointees for real political

[19]I have argued this at greater length in *The End of Liberalism* (New York: Norton, 1979), ch. 11.

149

trust. Even if they did not all have their private agendas, the process by which the top appointees are chosen and the reason for their selection, essentially wipe out the president's ability to trust them. By the time the president makes his cabinet and other top selections, it is too late for him to build a situation in which responsibility can be meaningfully distributed, whether to a few individuals or, especially, to a collective. This is a fundamental flaw in the American Constitution.

One reform that could very well improve on the president's opportunities to share responsibilities at an earlier stage would be to extend to its logical conclusion a ploy of Ronald Reagan's in 1976, which Walter Mondale copied to spectacular effect in 1984. Prior to the balloting for the presidential nomination, Reagan identified the person who would run with him as vice president. He even sought to make this step a rule for all candidates for the Republican nomination. (It was on this motion that Reagan lost in a show of force that confirmed the Ford nomination before the first nominating ballot.) In 1984, Walter Mondale implicitly followed Reagan's proposed rule by announcing his vice-presidential choice, Geraldine Ferraro, before the Democratic convention met.

It has long been customary for presidential candidates to pick their own running mate. Stevenson's delegation of that choice to the convention in 1956 was taken as a sign of his indecisiveness. But the rule Reagan proposed in 1976 is very different. Although he broke it himself in 1980 by announcing the choice of George Bush after the balloting for the presidential nomination was completed, the proposal makes a lot of sense. What would make even more sense would be extending its logic to require that all candidates for the nomination reveal the names of the twenty or more persons from whom their top appointments would be drawn. These persons would be then able to campaign during the pre-convention period and before the election, making themselves known as a group to the public, indicating by their combined characteristics the character of the administration they would comprise. Such a rule would not give them a political base independent of the president any more than the election of the vice president gives that person a base independent of the president. But it could produce a situation in which the president might be able to relinquish some of his need to keep the initiatives in his control at all times. The absence of such a collective situation, which can only be set up well before the election, simply underscores the instructional reason why presidents cannot relax. In early 1984, before they started dropping out, the eight candidates for the Democratic nomination gave off a very positive impression. Each had certain characteristics that would be desirable in an administration; each was in a sense a specialist in some particular area of national government. Throughout those early stages, it was clear to me that all eight of them would have made one good president. This is not because each was a pygmy who, standing on the shoulders of the others, would reach human proportions but because the eight of them, put together, might have been able to cope with an inhuman situation. One of the tests of qualification for president ought to be his or her ability to induce twenty or more credible leaders to agree at an early stage to serve in the administration.

Democratizing the Presidency

The third reason why presidents seem compelled to keep the initiative in the White House is that the masses have grown to expect it. The president is the Wizard of Oz. Appearances become everything. The legal powers and responsibilities focused so directly upon the presidency have contributed to myths about the ability of presidents to meet those responsibilities. And since the rhetoric that flows from the office so magnifies the personal responsibility and so surrounds the power with mystique, it is only natural that the American people would produce or embrace myths about presidential government. The myths are validated and reinforced by popular treatments of the presidency. The mythology of presidential efficacy is reinforced every time there is reference to "the president's capacity to govern."

Here in a nutshell is the dilemma: The more the president holds to the initiative and keeps it personal, the more he reinforces the mythology that there actually exists in the White House a "capacity to govern." Even if, like the Wizard of Oz, a president would like to give up the humbug and go back to Kansas, he would find rather quickly that the office itself is like the Tar Baby. It is difficult, if not impossible, to let go. Ronald Reagan has proved that: A conservative who wanted less government and less presidency ended up embracing the largest government in history and a continually expanding presi-

151

dency with all its personal humbug, as though he had wanted it that way, all along.

Democratizing Presidential Power

No political relationship is more intimate and more frequently reinforced in the United States than that between power and democratization: For every advancement of power, there seems to be an almost equal and opposite demand for more democratization. The demand may be phrased in terms of more representation, more participation, or more accessibility, but these all add up to more democratization.

The presidency illustrates or confirms this relationship better than any other center of power in America. Most noticeable is the president's continual appeal over the heads of Congress and the Washington community directly to the people—a continuation of presidential campaigning, in that the president continues to do all the things during his incumbency that he did to get himself elected. Once he has organized his mass base of popular support, he must do what he can personally to maintain it. The decline of political parties made this direct base necessary, but its very existence continually leads to the need for more and more democratic behavior on the president's part. He must not only communicate to but also receive messages from the public. That is to say, the president extends democratization by making himself more accessible—appearing to make himself more accessible—to the people. Pollsters in the inner councils of the White House continually take polls and sift resulting evidence, and the president gains somewhat more direct readings of the public by making regular visits around the country, despite great personal dangers to himself.

The need to maintain the initiative is directly related to democratization because of the new theory of democracy that puts the presidency at the center of democratic government. Everything the president does has to appear to be of, for, and by the people. This means that there must be many initiatives and every initiative must be defined as an expansion of democracy itself. His actions must be shown to confirm the theory of democracy and, in turn, the theory of democracy must be seen to guide his actions. Thus, every assertion of presidential power is likely to produce a reaction in the form of demands for more public involvement in some form or another, and presidents themselves tend to go through the ritual of trying to accompany each assertion of power with the appearance of greater public involvement.

Finally, democratization is deliberately sought by presidents for its possible payoffs in Washington. Europeans used to say "He who mobilizes the elite can mobilize the electorate." Presidents pursue the opposite policy, that of "He who can mobilize the masses may also mobilize the elite."

Once again, there is a dilemma. A president who feeds upon a theory of democracy may ultimately be devoured by it. If every initiative confirms democracy yet for all its show of power brings about demands for more democratization, the relationship between power and democratization may be a spiraling one. Economists treat the relationship of supply and demand as one that tends toward equilibrium. The relationship between power and democratization cannot be understood as an application of supply and demand. Equilibrium cannot be assumed. This relationship seems to behave according to principles all its own.

Implications — Costs over Benefits

Even a crude cost-benefit analysis of the plebiscitary presidency can be improved by separating domestic from foreign policy considerations. This distinction is important because of the Constitution's own approach to presidential power. The distinction is all the more important because cost must be weighed far more heavily in the foreign than in the domestic policy field. In both fields, however, the focus will be more heavily on costs than on benefits; part of my intention is to provide an antidote to the typical treatments of the modern presidency, which play so heavily on its benefits.

Domestic Policy and the Personal Presidency

As he was mixing the herbs for the potion Juliet was to take to make her appear to be dead, the friar reflected upon how good can come of evil and evil from good. It may be true in all really important things that benefits and costs are one and the same, where in proportion they are benefits and out of proportion they are costs. A presidency built on initiatives and democratization can be a source of great benefits to the society. It gives us the energy Hamilton said was needed in the executive. It makes the national government more sensitive to a variety of needs than it could otherwise possibly be. And it contributes an element of expansiveness, a tendency a government probably needs to have in a society as expansive as ours. Presidents, according to the First Law, may give up trying to succeed and resort to producing the appearance of success; the reputation for power may turn out to serve as well as the real thing. But if experience is any guide, presidents are neither casual nor frivolous about the initiatives they take and the proposals they make. Initiatives, democratization, and expansiveness seem to be correlatives. In proportion, these are obvious benefits. When they are out of proportion, the costs in money, in legitimacy, and in the risk of large-scale disaster are inestimable.

The Liberal Base

Still another element must be added before the accounts can be brought into balance: liberalism. The plebiscitary presidency has been built on a liberal base, just as much as it has been built on a democratic one. In fact, democratization, modern liberalism, and the modern presidency emerged together, with liberalism and democratization having a very yeasty effect upon each other.

Liberalism is individualism elevated to public philosophy. In brief, the liberal view is that since each individual has a moral code and no one moral code can be raised absolutely above another, all moral questions should be kept as much as possible out of the public realm. The freedom of each individual can be limited only at the points where the conduct of one person is injurious to another. Liberal government is one in which government coercion is obligatory as well as justified whenever a case can be made that some particular conduct in the society is producing harmful consequences. This points to the fundamental distinction between liberalism and conservatism in the United States: Liberalism is concerned with conduct deemed harmful in its consequences, and conservatism is concerned mainly with conduct deemed good or evil in itself. The liberal ap-

154

proach to government is a very rational one, appealing to the rational self-interest of all citizens. Any public policy proposal is a fit subject for the agenda in a liberal government if a plausible case, based on evidence, can be made connecting a particular harm or injury to a particular set of conditions. Conservatives are not against government. Quite the contrary, in a conservative government any conduct deemed fundamentally in violation of the community's moral sense should be controlled. If the conduct does not have serious moral implications, however, it can be left to the "private sector," more or less without regard to empirical arguments about harm. For this reason, conservatism is sometimes mistakenly associated with libertarianism when in fact libertarianism is a version of liberalism. Libertarians are simply liberals who believe that most arguments favoring intervention are not plausible and that most injurious conduct will correct itself better, more cheaply, and more thoroughly than the job could be performed by government intervention.

Liberalism as the primary guide to government was considered beneficial by a consensus large and stable enough to support the construction of the modern American national state. But liberalism, like any public philosophy, begins to expose its contradictions when pushed to its extremes. The virtues of liberalism then become its vices; the benefits become its cost. A reexamination of the definition of liberalism will show how this is possible. Since *all* conduct under some conditions can produce harmful consequences, liberal government must concern itself with *all* conduct, putting all conduct under surveillance, even though not all conduct will be subject to controls at any particular point in time. Pushed to its extreme, liberalism is unable to set clear, plausible, and consistent priorities among the various demands on government to deal with various kinds of conduct. Any demand for a public policy—if that demand is supported by a plausible theory about harmful consequences—has a rightful claim to serious consideration as a policy and a moderate-to-high probability of being adopted.

Liberalism Unrestrained

Liberalism and the modern presidency have become intimately interconnected in an upward spiral of costs because *liberalism tends toward its extremes where institutional restraints are weak, and the modern presidency was built at the expense of institutionalized re-*

155

straints. The absence of moral restraints in a liberal government must be compensated for by competition and counterpoise. The American Constitution is the classic liberal case of attempting to provide formal restraints against its own extremes. And Madison's defense is classic: "You must first enable the government to control the governed; and in the next place oblige it to control itself."[20] Where the presidency is concerned, the classic restraints were broken down by a succession of congressional decisions, a process well enough covered in previous chapters. No case is made, or can be made, that the American Separation of Powers and federalism are the only approaches to the institutionalization of restraints. The point is that when these were drastically weakened they were not replaced or supplemented by anything of comparable strength to contain liberalism within the bounds where its benefits outweighed its costs.

On a number of occasions since the end of the Vietnam War and Watergate, Congress has attempted to regain its place and to restore some meaning to the Separation of Powers. Reform of the budget process, already mentioned, was inspired largely by a congressional urge to restore balance between Congress and the executive. Occasionally Congress has crafted statutes with clearer statements of policy than usual and therefore narrower delegations of power to the executive. Reform of the committee structure supposedly contributes to more effective oversight. Although the changes flowing from the reforms have not been dramatic, they have also not been negligible. However, to the extent the reforms have improved Congress's position vis-à-vis the president, they have only turned the president more toward the mass public. Now that the "capacity to govern" has been shifted in theory and practice to the White House, any increases of congressional power—if not accompanied by a fundamental shift in theory—will be seen as congressional obstruction and interference.

The Supreme Court has done nothing significant to meet the constitutional need of liberalism for restraint through counterpoise. Thousands of pounds of newsprint have been devoted to analysis and criticism of the new "activist court," the "Imperial Judiciary." But a closer look will show almost the reverse of counterpoise. First, judicial review of the constitutionality of statutes and of government ac-

---

[20]Clinton Rossiter, ed., *The Federalist Papers* (New York: Mentor, 1961), No. 51, p. 322.

tions has been limited almost entirely to the policies, rules, and orders of *state* governments. Second, although the federal judiciary intervenes constantly in federal agency decisions, the type of review it engages in is not designed to restore constitutional balance and, thereby, constitutionalized restraints on liberalism. With a few exceptions, congressional delegations of power to executive agencies are broader than ever. When the judiciary intervenes in this process it may end up virtually rewriting the statute through its powers of interpretation. But statutory interpretation is itself a reaffirmation of Congress's right to turn over its legislative power to the executive. Moreover, although judiciary review may sometimes restrain or confine an agency, it more often pushes the agency toward an interpretation of its obligations and powers that is far broader than the agency's own. By thus identifying, confirming, and expanding statutory rights and by thus expanding or confirming already broad agency responsibilities, the federal appellate judiciary has maintained a role for itself in the era of big government not by providing constitutional balance but essentially the reverse, by raising expectations about what the executive branch can do, by enlarging many of those expectations into rights, and by expanding the scope and variety of remedies available for the rights so defined.

The decline of institutionalized restraints and of clear legislative rules has not been compensated for by any strengthening of informal restraints, such as programmatic political parties. Science might operate as a restraint if the requirements of evidence were rigorous enough. But today the liberal system is under great pressure to make a show of response to all arguments about injuries, their causes, and the policies that would eliminate them. All things considered, it seems rather clear that a presidential system, especially one constructed the way ours was constructed, pushes liberalism toward an extreme where it is difficult to develop a basis for saying no to any important arguments. Everything is good to do. There is no sense of priority and no procedure for establishing one.

Without a capacity to establish priorities among claims for policies, modern liberalism expanded in all directions, indiscriminately. It expanded the welfare state provisions until they were driving the economy at accelerating speeds toward insolvency. At almost the same instant, this modern liberal state produced a veritable binge of regulatory programs—called "new" or "social" regulation—each of which

157

was a response to a well-meaning demand to prevent injuries by changing in some fundamental way a basic sector or practice comprised of the behavior of millions of individuals. The ultimate goal was to reduce the actual costs of injuries in the society, in the sense that an ounce of prevention today was worth a pound of cure at a later point. But this connection could be made only because the liberal state had established itself as responsible for all injuries. Are all injuries equal, or are some more equal than others? This was not a question that could be confronted by a plebiscitary president, the political party of that president, or the governmental institutions around the presidency.

Although Lyndon Johnson may have been the most extreme case, again the most interesting is that of president Nixon, because Nixon was a partisan who presumably sought the presidency in order to oppose many of the things with which the Democratic party was associated. But instead, the first four years of the Nixon administration was a period of tremendous expansion of domestic policies and programs. The greatest single commitment to the expansion of Social Security since the original 1935 legislation was made in 1972, when Congress passed and Nixon enthusiastically approved the indexing of benefits. Moreover, this new system of indexing was enacted along with a whopping increase in the benefit base. It was the kind of commitment, made in utter disregard of obvious demographic changes, of productivity, and of inflation, that characterizes the plebiscitary presidency and its capacity to push liberalism to its extremes. The Nixon administration was also in office during the period in which virtually all the new regulatory programs were enacted, including some unprecedented in scale and coverage. At least forty major new regulatory programs passed Congress during the Nixon years. Nixon vetoed none of them, he favored many of them, and he implemented all of them conscientiously—including wage and price controls, probably the largest single peace-time regulatory program ever.

Although Ronald Reagan is a genuine conservative, he did not seek to reduce the presidency nor did he seek to restore constitutional restraints or to furnish new restraints to compensate for the absence of the traditional ones. From the start he took every opportunity to appeal to the people to moderate their demands and reduce their appetites for government services. But from the start President Reagan's expressed desire to get the government off our backs was com-

158

pletely phony. All his domestic budget cuts were neutralized by the great increase in the defense budget; and since a large share of the defense budget is spent for ordinary old patronage policies—the pork barrel—this conservative president had plenty of discretionary resources with which to placate the wealthier oligarchs in his party. He gave strong emotional support to such issues as the restoration of power to the states to reinstitute compulsory school prayer and to recriminalize abortion. If states adopted such laws following constitutional amendments, there would be a vast expansion of state government power over all parents in regard to their children's religious practices and all pregnant women and doctors in regard to unborn children. Even his commitment to deregulation was not genuine. He sought no legislation from Congress terminating or permanently reducing regulatory powers or jurisdiction. Instead he enlarged the powers of the presidency by putting all regulatory agencies under closer supervision to make them more sensitive to presidential preferences. In virtually all aspects of policy and personification he was equal to any liberal. Whereas liberals sought hegemony through science, this conservative president, from the start, sought moral hegemony. At no point did he oppose presidential hegemony itself. And just as liberal presidents sought mass support and rapport, so did this conservative. At no point did he ever oppose the plebiscitary presidency. It is the role he seemed most to relish. No president was ever better suited for it.

And all recent presidents, liberal and conservative alike, have failed equally to appreciate the need for a system of restraints and balances: A system dependent for its restraints on the persons who occupy the White House is a system without effective restraints at all. There are barriers, many barriers, to presidential success in governing. But the barriers are merely opposing interests, not constitutional restraints and limits. This is interest-group liberalism; it is a system of preferences, preferences without priorities.

These passages are not to be interpreted as opposition to liberal goals as such. I am personally quite sympathetic to most of them. My concern here is that American national government is being undermined by the lack of understanding among liberals about the system through which their goals can be pursued. Since they have not stopped to evaluate seriously the costs of the plebiscitary presidency, especially in its relation to liberal goals, they continue to expand

159

both; they have attempted to enhance the power of the one in order to accomplish more and more of the other when in fact they only planted the seeds of their own undoing. President Reagan changed the issues and provided a sense of priorities. As I have observed repeatedly, Reagan is the most ideological and programmatic president at least since FDR. Only time will tell if he will succeed in realigning American national politics around conservative principles. But there is a basis for doubt on the following grounds. (1) Reagan has done nothing to alter the liberal presidency. In fact he has embraced and confirmed it. (2) He has in fact been as *carte blanche* as the liberals, the main difference being that he has opened up his system toward defense rather than social policies. But his approach depends just as much as the liberals' on expansion. Naturally, conservatives, like liberals, prefer an expanding economy but are willing to accept as "the moral equivalent of an expanding economy" an expanding budget and an expanding deficit. With expansion one can defer the imposition of real priorities. As Reagan experienced stalemate with Congress, he attempted to maintain the sense of command and of the upholding of his priorities by the usual method of blaming Congress and by a pair of interesting innovations—support of constitutional amendments mandating a balanced budget and providing for the "item veto." But these are superficial gestures, if not downright phony. As gestures they convey an impression of a powerful president tied down by an irresponsible Congress. If adopted, they would enhance expectations about presidential capacity without contributing substantially to it. Neither Reagan's use of line-item veto power[21] while he was governor of California nor his own strong support of an expanded defense budget suggests that he could use the item veto to reduce the budget deficits substantially. And a constitutional requirement of a balanced budget, which amounts to an absolute prohibition against deficits, would work like any absolute prohibition, producing gigantic evasions and subterfuges. Such a constitutional deficit would in no way prevent plebiscitary presidents from creating illusions to cover their failures.

[21]Reporting Research Corporation, *The Quality of Earnings Report*, September 25, 1984, pp. 175-81.

Foreign Policy and the Personal Presidency

The modern American system for the conduct of foreign policy has come a long way since its beginnings during World War II. The enormous growth in the size and scope of the foreign policy establishment has been accompanied by impressive advancements in the professionalization of the diplomatic, military, and intelligence dimensions of foreign policy and also by a number of treaties and organizations dedicated to stable international relations. But this modern foreign policy establishment has been subject to at least two mischievous influences: (1) its long, pre-modern tradition and (2) its very modern presidency.

(1) The United States had a "traditional system" of foreign policy just as it had a traditional system of domestic policy. The former amounted to almost no foreign policy at all, because for more than a century we were a client state. This status enabled us to observe the principle of nonentanglement enunciated from the start by George Washington. It gave us freedom of action, especially in the Western hemisphere, and it left us at liberty to have as much, or as little, foreign policy as we wished.

Three types of institutional consequences flowed from this long era of client status: the intermingling of institutions of domestic and foreign politics; amateurism; and unilateralism. Each calls for a brief treatment.

Because the major powers were responsible for the conduct of most of the necessary international relations, American political leaders could use the world outside as a garbage dump for domestic conflicts. The tariff was, in effect, a means of displacing domestic conflicts. But as a consequence, we never did develop a distinction between domestic and foreign affairs, either in theory or in practice. Foreign policy was domestic politics "by other means." Only after World War II was any systematic attempt made to distinguish between domestic and foreign politics or policy. We began talking about how "politics stops at the water's edge," but this was more an expression of hope than a recognition of an established distinction.

Amateurism followed directly from this intermingling of domestic and foreign policy processes. Failing to make the domestic/foreign distinction, we also failed to develop a tradition of a separate foreign service composed of professional people who spent much of their adult lives in foreign countries, learning foreign languages, absorbing foreign cultures, and developing a certain sympathy for foreign (alien) points of view. Instead, we tended to be highly suspicious of any American diplomat or entrepreneur who attempted to speak for any such point of view.[22] No systematic attempt was made to create a professional diplomatic corps until after the passage of the Foreign Service Act of 1946. The same can be said of military personnel. We provided for no standing army and tended to revolt against the development of a professional officer corps topped by a professional general staff. It is not insignificant that the creation of the Joint Chiefs of Staff (JCOS) took place only during World War II and that we did not have officers of five-star rank until that time. (We chose to call a five-star general General-of-the-Army rather than Marshall, to prevent the first one from being Marshall Marshall.) The recency of all these titles and command posts is indicative of the preference for amateurism.[23]

Unilateralism is much better than isolationism as a defining term for American predispositions. Although there have been many isolationists in American history, we were never in any sense isolated from the world. Rather, we believed in the maxim "Go it alone." Thanks to our client status, we could practice what we believed. The great advantage of unilateralism was that we did not have to know very much about any other country in order to define and pursue our national interests.

Although World War II was the great divide, it was not the great divorce. America found itself a world power with its own client states. Institutions had been crafted or reformed to make a world role possible, including the JCOS, a professionalizing Foreign Service, a new Department of Defense, the CIA, and the political training as well as the professionalization of military officers. But traditional values, institutions, and practices were not cast off. Domestic pluralism continued to dominate foreign policy-making. Amateurism and distrust of professionalism continued to prevail. And, while unilateralism may have grown weaker, there remained a continuing distrust of or

[22]E. E. Schattschneider, *Politics, Pressures and the Tariff* (Englewood Cliffs: Prentice-Hall, 1935).

[23]For professionalization in the State Department, see John E. Harr, *The Professional Diplomat* (Princeton: Princeton University Press, 1969); for the military, see Morris Janowitz, *The Professional Soldier* (New York: The Free Press, 1960, 1971).

impatience with diplomacy. We permitted ourselves to become a world power but did not commit ourselves fully to all the requirements of that role. The instruments of foreign policy created during the postwar period are all indicative of our ambivalence between traditional values and demands for new ones. For example, the commitment to the United Nations was indeed a commitment to a modern, comprehensive peacetime involvement in world affairs, but, as with Wilson and the League of Nations, we viewed the UN as a way of avoiding diplomacy. As Wilson had put it twenty-five years before, the goal of world organization was "open covenants openly arrived at." Another example of ambivalence is our commitment to collective security in a variety of multilateral treaty arrangements. Such involvement is definitely a rejection of George Washington's warning in his Farewell Address; but the structure of collective security, in its effort to make relationships among the members automatic, ultimately aims at an escape from continuing diplomacy. It is a dangerous route to escape, in that if an attack on any member of a multilateral mutual defense treaty is defined as an attack on the United States, then we have put the trigger in the hands of the weakest ally and have left the decision to provoke its use in the hands of the adversary. Even the atomic bomb, as a kind of doomsday weapon, serves to obviate the finer points of diplomatic relations. And the same can be said of our two most important instruments of economic foreign policy, the Bretton Woods international monetary structure and the Marshall Plan. Both were aimed at obviating diplomacy in the normal political sense; and to underscore that intention, both, like the Atomic Energy Commission, were with conscious intention placed outside the State Department bureaucracy and beyond the reach of State Department authority.[24]

Those who think the transition from the traditional to the modern system of foreign policy was painless need only to be reminded of McCarthyism. Nevertheless, a modern system did evolve, with the president at the center capping a professional foreign policy establishment. During the 1950s, despite McCarthyism, there was growing recognition that foreign policy must be separated from domestic and that presidents and diplomats must be trusted with discretion to use

[24]An expansion of this interpretation will be found in Lowi, *The End of Liberalism*, ch. 6.

163

American resources to maintain peace as well as to advance American national interests. The president was finally victorious over Congress in the "struggle for the privilege of directing American foreign policy."[25]

However, the spell of tradition has never been completely cast off. Domestic pluralism continues to be very much the pattern of politics in foreign policy, to such an extent that we still have no integrated "foreign ministry." Even after a full generation of international involvements and extensive experience, the United States still cannot speak with a single voice. No one doubts the superior position of the presidency, but the president lacks the capacity to prevent agencies in the foreign affairs field from having and conducting their own foreign policy. The State Department has never been able to become a foreign ministry in the sense of incorporating all the important agencies and functions relative to diplomacy and foreign policy. The Pentagon has a larger number of military personnel stationed abroad than the State Department has diplomats. The Treasury Department has its own representation abroad, and even it cannot prevent the Special Trade Representative from operating in separate spheres. The same, albeit to a lesser degree, is true of the departments of Agriculture, Labor, and Commerce, all of which have significant ties with their counterparts in other countries. Unification of the policies of all these and other agencies with foreign interests is difficult enough politically but compounded still further by various laws that give them a legal right to engage in international relations. Nothing has to be routinely cleared with the secretary of state. In fact, the valiant efforts on the part of Secretary of State Alexander Haig to make his office the clearing house and command post for all foreign policy under the Reagan administration led only to his failure and resignation. The fact that neither President Reagan nor his predecessors wanted a strong secretary of state to succeed in becoming a head of a true foreign ministry brings us back to the plebiscitary presidency. It will turn out to be no paradox that plebiscitary presidents want unity— and they don't want it.

(2) The heavy weight of tradition has made a major direct contribution to the problems of conducting American foreign policy. It has

[25]E. S. Corwin, *The President: Office and Powers*, 3d. ed. (New York: New York University Press, 1948), p. 171.

also made an indirect contribution in enhancing the second mischievous force in foreign policy, the plebiscitary presidency. Lack of institutional unification has had to be compensated for by emotional or charismatic unification, a substitution that requires strategic use of the plebiscitary aspects of the presidency. As I observed earlier, the president must somehow mobilize the electorate in order to unify the elite.

What remains is to spell out the implications of these patterns for presidential behavior. Here, then, is another "behavioral model." It is composed of at least four clusters of predictable characteristics. In order to convey the impression that these are stable clusters of behavior, applying to all presidents regardless of party or personality, I have called them *syndromes*.[26] The four syndromes easiest to identify and describe are: the star or celebrity syndrome; the anti-diplomacy syndrome; the administrative pluralism syndrome; and the oversell syndrome. I would not want to leave the impression that these are the only types of characteristic behavior patterns. They may not even be the best sort of classification. But they are sufficient to pursue to a conclusion this important discourse regarding the potentialities of the connections between modern government, the political system created by that modern government, and the problems fed back upon that government by what I consider an inadequate adjustment of the political system to the government.

The Star Syndrome

If the president is already under some kind of compulsion to maintain the initiative in the White House, he is *least* willing to share, initiatives in the foreign policy field. No star was ever more jealous of the light.

The National Security Act of 1947 recognized the need for a presidential capacity to take and maintain foreign policy initiatives. Informally it was called the Unification Act. It created the National Security Council, with its important staff, for the purpose of providing the president with the capacity to make a central decision and to coordinate its implementation among the relevant departments. The desire for unity under the presidency was also reflected in the orga-

---

[26]A syndrome is a set of concurrent symptoms—usually with reference to components of a disease.

nization and placement of the CIA, as the international intelligence servant of the National Security Council. However, the president has gone much further than the letter or spirit of the National Security Act by centralizing initiatives still further into the White House and unto himself. At least since Kennedy, and possibly since Eisenhower, presidents have chosen to be "their own secretary of state."[27] Each has chosen a relatively weak person to hold the title, weak in the sense that he lacks independent stature and independent bases of political support. And the secretaries of state are willing to maintain a subordinate role, or else they are relatively quickly cashiered. Dean Rusk remained slavishly loyal throughout his long period of service to Presidents Kennedy and Johnson. Thomas Cronin attributes to President Johnson the following comment: "I'll always love Dean Rusk, bless his heart. He stayed with me when nobody else did."[28] Secretary of State William Rogers had been a close friend of Richard Nixon's and was willing to be as loyal and subordinate as Nixon required in order to run foreign policy for himself from the White House—with the help of Henry Kissinger, his special assistant for national security. Cyrus Vance was forced to resign from office the first moment there was a serious disagreement between himself and President Carter.

One apparent exception to this pattern, Henry Kissinger, actually confirms the rule. Kissinger rose to power in the White House by helping to make possible President Nixon's performance as his own secretary of state. Toward the end of Nixon's tenure, Kissinger was appointed secretary of state and stayed through the Ford administration as the strongest and most independent and creative holder of the position at least since John Foster Dulles, and probably beyond that. But Kissinger in effect captured the State Department for the White House and from the White House.

Ronald Reagan also fits the mold. For Reagan we should probably refer to White House strength and the guidance of a strong staff,

[27]Although John Foster Dulles had the reputation of being the strongest and most independent and creative of modern secretaries of state, new research, especially that of Professor Fred Greenstein, is indicating that Eisenhower was the precursor of the modern pattern of being his own secretary of state. Dulles was much more his servant than was understood at the time. See Fred Greenstein, *The Hidden Hand Presidency: Eisenhower as Leader* (New York: Basic Books, 1982).

[28]Thomas E. Cronin, *The State of the Presidency*, 2d ed. (Boston: Little, Brown, 1980), p. 12, attributed to former Johnson crony Bobby Baker.

rather than presidential strength. Nevertheless the pattern is still that of his predecessors. For example, the president or the White House pushed Secretary of State Haig from office for trying to be a strong force. The earliest presidential actions in 1981 included direct sale of the highly strategic AWACS airplanes and technology to Saudi Arabia, lifting of the wheat embargo on the Soviet Union, and the rejection of SALT II, all without consultation with the State Department. Evidence of White House dominance includes the sending of Secretary of State Shultz to Lebanon before any diplomatic groundwork was prepared, then the dispatching of the Marines as a peace force, followed by the elimination of their neutrality and a commitment to the Gemayel government. Evidence includes also the Grenada invasion and the commitment to an overt/covert CIA sponsorship of military action in Central America. George Shultz, Reagan's second secretary of state, was given no enhanced power or trust; his role was mainly one of mediator among the several major participants in foreign policy. President Reagan fits the mold most comfortably in his ability to associate himself with international events that bear positively on his general public approval rating but have very little direct cost attached. His ability to play off the annual economic summit meetings, his ability to play on the revulsion against the Russians for shooting down the Korean Air Lines plane, and his talent for pursuing the right international adventures and trips, such as Grenada and Normandy, are second to none who have ever occupied the office of president. Reagan is truly a Great Communicator. For a plebiscitary president, this is the functional equivalent of a foreign policy.

The Anti-Diplomacy Syndrome

Although distrust of diplomacy is a traditional American attitude, the significant point here is that it has continued into the modern atomic era, and it continues not only among the unsophisticated masses but also in the minds and hearts of plebiscitary presidents.

More is involved in the anti-diplomacy syndrome than merely a persistence of the traditional homespun idea that diplomats are elitist and potentially disloyal. Presidential distrust of and impatience with diplomacy are built into the presidential system as well as into presidential psychology. Presidents simply cannot relinquish enough of their own authority to permit a process such as diplomacy to develop an independent professional force. Although they often

167

rely on the foreign service and on the international military bureaucrats, as soon as political relationships with any particular country begin to intensify presidents show a strong tendency to withdraw the issue from the diplomats and from diplomacy itself. The president does not merely pull the issue upstairs to the secretary of state. Rather, he withdraws it to the White House, turning it over to the special assistant for national security or to an envoy appointed for the particular role. When a special envoy is sent abroad to represent the president, that envoy holds a status higher than the local ambassador. The ambassador becomes the servant of the envoy, and the embassy becomes the envoy's pied-à-terre. This displacement of ambassadors as soon as the stakes go up does not well serve the long-term improvement of the diplomatic corps or the long-term interest of the nation. Many people have complained about the American tradition of appointing political hacks to major ambassadorial posts. Demeaning and discouraging as it is, I doubt it is as demeaning and discouraging as the less-noticed, less-criticized practice of temporarily removing career *or* political ambassadors from a foreign policy issue as soon as it begins to heat up.

Presidents are distrustful of diplomacy and impatient with it for reasons beyond the tendency of stars to resist sharing the limelight. The president cannot permit the development of an independent foreign ministry that would prevent him from reserving the option of individual and dramatic action whenever he feels he needs a foreign policy fix. Although he cannot use this option as often as he might wish, he must have available to him from time to time the opportunity to prove his capacity for governing world events. For a true diplomat, the measure of success in any international relationship is its *absence* from the front pages of the newspapers. A president can abide this kind of success only so long. For the diplomat, peace can be measured by the absence of conflict and the virtual bureaucratization of relationships between countries. Presidents, especially plebiscitary presidents, get no credit from that kind of peace. For a plebiscitary president, peace requires advancement, and dramatic moves against the advancements of adversaries. Presidents need credit, and credit comes from action, not from the absence of it. Diplomacy and plebiscitary presidencies are natural enemies. The real need of a plebiscitary president is the capacity, and the reputation for the capacity, to produce on demand for his mass constituency

—or to create the appearance of—results in foreign policy. In contrast, a bureaucratized foreign ministry tends to avoid specific results, especially dramatic results, and to prefer continuity of its processes and ambiguity of outcomes in order to protect the continuity of the processes of other countries. For a mature foreign ministry, the worst outcome of any endeavor is, of course, unambiguous defeat. But second in dread only to that is unambiguous victory. Plebiscitary presidents thrive on unambiguous victory, or its appearance.

The Administrative Pluralism Syndrome

This syndrome is related to the previous two but is important enough to deserve separate analysis. Administrative pluralism in foreign policy is an obvious and undeniable trait, as I have already observed. Not only does the Defense Department have more people serving abroad than the State Department does; for most presidents, the secretary of defense is equal in importance for foreign policy to the secretary of state. And the Treasury Department is not only another important foreign policy agency; some strong secretaries of the treasury have enjoyed coequal status with state and defense. Other departments and agencies have a legal and formally recognized right to engage in international affairs within their jurisdictions. And cases abound where one department or agency makes a relatively important commitment without the knowledge of the secretary of state, sometimes to the embarrassment of the country. One of the more important examples was that of President Nixon during the 1971-72 international monetary crisis, in which he used the Treasury to terminate the Bretton Woods international monetary structure without involving the State Department at all. Resumption of the sale of wheat to Russia was a deal made by President Reagan and his secretary of agriculture without the full knowledge of the secretary of state. The sale of the AWACS planes to Saudi Arabia was an exclusive for the Pentagon. A very significant proportion of the $400 billion worth of international debt and an especially large proportion of that debt held by Third World countries result from projects encouraged by and credit extended by various developmentally oriented U.S. agencies without any coordination whatsoever. The largest debtor nations, such as Mexico and Brazil, have been subjected to a bewildering array of U.S. representatives encouraging them to go into further debt.

Since dependence on bureaucracy is inevitable, the president seems to search for safety in numbers, so that no one bureaucracy or one process becomes competition for foreign policy power or a drag on presidential flexibility. The maintenance of multiple foreign policy agencies gives the president a larger range of options for maintaining the appearance and possibly even the reality of delivering results in foreign affairs. But, just as the absence of political parties makes the president a mass leader but vulnerable to those masses, so pluralism in foreign policy enables him to build upon agency and corporate interests but at the same time makes him the potential prisoner of their claims and commitments abroad. Pluralism was not a problem in foreign policy as long as America was a client state. Pluralism was not a particular problem for a world leader in an international system without atomic bombs and intercontinental delivery capacity. But pluralism becomes a significant problem where world leadership and atomic threats require international stability and continuity.

Lying in State—The Oversell Syndrome

In an earlier work, I developed a notion of "oversell" in American foreign policy as a natural and predictable outcome of liberalism, part of the linkage liberalism has encouraged between pluralism and foreign policy.[29] I continue to hold to that interpretation but now see the need to augment it with the idea of the plebiscitary presidency. A product itself of liberalism (as I argued in Chapter 5), once the plebiscitary presidency was fully established it added immensely to the predictable consequences of liberalism. Such are the president's channels of mass communication that he must simplify and dramatize his appeals, whether the communication deals with foreign policy, domestic policy, or something else again. Almost every initiative is given a public relations name. Every initiative has to be "new and improved." Every initiative has to be a response to "threats to the national interest." Did anyone ever hear of a president trying to belittle an action or a challenge? Can anyone remember an instance where the president proposed something that was not absolutely vital to our national interest?

Quite to the contrary, each challenge must be escalated. Conflicts of interest abound among nation-states, even among historic allies.

[29]*The End of Liberalism,* ch. 6.

170

Despite our "special relationship" with England and Israel, our interests conflict with theirs at numerous points. Conflicts of interest frequently are so serious as to destabilize relations among Common Market countries. The Soviet Union has serious conflicts of interest with Poland, its most important satellite. Conflicts of interest are the normal stuff of diplomacy. But the plebiscitary president is under pressure to take some of these conflicts of interest and convert them into threats to the national interest. There is also pressure to take some of these threats to the national interest and move them up another notch, to be vital threats to the national interest or threats to vital national interest. Everywhere countries can be arranged in dominoes, and wherever they are, the last domino is the United States. If we don't stop them there, they will be in San Francisco or Miami by sundown. Even where a low-key definition of our national interests might justify a direct involvement with a country or its internal conflicts, that ordinary interest does not seem to be sufficient for maintaining the president's popular support. It has to be pushed up at least one step on the ladder of escalation. Whether it is the value of American investments or a friendly ruler that might be at stake, the president still has to find a commie in the woodpile. And logically, as the definition of the conflict escalates, the president may well find himself committed to an escalated real involvement, not only moving up the scale of intensity but moving from diplomatic to military steps.

Preference for overselling the threat is not associated with a particular personality type. No one resorted to overselling threats more frequently and more eloquently than active-positive John Kennedy, but active-negative Johnson and Nixon were his near-equals, and so was passive-positive Ronald Reagan. Kennedy saw us in peril from a missile gap and was fascinated by the probable relationship in small countries between insurgent-type civil wars and involvement by Chinese or Russian agents. Lyndon Johnson systematized this connection with arguments that the Vietnam War was a proxy war in which the spread of Soviet/Chinese communism had to be stopped once and for all. No matter that by the mid-1960s the Soviets and the Chinese were at vicious odds with each other; the president's public definition of threats did not allow for such refinements. Despite Richard Nixon's final recognition of the China/Russia split and the playing of the first "China card," he kept us in the Vietnam War for another four years on the grounds that anything short of an "honorable" settlement would destroy our credibility and give rise to other Vietnams around the world. And, despite over a decade of full acceptance of an independent China, Ronald Reagan has reverted to the idea of a bipolar world in which an "evil empire" is threatening wherever national movements and civil wars are taking place.

At other times presidents have shown a preference for the other side of oversell, the solution. Our "window of vulnerability" (the threat oversold) can be closed (for all time?) with the MX missile or the space machinery, or the poison gas, or the resumption of the arms race. It is here that we get our delicious Madison Avenue names and titles for foreign policies. A Caribbean Basin Initiative would turn the economic tide in that whole region and at the same time put an irresistible economic squeeze on Cuba. That policy was a repeat of the Alliance for Progress which, nearly twenty years earlier, oversold to such an extent that Kennedy sounded like a revolutionist to the governments of recipient countries. And, similarly, the modest Jimmy Carter contributed to the eventual troubles of his diplomatic arrangements between Israel and Egypt by making so much of the Camp David Accord and the Spirit of Camp David that expectations for the solidity and scale of success were out of all proportion.

One case will illustrate that these kinds of excesses are not examples of the superficial and the whimsical but are basic to the presidency and the relationship between the office and the people. That is the Iranian hostage case. After the Iranian revolutionists stormed the American embassy in Tehran and took the fifty-odd embassy people as hostages, President Carter's general approval rating jumped from 32 percent to 61, probably the highest single jump in the history of polling. Once the hostages had been taken and they were in the hands of dedicated and possibly hysterical revolutionaries, the best counsel was to hold fast and to watch the progress of the revolution in Iran and use the best available lines of diplomatic communication to try to keep the situation there from going crazy. As days passed, however, pressures on President Carter personally to do something about the hostages were incessant. And mounting. From time to time reassurances were issued but to no avail. Secretly, planning had already begun for what was to become the ill-fated helicopter rescue. Once the adventure was aborted and the secret revealed, President Carter naturally accepted responsibility for the plan and its failure but at the same time insisted that it was a "humanitarian" mission so well conceived that without the series of accidents, it would have been carried out without a casualty. Note the oversell tendency even after the fact, but note more seriously the futility of the gesture. Whatever the plan, it is undeniable that, at some level of probability, the president had endangered the lives of the hostages, the rescuers, and hundreds of Iranian bystanders. Given how quickly several thousand frenzied Iranians gathered around the American embassy compound following minor provocations, one can imagine the response to radios and loudspeakers announcing in panic the invasion of Tehran by a fleet of helicopters and an indeterminate force of American soldiers.

No president makes an international move casually. A peace-loving, religious man like Jimmy Carter did not take the risk of the Iranian rescue mission merely to give himself a convenient lever to move American public opinion. The leverage worked the other way: Public opinion had forced upon the president an act of the sheerest adventurism. On the other hand, like all plebiscitary presidents Carter was not incapable of rhetorical excesses. For example, it was Carter who characterized the Russian invasion of Afghanistan as our "most serious crisis since World War II," when the same invasion could just as well have been seen as a reflection of the crumbling of international socialism and the profoundness of Soviet fears of China.

Rhetoric—as any angry ape will testify—is preferable to action; but the relationship between rhetoric and action is a problematic one. Mass pressure on plebiscitary presidents requires results, or the appearance of results, regardless of the dangers. Thus, while there is a difference in principle between diplomatic and military approaches, escalation of the definition of conflicts can reach such a height that it wipes out that difference. Oversell is the rhetorical equivalent of militarism.

Costs and Benefits—Mainly Costs

August 1984 was the tenth anniversary of the culmination of Watergate and the twentieth anniversary of the Tonkin Gulf Resolution, the virtual declaration of war on North Vietnam. Both were grim reminders of the pressures that have led plebiscitary presidents to deceive, systematically, the public and the Washington community. Even Machiavelli counseled the prince that truth was preferable to deceit, except where the maintenance of the state itself was at issue. The Tonkin Gulf Resolution and Watergate were both instances in which deceit actually put the state at issue. Only a long and intricate chain of causation could lead from Hanoi or from the Democratic National Committee headquarters to revolution. Yet, although John Kennedy, Lyndon Johnson, and Richard Nixon were very different characters operating in very different world and domestic contexts, they all came to view the presidency and the state as one and the same— bringing to mind the assertion of Louis XIV, "L'état, c'est moi." Plebiscitary presidents have all the disadvantages of monarchy with none of the advantages. They must live on appearances and have contingency plans for deceit, yet they are not part of a protective tradition of a ruling class tied by history and religion to the system of governance.

As presidents have come to view their office as tantamount to the state, they have tended also to view barriers and obstructions to their activities as tantamount to disloyalty. As the presidency grew, so did the practice of using the FBI, the CIA, and other agencies to engage in surveillance of "subversive and extremist" individuals and groups, even in times of peace. Ample evidence exists that presidents in the 1980s continue to view all social disorder as tied to the presidency. Very shortly after Reagan's election, he pardoned the two former FBI agents who had been convicted of illegal uses of power against several political activists. The pardon was appropriate, according to Reagan, because the illegal activities were engaged in "not with criminal intent," but "on high principle to bring an end to terrorism." He hoped their pardon would restore the integrity of the FBI and underscore the dangers of subversion and extremism, to which was added domestic terrorism. After some months of work on a new executive order concerning domestic intelligence activities, a final version was produced that permitted all federal government intelligence agencies to "use such techniques as electronic surveillance, unconsented physical search [breaking and entering], mail surveillance, physical surveillance, or monitoring devices," provided that the attorney general approves the use as conforming to guidelines which "shall protect constitutional and other legal rights and limit use of such information to lawful government purposes." Henceforth, more agencies than ever can maintain surveillance over citizens.

The Bottom Line

One of the more thoughtful essays on the twentieth anniversary of the Tonkin Gulf Resolution proposed three lessons to be learned from the experience. First, although Congress can be deceived, the eventual cost of the deception is inestimable. Second, Congress must define more clearly its relationship to the president, including making firm its own obligation never to enact laws and resolutions that can be interpreted in ways opposite to its real intent. Third, even in foreign policy, the system cannot work without a separation of powers, but one based on good will and not distrust.[30] Worthwhile as these lessons are, they are incomplete and can be extended. First, without a constitutional balance the presidency flies apart. Second, deceit destroys the balance, because deceit destroys good will. Third, the costs of the plebiscitary presidency will always outweigh the benefits because deceit is inherent in the present structure. Since more is demanded than can ever be delivered, and since the payoff is pinpointed personally on the president—that's where the buck stops—deceit will always be used to save the president as well as to defend the fundamental interests of the state. No big government can afford this—least of all a world power with atomic capacity. Governmental incapacity and atomic capacity are the ticket to annihilation.

[30]Allan E. Goodman and Seth P. Tillman, "Debris from the Tonkin Resolution," *New York Times*, August 5, 1984, p. E21.

175

7

Restoring the Balance

> In framing a government . . . the great difficulty lies in
> this: You must first enable the government to control
> the governed; and in the next place oblige it to control
> itself. A dependence on the people is, no doubt, the pri-
> mary control on the government; but experience has
> taught mankind the necessity of auxiliary precautions.
>   —James Madison

The tortured logic of Watergate calls to mind the
notes from an apocryphal biology lab report:

Detached right wing and legs from fly. Commanded it to fly. It flopped
about on the dish.

Detached left wing and legs. Commanded fly to fly. No movement.

Findings: When you detach all wings and legs from a fly, you impair its
sense of hearing.

Ten years after Watergate the received wisdom seems to be that it
was a low point in the history of the presidency and a high point in
the history of the genius of the American system for self-correction.
For the first time in American history, a president was forced to resign from office. For the first time in American history, a president
had personally committed crimes for which he would almost certainly have been proved guilty if he had not avoided impeachment by
resignation and avoided trial by the timely pardon granted him by
his hand-picked successor. Yet, "Watergate was potentially the best
thing to have happened to the presidency in a long time," wrote Ar-

thur Schlesinger, expressing a view held by many. Removing the president and putting most of his White House staff in jail may have shut the evil genie up in the bottle again for as much as fifty years.[1] All our "imperial presidency" needed to bring it into line was a single blow against misuse, proving that transgression against the Constitution and the laws will be exposed and punished. Fear of exposure and punishment will keep future presidents in line.

An examination of the specific results of Watergate will simply not sustain that kind of conclusion. Ten years of perspective ought to have reduced the scale of Watergate's importance and introduced an element of sobriety in the weighing of the good that came from the punishments of wrongdoing. I frankly do not think the argument about Watergate's benefits was sustainable even in 1974, but in any event, a proper understanding of the presidency today requires a more balanced, therefore a more skeptical, assessment.

Before jumping to any larger conclusions, such as the fly's loss of hearing, let us review the direct lessons that can definitively be learned from the outcome of Watergate. *If you are president*: Don't commit a crime. Don't encourage members of your staff to commit a crime—that is itself a commission of a crime. Don't keep records—written or on tape—of actions or discussions remotely connected to the commission of a crime. Dispose of any such records well before allegations of possible crimes can be made, because executive privilege does not protect confidential records that bear on such allegations. *If you are a member of the president's staff*: Don't burgle for the president. Don't engage in forgery for the president. Don't engage in illegal wiretapping and electronic surveillance for the president. Don't lie for the president, and in particular don't permit your president to encourage you to lie. Don't encourage or participate in the obstruction of justice. Don't destroy evidence. Don't offer or accept bribes. Don't try to encourage persons or government agencies to engage in actions that violate federal laws. And if any of these activities should take place, be absolutely certain of deniability—that proof can be rendered up that the president was truly and absolutely ignorant of the illegal activities that were taking place.

In other words, no substantial direct lesson can be learned from

[1]Arthur Schlesinger, Jr., *The Imperial Presidency* (New York: Popular Library, 1974), p. 396.

Watergate except not to engage in illegal activities or be caught doing so. No general lesson can be drawn about the imperial presidency or the plebiscitary presidency that could not have been drawn before Watergate or in ignorance of its events and results. No new Ervin committee or any other source of inside dope is needed to give us facts about how presidents must behave in order to meet the necessities of that office. For the same reason that the English racing car driver could predict the outcome of the Grand Prix du Roc, we can know from our general sense of the presidential track that, except for the violation of a few criminal provisions, the Watergate case is confirmation of and consistent with the nature of the modern presidency, not an aberrant episode. In every respect other than the extent of illegal activities, there is a Watergate of some kind everyday in the life of a president. The scale of presidential power and of mass expectation about presidential power is so great that presidents must, as in Watergate, attempt to control their environment to the maximum, especially those aspects of it that might tend to be barriers in the way of meeting presidential responsibilities. Those responsibilities are so pressing and so close to unmeetable that presidents must have vast contingency plans to make up the difference between expectations and realities. In order to avoid the full impact of the Three Laws of Politico-Dynamics enunciated in Chapter 1, presidents must first and somehow find a way to control events themselves. But because of the Second Law, the near certainty of failure, presidents must have contingency plans for what to do if they cannot control events. This means they must have contingency plans for controlling the news about the events. That requires an army of public relations people to put the best possible interpretation on whatever is reported as news—that is, to try to create the appearance of success. But since the White House cannot control the way events are interpreted as news, there must also be contingency plans for controlling what gets into the public domain in the first place. To this end, not only are an army of people to do public relations needed; there must also be "plumbers" armed with whatever devices of administrative control can be made available. These contingency plans are a perfect parallel to Watergate events and motivations—but carried on by people who learned from Watergate how to do it all without engaging in criminal acts.

The events of Watergate can be considered a culmination and a corrective only if one assumes that Watergate was a case of personal usurpation. Some believe it to have been just that. Schlesinger contributed to this interpretation in 1974 with his important analysis that treated the shift to the imperial presidency as the result of a "capture by the presidency [of] powers reserved by the Constitution and by long historical practice to Congress."[2] But if—as I have tried throughout the book to show—the modern presidency is not built on personal usurpation, then no personal punishment like the Watergate convictions can abate it, for fifty years or for one year. In the first place, the modern presidency, whether it is defined as imperial or plebiscitary, was very largely the construction of the United States Congress, with the complicity of the federal courts. Second, that construction began with domestic policies during the New Deal and afterward, not with foreign policies. Third, the theory of presidential government was already in place and legitimized well before we became a "national security state." Fourth, although there may be many specific cases of usurpation by modern presidents, these are extreme actions in pursuit of powers and responsibilities by and large willingly and voluntarily delegated to the president by Congress. For example, until Watergate, the clearest case of presidential usurpation was probably the 1952 steel seizure case,[3] and there the Supreme Court told President Truman, even as they were turning him down, that he could probably legally and constitutionally have seized the steel mills if he had relied upon emergency powers granted the presidency under several *congressional* acts rather than claiming inherent presidential powers. In effect, the Supreme Court was giving the president guidelines on how to act extremely without behaving unconstitutionally or illegally. Although President Nixon disregarded the Court's guidelines, no case can be made that he was aberrant, illogical, or psychopathological. Quite the contrary. When one understands the assumptions under which he was operating, the only meaningful conclusion is that Nixon was consistent, logical, and normal. To examine those assumptions is in an important sense to review the previous six chapters.

[2]Ibid., pp. 10–11.
[3]*Youngstown Sheet & Tube Co.* v. *Sawyer*, 343 U.S. 579 (1952).

The Imperial/Plebiscitary Presidency

Richard Nixon was brought up on the imperial presidency and had no serious misgivings about it. Imperial meant something established, neither extreme nor extraordinary. Schlesinger could conceive of an imperial presidency precisely because it was already a real thing and not a figment of his or of Richard Nixon's imagination. Schlesinger chose the characterization *imperial* because it connotes a strong state with sovereignty and power over foreigners, as well as rank, status, privilege, and authority, and it also connotes the president's power and responsibility to do whatever he judges necessary to maintain the sovereignty of the state and its ability to keep public order, both international and domestic. The imperial presidency turns out on inspection, therefore, to be nothing more nor less than the discretionary presidency grounded in national security rather than domestic government. Characterizing the presidency as plebiscitary is not at all inconsistent; it is an attempt to capture the same factors and at the same time to tie them to the greatest source of everyday pressure on the presidency—not the Soviet Union, not world leadership, but the American people and their expectations. Nixon's understanding of this situation in all its aspects was probably more extensive and complete than that of any other modern president. He understood it to a fault. And he spoke and acted as though his understanding of it was exactly the same as that which has been portrayed in this book. If so, he was operating logically and sanely under the following assumptions:

The first assumption is that the president and the state are the same thing, that president is state personified. The second is that powers should be commensurate with responsibilities. Since most of the responsibilities of state were intentionally delegated to the president, there is every reason to assume that Congress and the people intended that there be a capacity to carry them out.

The third assumption, intimately related to the second, is that the president should not and cannot be bound by normal legal restrictions. To put this indelicately, the president's actions must be considered above the law or subject to a different kind of law from those of ordinary citizens. While not free to commit any crime merely for the sake of convenience, the president nevertheless cannot be constantly beset by considerations of legality when the state itself is or seems to be at issue.

The first three assumptions lead inexorably toward a fourth, which is that any *deliberate* barriers to presidential action must be considered tantamount to disloyalty. Barriers to presidential action can be tolerated up to a point, and it is probable that most presidents, including Richard Nixon, have prided themselves on their uncommon patience with organized protests, well-meaning but embarrassing news leaks, journalistic criticism, and organized political opposition. But there is a point beyond which such barriers cannot be tolerated, and as that point is approached, confidential knowledge of the identities and contentions of the organizers of obstructions must be gathered. When the intentions of these organizers are determined, to the president's satisfaction, to be malicious, it would be foolish for the president to wait until they are fully set in train.

If these assumptions only barely approximate Nixon's understanding of the presidency, then his actions, including his crimes, are entirely consistent and rational, quite possibly motivated by the highest sense of public interest. To reach that conclusion, however, is not to exonerate Nixon but only to bring the system and all its presidents into question. The Tonkin incident involved a much greater deceit than Watergate. And Nixon's connection between himself and the state was never so intimate as that made by President Johnson, who was even able to define the Vietnam War in personal terms: "I won't be the first to lose a war."

"Lying in state" is common practice. Presidents operate on the brink of failure and in ignorance of when, where, and how failure will come. They do not and cannot possibly know about even a small proportion of government activity that bears on their failure. They can only put out fires and smile above the ashes. They don't know what's going on—yet they are responsible for it. And they feed that responsibility every time they take credit for good news not of their own making. The best recent example is President Reagan's claiming credit for the 1984 rise in average national SAT scores.

"Lying in state" is justifiable when the fundamental interests of the state are in peril: when there exists a palpable threat to public order or to diplomacy in situations where premature popular demands could contribute to war. But modern presidents, among whom Richard Nixon is only one, perceive vital threats to national interests earlier and more often than ever. The threats don't have to be real—and usually aren't. Presidents don't have to believe they are real—and probably don't. Their main obligation is to preserve the myth that they are reserving themselves for the big decisions. This permits them to remain ignorant of most of what is happening; it permits them to leave most of the decisions to staff and most governing to administrators. This is presidential government. *This is presidential government?* It has frequently been observed that one of the main functions of a presidential press conference is the opportunity it provides to brief the president in order to keep him abreast of what is going on. What is presidential government between press conferences?

The presidency has great powers. The president is their victim. And so, unless we act, are we.

Reform: Some False Starts and Panaceas

The decade of 1962-72 was one of the most remarkable in the history of American government. It began in almost unprecedented optimism and ended on the eve of despair. It was a period of unprecedented prosperity and of deep decline in respect for all big institutions, including corporations. It was a decade of tremendous public policy expansion and also a decade in which one president was disgraced and another was about to be deposed. (That still another was assassinated does not appear to have contributed directly to the sense of distrust of authority that was to begin after 1964. In fact, following JFK's death, the public embraced all the more the programs that contributed to the great expansion of the national government. The New Frontier programs that had bogged down in 1962-63 sailed through in 1964.)

The connection between expansion of government and crises of authority did not go unnoticed. During the 1970s a number of important changes were made that were intended, in one way or another, to restore balance between president and Congress. They simply were not adequate to attain that end, however, because they failed to meet one or more of the following criteria: (1) An appropriate reform would have to deal effectively with the excessive personification of American government in the presidency. At a minimum this would require

182

deflation of public expectations about the capacity of presidents, as individuals, to govern without collective responsibility. (2) A good reform would have to deal with the plebiscitary nature of the presidency. Personification would be less of a problem if the only constituency were Congress and the Washington community. Therefore, a good reform would cool if not break up altogether the love affair between the masses and the president. (3) A good reform would contribute to constitutional balance. Such balance does not have to take the form of the original Separation of Powers, although much can be said for that. As long as the American system rejects a single moral code, however, it must respect Madison's admonition that "auxiliary precautions" are necessary. The approach does not have to be Madison's, but the reform must be judged according to whether it improves the prospect of balancing power against power, ambition against ambition. Two of the most ambitious attempts to increase congressional power vis-à-vis the president—the War Powers Resolution and the Congressional Budget and Impoundment Control Act—failed to bring about any such improvement.

The War Powers Resolution

The War Powers Resolution was passed in November 1973, by a Congress that wanted to put an end to what its members deemed usurpation, the assertion of presidential power to make presidential war. The purpose of the resolution was to guarantee that the president could not commit troops for more than sixty days (or ninety under special conditions) without a congressional debate resulting in congressional approval. Sec. 3 provides, hopefully, that the president will "in every possible instance" consult with Congress before introducing armed forces into hostilities or "into situations where imminent involvement in hostilities is clearly indicated." Sec. 4 provides that the president will report his actions to Congress and continue to keep Congress informed. Sec. 5 provides that the President must terminate any such use of armed forces within sixty calendar days of submitting his report unless Congress has declared war or has enacted a specific authorization for the use of those armed forces. Since presidents in the past have claimed that congressional appropriations amounted to a retroactive approval of the use of armed forces in hostile situations, Sec. 8 provides that no such interpretation of an appropriation is warranted, unless explicit provision for the particular use of armed forces is included. Sec. 8 also denies to the president the opportunity to interpret from any mutual security treaty an advance authorization for the use of armed forces.

The purpose of the War Powers Resolution was to "fulfill the intent of the framers of the Constitution" (Sec. 2) by reintroducing a balancing role for Congress. The resolution is in largest part a failure, however, in at least two respects. First, it does not give Congress any substantial powers to check the president or any substantial new opportunities to participate in foreign policy that it did not already have or could not exercise without the resolution. Second, presidents since 1974 have not regarded themselves as bound by the resolution, at least not in the sense Congress seems to have intended. Indeed, they are able to disregard the provisions with impunity, and they seem to have every incentive to do so. It is for the president to decide whether there is a probability of hostilities, and where the troops are introduced. And no president is likely to admit a mere resolution overrides an obligation in a treaty, as he interprets it. Also subject to presidential interpretation is the requirement of consultation "in every possible instance." Congress even put an additional limit on itself by providing that it could not use the "subsequent restraint" of a condemning joint resolution if it had already approved an action through a specific statutory authorization. (Subsequent restraints are in any case severely limited because few members of Congress would be willing to be responsible for cutting off appropriations to support American troops abroad if the president insisted on stationing them there and maintaining them.)

Even the president with the weakest constitutional authority in American history, the appointed Gerald Ford, was able to play fast and loose with the War Powers Resolution within a year after its passage. Among the several instances in which Ford avoided applying it, the most important was the *Mayaguez* incident in 1975. On May 12 the U.S. freighter *Mayaguez* was boarded by Cambodians and taken to the island of Kho Tang. Denouncing the seizure as "an act of piracy," President Ford ordered up a naval blockade, sinking and damaging several Cambodian boats. On May 14 he dispatched eight hundred troops to Thailand and immediately authorized a rescue operation involving bombing and invasion. Ultimately, forty-one Ma-

184

rines were killed and fifty more were wounded, along with an unde-
termined number of Cambodians, and all in vain because the American captives had shortly before the attack been released and sent
across the border into Thailand. At no point during the incident's
unfolding did President Ford observe the provisions of the War Powers Resolution. Even when he did choose to report to Congress, he
based his actions on his authority as commander-in-chief and therefore saw no need to observe the provisions of the resolution. Toward
the end of his term as he reviewed the six incidents of foreign involvement where presumably the War Powers Resolution was appli-
cable, Ford argued that he "did not concede that the Resolution itself
was legally binding on the President on constitutional grounds."[4]

Jimmy Carter entered office opposed to an imperial presidency.
Yet he also evaded the application and intent of the War Powers Resolution, particularly in his dealings with Iran. Carter's actions tended
strongly to confirm an argument made at the time that, rather than
limiting a president's involvement in foreign hostilities, the resolution might actually have served to encourage presidents to initiate
some military action during the sixty-day grace period when legislative approval is not required. In effect, the resolution gives the president blanket power to use military force for sixty days, without legislative authorization; in other words, this provision "legitimizes a
war-making power that heretofore had been based on customary
practice and precedent."[5]

Budget Reform

The Congressional Budget and Impoundment Control Act of 1974
also had as its intention the restoration of a balance between the
president and Congress. The purpose of the act was to centralize the
budgetary process in Congress and to bring appropriations decisions
closer to revenue decisions. The act created a House and a Senate
Budget Committee and a new staff agency, the Congressional Budget

---

[4]Quoted in Raymond Tatalovich and Byron W. Daynes, *Presidential Power in the
United States* (Monterey, Cal.: Brooks/Cole, 1984), p. 332. The six cases were: three evacuations from the Indo-Chinese peninsula in 1975; the *Mayaguez* incident; and the two
evacuations from Lebanon in 1976.
[5]Ibid., p. 363.

Office (CBO). It also created an entirely new schedule for budget deci-sions and a new set of procedures for moving the budget along from phase to phase. The CBO was set up to give Congress the expertise and the research staff necessary to make the whole process work in-dependently of the president and OMB. The guts of the new process was to be the annual Concurrent Resolution, to be passed by the House and Senate by May 15, setting forth budget outlays, new bud-getary authority for particular programs, projections of future com-mitments, estimated revenues, and the level of taxation for the next five fiscal years. This resolution was intended to govern all appropria-tion decisions, which accordingly would be made in light of estab-lished budgetary ceilings and of available revenues. By September 15, a second Concurrent Resolution, taking into account the debates and decisions on the various appropriations and revenue bills, is supposed to be passed. Once adopted, this resolution is binding on Congress, preventing enactment of any spending bill beyond the ceil-ings or adoption of any tax measures which alter the revenue esti-mates. "Reconciliation" of any legislative action in conflict with the second Concurrent Resolution is supposed to be completed by Sep-tember 25, in time for the new fiscal year, which since 1974 has begun on October 1.

There are few disagreements with the contention that the re-formed budget process is an improvement. The CBO has turned out to be a definite asset for Congress and a tremendously important source of fiscal information independent of and often in contention with that of the White House and the OMB. However, there are few who would argue that the new arrangements have substantially changed the imbalances of power between the executive branch and Congress. Even where Congress permits itself to be influenced by its own ceilings as established in the first Concurrent Resolution, the second Concurrent Resolution has been late every year since the first year (1976) and is therefore not available at the most significant times when commitments are made. Moreover, Congress has not yet been able to use the reformed budgetary process to improve its ability to make real "program budget" decisions, wherein priorities between and among programs and appropriations are actually set.

The real test of the reformed budget process came with Ronald Reagan. President Reagan's commitment to reduce the size of the na-tional government made the budget process more important than ever. Major policy decisions involving substantial cuts, especially in welfare and other service programs, were ultimately translated into budgetary decisions. In an unusual move, Reagan's assistants in the White House conspired with his supporters in Congress to incorporate all of the executive budget proposals into a single bill, called a Reconciliation Bill, adopting the language of the Budget Act. This forced Congress to accept the Reagan budget priorities and thus to accept the executive budget on the president's terms, just as had happened under the strongest executives *before* the passage of the 1974 act. As a result, members of Congress could not influence the budget in the usual way, by separating out particular things to bargain on. And the budget was made into a popular issue, which forced members of Congress into the position of voting for or against bigger budgets and for or against a very popular president.[6]

President Reagan did not repeat this strategy or gain the same successes with his later budgets. In fact, president-Congress relations in his second, third, and fourth years were more like war in the trenches. But whether presidential goals are attained or not, there is nothing about the present budget process itself that anywhere nearly meets the criteria for meaningful reform set forth above. Assessment of the budget reform's success in reducing constitutional imbalances can best be made in the words of the most outstanding and respected student of the budget process:

> [N]either Congress nor the President can effectively budget if most spending decisions are made outside the budget process. . . . [T]he fact that three-quarters of total expenditures are deemed to be uncontrollable [entitlements provided by law, "off-budget" commitments in loans and loan guarantees, etc.] means that the amounts cannot be determined through budget decisions alone but can be controlled through other actions such as legislative changes in existing laws. In effect, budgeting is subordinate to other resource allocation processes which lack its routines and sensitivity to the relationship between claims on the budget and available resources. . . . As a result, while the Government's control of the "administrative budget" is adequate, its control of the political budget is not. . . . *Tinkering with the machinery of budgeting will*

---

[6]Allen Schick, "How the Budget Was Won and Lost," in Norman Ornstein, ed., *President and Congress: Assessing Reagan's First Year* (Washington: American Enterprise Institute, 1982), pp. 25–26. For an updated assessment by Schick, see "The Budget as an Instrument of Presidential Policy," in Lester Salamon, ed., *Governance: The Reagan Era and Beyond* (Washington: Urban Institute, 1985).

187

not solve the problem of control nor will it restore the process to the status it once had. Budgeting is not designed to cope with the issues it now faces.

The problem is not solely one of budgeting, but goes to the heart of governance. . . . When the federal government effectively governs, it will again have the capacity to budget.[7]

An Old Panacea, Wisely Resisted: One Six-Year Term

War Powers provisions and added congressional budget controls righted no fundamental wrongs. Balance did not replace imbalance. Congress continues to delegate and defer, preferring as always to fight little battles rather than confront constitutional causes. The president continues to be plebiscitary, and presidential behavior continues to show the stresses of that situation. Parties continue to live, and decline, at the periphery. Members of Congress continue to rely, and increasingly, on PACs, pushing parties further to the periphery. And the people, *en masse*, continue to vacillate between excessive expectations and unwarranted indignation. No wonder some of us are tempted from time to time to revive old proposals, especially if they look like panaceas. The panacea that will not die but will not, as yet, be accepted, is the constitutional provision limiting presidential tenure to one six-year term.

This remedy for excesses of presidential power is as old as the presidency itself. A nonrepeatable term was considered at the Constitutional Convention and was proposed in Congress as early as 1821 or 1826, depending on which presidential historian you consult. Although there is no open and shut case either way regarding this proposal, something important ought to be learned from the fact that it has been so attractive to so many people yet always falls short of being adopted.

The points in favor of the single six-year presidential term can be outlined simply and briefly. It would enable the president to devote all of his time to the job. Many a staffer and president-watcher has observed that a president begins his reelection campaign shortly after his inauguration. Moreover, the argument goes, the president

---

[7]Schick, "The Budget as an Instrument of Presidential Policy," quoted from the typescript, pp. 45–46; emphasis added.

would be free of partisan consideration and could be the leader of all the people. The single six-year term proposal enjoyed a particularly strong revival in the mid-1970s because of the assumption that Watergate would not have occurred at all if the Nixon people had not been so obsessed with reelection.

Everything that can be said in favor of the single six-year term boils down to the single argument that politics should be taken out of the office. As James MacGregor Burns observed, this issue is indicative of the ambivalence of the American people, including American presidents, toward the presidency itself and all its power. Every president between Harry Truman and Jimmy Carter, with the possible exception of Dwight Eisenhower, seems to have at one time or another favored a severe constitutional limitation on presidential tenure.[8] They may later have switched their positions, but that in itself is indicative of ambivalence toward the power and the potential imbalance in the office.

The case against the single six-year term reform is more complex but at least equally compelling—considerably more compelling to some people. First, any constitutional limit on the number of terms that can be served is a violation of democratic principles, which favor accountability through election, of which reelection is an essential part. On this ground the Twentieth Amendment, limiting presidents to two four-year terms, was also an extremely dubious reform. Second, even if we can justify an exception to the principle of accountability through election, it is impossible to determine the ideal length of the single term. Woodrow Wilson made this point in his case against the single six-year term, "Four years is too long a term for a president who is not the true spokesman of the people [and] is too short a term for a president who is doing, or attempting, a great work of reform, and who has not had time to finish it."[9]

Another strong argument against the single six-year term is that it would remove the presidency still further from party politics and thrust it still further into mass politics. Adoption of important policies requires a long and involved process of mobilizing support. Pres-

---

[8]James MacGregor Burns, *The Power to Lead: The Crisis of the American Presidency* (New York: Simon & Schuster, 1984), pp. 181–82.

[9]Quoted in Thomas E. Cronin, *The State of the Presidency*, 2d ed. (Boston: Little , Brown, 1980), p. 356. This is an excerpt from Cronin's own excellent assessment of the single six-year term.

idential leadership is needed, but the role it plays here is not simple. Freedom from reelection cannot alter that but can change the process, reinforcing the plebiscitary character of the presidency by freeing the president from party but not from popularity.

It is also persuasively argued that a president elected to a single six-year term would still have a gigantic bureaucracy to confront. As unwieldy as that gigantic bureaucracy is, it is more responsive to a popularly supported president and an enthusiastic Congress than to anything else.

While all those points are worth making in an evaluation of the single six-year term, it is curious to me that one of the most telling points against the single, nonrepeatable term has not been advanced. Its absence can perhaps be attributed to the lack of political scientists raised in southern states. This kind of constitutional limitation on elections is generally a product of systems with weak or nonexistent political parties. Since there is no party continuity or corporate party integrity in such systems, there is no basis for putting trust in the desire for reelection as a safeguard against bad management. Better under those conditions to operate on the basis of negative assumptions against incumbents. I do not know if the earliest proposal for a single, nonrepeatable term was made in the 1820s because that was a period of severely weak political parties. But I do feel confident that this is a major reason, if not the only reason, that such a proposal has been popular since the 1940s. And though the association of the nonrepeatable election with weak political parties is not in itself an argument against the limitation, the fallout from this association does contribute significantly to the negative argument. To put the matter bluntly, single-term limitations are strongly associated with corruption. In any weak party system, including the national presidential system, the onus of making deals and compromises, both shady and honorable, rests heavily upon individual candidates. Without some semblance of corporate integrity in a party, individual candidates have few opportunities to amortize their obligations across the spectrum of elective and appointive jobs and policy proposals. The deals tend to be personalized and the payoffs come home to roost accordingly. If that situation is already endemic in conditions of weak or no parties, adding to it the limitation against reelection means that the candidates and officials, already prevented from amortizing their deals across space, are also unable to amortize their obligations across time. This makes for a highly pressurized situation, where all the deals have to be personal and immediate. And it is a highly corrupting situation, turned from bad in the absence of a party ticket to worse in the absence of the time perspective produced by the prospect of reelection. As I implied earlier, the two-term limit we have now ought to be repealed.

The single six-year term for presidents is a reform comparable to the party and campaign finance reforms of the 1970s. It is an effort to compensate for the absence of a viable party system, but it is a compensation ultimately paid for by further weakening of the party system itself. Observers, especially foreign observers, have often noted that one source of weakness in American political parties is the certainty of election every two or four years. This, they say, is already an unjustifiable limitation on the electoral process, not only because any artificial limitation on elections is a violation of democratic principles but also because when elections are set in a certain and unchangeable cycle, political parties do not have to remain alert but can disappear into inactivity until a known point prior to the next election. In contrast, parliamentary systems in which elections can be called essentially at any time, depending upon political advantage or the maturation of a certain issue, require relatively continuous alertness on the part of party leaders, party candidates, and party workers. To rigidify matters by going beyond the determinacy of the electoral cycle to add an absolute rule of one term would hang still another millstone around the neck of already doddering political parties.

I can only hope that the addition of this argument to the negative case will contribute to a definitive and final rout of the single six-year term as a reform. At least one thing can be learned from the career of George Wallace. Although he sought the restoration in Alabama of the right of reelection for the wrong reasons, it is nevertheless true that he sought it at a time and achieved it at a time when Alabama had once again reentered the ranks of states with active and competitive party systems. The limitation on reelection is an idea whose time ought never to come.

Another Approach: Reform the Reforms

Virtually every treatment of the modern presidency, including this one, is respectful of the relationship between the selection process and the nature and conduct of the office. The present selection arrangements are themselves the products of reforms, reforms whose principal motivation was the enhancement of some desirable presidential characteristic—more democratization, more power, more accountability, and so on. This long tradition continues.

One of the most important reform proposals is that of a national direct primary for nominating presidential candidates. This suggestion is not new; like any advocacy of direct primary, it comes out of the anti-party tradition beginning in the 1890s. The proposal for a national direct primary returned to popularity in the 1970s not only because opposition to conventions continues but also because of disappointments with the results of state primaries for choosing delegates to conventions. All such concerns would be obviated if the national nominating conventions were replaced with a single direct nominating primary to select the presidential candidate for each party. The typical reform proposal provides for the national primary in August preceding the November presidential election. If no candidate receives, say, 40 percent of the primary vote, a second or run-off primary between the two leading candidates is to be held a week or a month later. Other provisions deal with the number of signatures on qualifying petitions, the number of states in which signatures must be obtained, the qualification of voters to participate in each of the national primaries, and so on. A typical compromise in these proposals is to provide for a national convention to select the vice presidential candidate and to adopt a platform.

The main advantages of such a reform are fairly obvious. The national primaries would be far more open and public than any other method of nomination. They would eliminate the risk of choosing a "dark horse," that is, a presidential candidate unknown to a large part of the public, initially supported by only a minority of activists. Other great advantages would be the reduction of the inordinate length of the selection process and the elimination of the tremendous cost of campaigning in state after state from January through June. A related advantage would be that the method would cut down or perhaps even eliminate the "bandwagon" effect whereby a few unexpected successes in early primaries can produce a momentum difficult to resist later on, even though the candidate, like Jimmy Carter, started out as a distinct minority candidate.

But the disadvantages more than counterbalance the strong points. The greatest drawback, at least in the eyes of most people, would be the likelihood that the direct national primary would deal a death blow to a national party system. A second, and related, problem is that national primaries would be heavily biased in favor of candidates already fairly well known and recognized by the public. There would be no opportunity for others to gain public recognition through their performances in a sequence of state primaries. Third, and to me most important, the direct national primary would reinforce and enhance the existing system's tendencies to strengthen and encourage the plebiscitary presidency. With all its present weaknesses—especially the fact that delegates are merely amassed, covered in detail in an earlier chapter—the present delegate selection process at least provides an opportunity for middle-level activists to play a role and contribute to some modicum of party presence at a national level. Without that intermediate process, the phenomenon of flux would be even more prominent. The mass base of the president would be even more direct and unmediated than it is today. Here is another of those cases where a reform can achieve the opposite of what many of its supporters want to achieve.

Partly in the hope of avoiding that pitfall, some of the most recent proposals for reform have been aimed directly and unapologetically at deliberate restoration of party organizations and the two-party system. One of those, aimed at restoring the convention system, provides that up to one-third or even one-half of the delegates be chosen by state party leaders without going through a public selection process at all. The argument is that this would permit some of the real coalition building that was once a natural and essential feature of party government. Another such proposal is that of a preprimary convention, a system of selection in which delegates chosen by state caucuses or conventions would go to a national preprimary convention to cast their ballots, either as unpledged individual delegates or as members of unified state delegations. One or more ballots would be cast at the convention, but the candidate with a majority would not be declared the nominee if any second candidate received as much as 25 percent (or some other specified percent) of the delegate votes. In that event a national primary would then be held, in order to determine on a popular basis who the nominee would be. Another equally imaginative proposal is to permit delegates to be selected in any manner the states provide but not to permit them to be pledged to vote for a specific candidate at the convention. Such a collection of several hundred uninstructed delegates would be able, it is argued, to deliberate to form real coalitions as parties did in the good old days.

Whatever case might be made for each of these proposals and others like them, it is extremely doubtful that they could revive the two major parties to a state in any way comparable to that they once held. If I am correct in my contention that most anti-party reforms of the past were more a reflection than a cause of party decline, then a reversal of the original reforms would not reverse the downward trend. But even if these reforms were direct causal agents, there is no guarantee at all that reforming these reforms would restore the parties to the *status quo ante*. Many other conditions now exist—especially big government itself—which are inhospitable to parties and especially to the two-party system. Over and above all reforms and reformed reforms, these new conditions have to be confronted before there can be any developments toward party government and, by that means, the restoration of some constitutional balance.[10] Moreover, it is a chicken/egg situation. Even if a clear case can be made that one of the new reforms or a reformed reform would contribute directly to party restoration, strong parties would already have to exist before any of these reforms could be implemented and sustained. For example, any unified national system of presidential selection would require enough organized support at the national level to impose uniform registration and selection rules on all the states. It is difficult to imagine this being possible without the preexistence of fairly unified parties in Congress and around the president and major presidential candidates. Political parties that are already too weak to fight off anti-party reforms are not the kinds of institutions that can enact new legislation making them strong enough to resist and reverse the anti-party trend.

Proposing the Unattainable: A Presidential Cabinet

Clearly one of the most desirable reforms would be a real cabinet around the presidency. A cabinet combines the advantages of a sin-

[10]The best evaluations of the recent reforms and reform proposals will be found in James W. Davis, *National Conventions in an Age of Party Reform* (Westport, Conn.: Greenwood Press, 1983), ch. 8; and Nelson W. Polsby, "Reform of the Party System and the Conduct of the Presidency," in James Sterling Young, ed., *Problems and Prospects of Presidential Leadership in the 1980s* (Lanham, Md.: University Press of America, 1982), pp. 103-11.

gle chief executive with those of a plural executive. A cabinet would cut down, without eliminating, the personification of government in the plebiscitary presidency. Any number of advantages flow from the introduction of collective responsibility.

Unfortunately, this proposal runs afoul of a law governing all reform proposals: *There is an inverse relationship between feasibility and effectiveness.* As I suggested earlier, a small step toward the development of a cabinet might have been taken after 1976, when Ronald Reagan identified his vice presidential running mate before the balloting and proposed that such a step be made a rule of the Republican party. If this same principle were expanded slightly, a true cabinet might develop. The important part of the early naming of appointees would be to identify the group *as a group* and to associate the members with the president and with the electoral process. This practice would give voters a much better sense of the shape and direction of the eventual administration, and at the same time it would provide the president with a true basis for sharing his responsibilities.

Effective as a cabinet would be, it is not feasible as long as the political parties are as weak as they are. Preelection identification of top appointees might help restore some strength to the national political parties, but a number of other conditions favorable to strong parties would also have to prevail. The point is that a cabinet is an instrument of party government and is difficult to conceive or construct without a minimum of party continuity and organizational integrity. At the present time, both the major parties fall below this minimum.

Real Reform: Toward a More Responsible Multiparty System

Time and again my analysis of presidential pathology has encountered the decline and continued weakness of the party system. The plebiscitary presidency is virtually defined by the contrast of mass democracy with party democracy. Cabinets are hard to conceive without parties. Presidents are exposed to unconscionable stress, impossible mass expectations, and incessant interest group pressures without the mediating influence of political parties. In 1950, the Committee on Political Parties of the American Political Science Association was already able to observe that the weakness of the party system "is a very serious matter, for it affects the very heartbeat of American democracy. It also poses grave problems of domestic and foreign policy in an era when it is no longer safe for the nation to deal piecemeal with issues."[11]

But the American Political Science Association committee went wrong in its assumption that the restoration of American parties and party government meant restoration of the *two-party* system: "The fundamental requirement of accountability is a two-party system in which the opposition party acts as critic . . . presenting the policy alternatives that are necessary for a true choice in reaching public decisions."[12] Committee members accepted this proposition *despite their explicit recognition* that the two-party system never gave America cohesive policies, coherent programs, *or* collective accountability. And almost all the published responses to their important report, even those that otherwise criticized it, embraced the parts concerning the virtues of the two-party system.

The two-party system is a good source of examples of myths in politics. A myth is not a falsehood. A myth is a statement or a belief about reality that does not depend upon the truth to be accepted. A myth may be true or based on truth; the closer the myth is to the truth, the more durable it is likely to be. Nevertheless, the mark of the myth is acceptance for reasons other than evidence. Plato was probably the first thinker to recognize the political importance of myths and their value in building and maintaining a republic.

Without any difficulty I have identified nine of the myths that support the two-party system. They are not an exhaustive inventory, but their exposure will help to prepare the way for a move in another direction.

Nine Easy-to-Spot Myths about the Two-Party System

Myth 1: American democracy is based on the two-party system, and we have been operating continuously under that system for almost our

[11]American Political Science Association, "Toward a More Responsible Two-Party System," supplement, *American Political Science Review*, 44, no. 3, part 2 (September, 1950), p. v. Portions of this section were first published in Lowi, "Toward a More Responsible Three-Party System," *PS*, 16 (Fall 1983), 699-706.
[12]APSA, "Toward a More Responsible Two-Party System," pp. 1-2.

entire history. American democracy is inconceivable without the two-party system.

The two-party system does indeed go back a very long way in American history, and there is ample evidence to support a non-mythological argument that it has made a significant contribution to the country's development. However, the golden age of the two-party system was the nineteenth century, and that age ended rather abruptly in 1896, when the southern states became exclusively one-party systems dominated by the Democrats and to a lesser degree the northern states became one-party systems dominated by the Republicans. Even in some important states where the two parties competed directly, the counties in one part of the state were one-party Democratic systems, and those in the other part were one-party Republican systems. Therefore, while nationally the two-party system seemed to dominate into the twentieth century, the truth was that *we were governed mainly by two competing one-party systems,* not a bona fide two-party system. This situation of two competing one-party systems prevailed at the national level and within many states from 1896 into the 1950s, when the Republican party began making serious inroads into the Democratic south. But by that time the two political parties were internally so weak that the two-party system President Eisenhower reintroduced was hardly a shadow of its nineteenth-century ancestor.

> *Myth 2:* The two-party system must be defended at all costs because, as with competing enterprises in a market economy, the competition between the two major parties yields great though unintended public benefits, such as: a higher rate of participation than in systems without two competing parties; automatic majorities, so that Congress and the president can get on with the job of governing after the election is over; greater effectiveness and decisiveness in government; and therefore a larger degree of government legitimacy because of a continuity between the electorate and important policies.

If all these benefits genuinely did result, a person would be a real subversive to support anything other than a two-party system. But a closer examination quickly turns these contentions into nonsense. Two-party competition has not had an appreciable regular positive effect on voter turnout since the late nineteenth century. Two-party

197

competition cannot even explain the dramatic increase in the political participation of blacks in the south. Blacks were effectively enfranchised by laws passed in Congress with *non*partisan northern majorities, imposed on southern states. And one of the most dramatic scenes of increased political participation has been the city of Chicago, not a famous case of two-party competition.

Belief that the system provides automatic majorities flies in the face of the fact that Congress for the entire twentieth century has operated on the basis of coalitions among voting blocs. Except for an occasional honeymoon, such as Reagan's in 1981, there has been very little party cohesion in recent decades, and every major legislative campaign requires the development of a coalition of voting blocs virtually from scratch. What produces automatic majorities is the presentation of alternatives in stark yes/no forms—and that takes intellectual creativity and legislative draftsmanship. Any number of blocs and parties can play, and majorities will be produced as long as members can only vote yes or no. Party leaders are important in Congress, but their functions would not be rendered impossible by the mere presence of members of more than two parties.

And as for legitimacy, given the overwhelming evidence in the public opinion polls of the past twenty years, as seen in the earlier chapters, it is hard to imagine that we could do any worse for legitimacy with a multiparty system. The dramatic decline of trust coupled with the dramatic increase in the percentage of voters who refer to themselves as Independents—during the very two decades in which two-party competition was restored to many of the states—ought to bring at least some discomfort to the defenders of the myths of the two-party system.

Myth 3: The two-party system is natural; it is American, it is the only system consonant with America's historic electoral system—the single-member district system.

The fact is that the two-party system is not natural and requires laws to foster and protect it. Even the historic place of the single-member district system is mythological. In the first place, the most important single-member district of all, the state, existed only for governor. U.S. senators were not elected directly by the people until 1914. In the second place, all during the formative years of the nineteenth century, there were significant numbers of *multiple*-member districts. In 1842, Vermont was the only state, among twenty-six, where all state legislators were chosen one to a district. In all the states during the nineteenth century, all or most members of Congress represented multiple-member districts.[13] Although Congress attempted to change this situation in the 1870s with laws requiring single-member districts, multimember districts were slow to disappear. In 1912, when the forty-eighth state entered the Union, multiple-member districts were still numerically dominant in legislatures in at least half the states, even more than half of the original thirteen states. In 1955, over half (58.3 percent) of the districts of the forty-eight state legislatures then existing were multiple-member districts. By the mid-1970s most districts (92.8 percent of state senatorial and 80.5 percent of state assembly districts) were single-member; but even so, 42 percent of the members of the state assemblies were elected from multimember districts.[14]

Although it is true that the two countries with the most widespread practice of single-member district representation — the United States and Great Britain — have had the most extensive experience with two-party systems, their experiences do not confirm the myth nearly as strongly as has been believed. Great Britain has operated under a *three*-party system for a good proportion of the twentieth century. And its present party system is doing its best either to disintegrate or to re-form into a three-party system. In the United States, the extensive experience with *one*-party systems suggests that the single-member district system of representation is capable of discouraging a weak *second* party just as it has been capable of discouraging third parties.

Recognition of these facts opens up several possibilities: If the number two is not sacred, need myths and laws continue to overwhelm third parties? (I am not advocating any particular number, but for reasons I give below, three-party systems are more likely to develop than systems with more than three.) First, a third party can survive in single-member districts if it can split off enough votes to be an occasional winner, or a threat to win — so that the psychology of

---

[13]Maurice Klain, "A New Look at the Constituencies: The Need for a Recount and a Reappraisal," *American Political Science Review*, 49 (1955), 1105-1119.

[14]Alan Rosenthal, *Legislative Life: People, Process, and Performance in the States* (New York: Harper & Row, 1981), p. 15.

the wasted vote is avoided. Second, a third party can extend its survival by joint nomination—that is, by nominating some of the candidates of one of the other two parties. This is one of the major secrets of the success of the Liberal party and the Conservative party in the state of New York. Third, to the extent the single-member district system does discourage more than two parties—and this is a stronger tendency where the chief executives are also elected in a winner-take-all plurality system of elections—there will be some districts in which the third party survives and one of the two previously major parties declines. These possibilities in turn raise the probability that even if three party organizations actually co-exist in only a few individual districts, there would still be a three-party legislature. And that would improve the probability of three-party competition for the governorships and the presidency, in which the winners would be elected by pluralities far smaller than majorities. Such outcomes would contribute significantly to the deflation of the plebiscitary chief executive. More will be said of this below.

Myth 4: A vote for a third-party candidate is a wasted vote.

Myth 5: A vote for a third-party candidate is a mischievous vote, more powerful than a vote for one of the major party candidates, because it helps elect the worse of the two major candidates.

These two myths are taken together because they give contradictory arguments against supporting a third party and thereby prove that myths need not be consistent to be effective. Take number 5 first. It operates on the very questionable assumption that one of the major candidates is clearly better than the other. But what are voters to do if they have concluded that *both* major candidates are worse? Recognizing the absurdity, many voters become nonvoters. Since nonvoting is stigmatized, nonvoters are usually quiet, thus depriving their nonvote of the influence it should have. Nonvoting, when done loudly, is an important form of participation. But by the same logic, so is a vote for a candidate for a third party, which is the short answer to myth 4. A vote for a third party candidate is *never* wasted. If the vote is for a dissident party, it is a protest vote that can instill considerable anxiety in the leadership of the major parties. If the vote is for a programmatic third party, a more substantive message is sent; and history shows that these messages are almost always received by the leaders of the major parties. There is still another type of third party, and a vote for it would be the most effective of all—if a party of that sort were made available. This is an *electorally* based third party: a third party just like the two major parties, just as pragmatic, just as concerned with winning elections. Creating such a party on a national scale has not been tried seriously since the Progressives tried it in 1912. The very presence of such a third party would make a fundamental difference to the political system.

Myth 6: If some third-party candidates got elected to Congress, there would be havoc. Their presence would foul up the allocation of committee assignments, and all during the session their presence would remove from the more important two parties the automatic majority that makes decisive legislation possible. There would be resort to bloc voting and balance-of-power politics.

The general case made earlier about the nonsense of automatic majorities applies to the particular instance of Congress. As for the complicating effect of third-party members on committee assignments, surely the task, though more complex, would be far from impossible. And once Congress got itself organized with third-party members in their assigned committees, why should three blocs calling themselves by party names complicate congressional coalition-building any more than the present multiple-bloc structure complicates it? The presence of a significant third-party delegation in Congress might very well ease the burden of legislative leadership inasmuch as the conferences and caucuses of the two major parties could more readily and clearly develop and maintain distinct policy positions. Many party leaders cultivate the two-party system mythology precisely because they want to avoid the collective responsibility inherent in cohesive parties.

Myth 7: If a third party elected some members of Congress and also received some electoral votes in close presidential elections, then there would be a real calamity—a constitutional crisis where the lack of an absolute majority in the electoral college for one candidate would require selection among the top three candidates by the House of Representatives, with each state having one vote regardless of its size.

Myth 8: Even if the presence of an important third party did not have an apocalyptic effect, it would hold a balance-of-power position giving it an influence far out of proportion to its size.

One important myth not counted here because it is not directly pertinent to the two-party system is that American democracy is so fragile that the slightest constitutional jolt will have an apocalyptic effect. Defenders of the status quo will always invoke the specter of constitutional crisis although constitutional crisis is contemplated by the Constitution itself. There is hardly any doubt that the regular presence of more than two parties would transform the present selection system, just as the new party system of 1800 transformed the original selection system, producing the Twelfth Amendment and the undermining of the original intent of the Electoral College. It is also true that if a third party candidate were regularly present, the two major candidates would have to do some very serious bargaining with the third party at times when they fell short of an absolute majority of electoral votes. That bargaining would lead to fundamental compromises with the platform as adopted the previous July or August and developed during the campaign. But, as for Myth 8, why should the added intensity of bargaining give a third party such a disproportionate influence? What is to stop the candidates of the two major parties from compromising with each other? This ability to compromise "across the aisle" is often identified as one of the virtues of American politics. There is no reason to assume this virtue would disappear in the presence of more than two parties.

If a third party should establish itself, Americans would not long tolerate so unrepresentative a system as that called for by the Twelfth Amendment, in which each state, regardless of the size, has only one vote in the House of Representatives. The result would probably be the adoption of a constitutional amendment providing for the abolition of the Electoral College and/or the removal of the original provision that the House of Representatives would vote according to states. However, during the time Congress would need to pass a new amendment and the states to ratify it, a serious revaluation of the presidency would be set in train. One aspect of that revaluation would involve a move by Congress back toward the center of the president's constituency, intervening between president and masses. Another aspect would be confrontation of the fact that presidents even today are elected not by real majorities but by minorities— which we call pluralities. Finally, if a third party did succeed in establishing itself, and if that did bring forth a constitutional amendment, that amendment would either have to provide for a national election—in which the victory would definitely be a matter of mere plurality—or the new amendment would have to provide for a run-off election between the two leading candidates; and *a system with a run-off election turns out to be much more conducive to a multiparty system than our present single-member district plurality system*. Either way, therefore, a serious third-party presence would profoundly alter the selection system and bring presidents down a notch or two.

Myth 9: Without his own party base, the president would not be able to govern.

This is a myth from the past that is becoming a scientifically validated reality of the present. When presidents had a party base, they weren't governing. Once the governmental system was reconstructed to depend on the president's capacity to govern, there was no longer a party base. And sure enough, without that party base, they can't govern.

Nothing about the present American party system warrants the respect it receives. Presidents need a party and have none. Voters need choices and continuity and rarely have either. Congress needs cohesion and has little. Although almost everyone recognizes that party organizations in the United States have all but disappeared, especially from the national scene, most people nevertheless assume that this is merely a momentary lapse and that the two-party system is the American way. But this moment of lapse is now three or four decades in duration. It should be clear by now that big, modern, programmatic governments are not hospitable to two-party systems, anywhere in the world. A two-party system simply cannot grapple with complex programmatic alternatives in a manner that is meaningful to large electorates. Modern programmatic governments do need political parties, just as much as traditional patronage governments needed them. It is not party systems but the two-party system in particular that no longer can suffice. No amount of tinkering by well-intentioned reformers can revive the two-party system. Most efforts to do so have turned out to be counterproductive.

A multiparty system will seem alien on American soil only as long as the two-party system is taken as the only true, American way to govern. But in our epoch, that is almost the same as saying that the sun daily crosses the sky as a heavenly chariot of fire drawn by two giant horses. It is the two-party system that has become the alien phenomenon. The presence of other real parties with a real electoral base and a real presence in state legislatures, in Congress, and in the Electoral College, could clarify the policies, programs and the lines of accountability of the two major parties by reducing their need to appear to be all things to all people. The scale of their coverage and commitments could be narrowed. And most important, presidential candidates would no longer have to appear omnicompetent. Parties could present real choices, especially after everyone begins to recognize that the compromises would take place in the legislature, after the election.

Actually, the prospect of a constitutional crisis over the election of the president turns out to be one of the best arguments *in favor* of a multiparty system. There is virtually a consensus on the proposition that the presidency has gotten too big. The last two presidents won by running against the big presidency and the big government for which the presidency is responsible. Most people now agree that the presidency is too exposed to the mass public and too heavily burdened by personal responsibility for putting the whole world to rights. The presence of a third important party capable of obtaining seats in the House of Representatives and a few electoral votes would hardly throw every presidential election into the House of Representatives. Its presence *would,* however, force each of the candidates for the nominations of the two major parties to look to the House of Representatives as the place where the real election *might take place.* This would transform the presidency because Congress would become the president's direct constituency. A stalemate in the Electoral College would not have to happen every four years. The likelihood of its happening would be sufficient to require every presidential candidate to have a contingency plan for such an eventuality. This necessity would tilt the recruitment process even more than at present toward congressional personnel, but more important, it would force each presidential candidate and each president to build and maintain a congressional constituency. That is precisely the relationship embodied in the original plan of the Constitution before the two-party system captured the Electoral College. During the century of real two-party democracy, it was probably very good that the presidency had an independent, democratic popular base in the United States. But when the president's base is no longer a party base but a loose mass base, the situation is altered. A multiparty system would give the presidency a base both in Congress and in a party. It would also bring the presidency back toward human scale by providing an adequate, democratic basis for real collective responsibility.

It bears repeating here that if a three-party system were established in the national government of the United States, there would be a serious move to abolish the Electoral College or change the provision that the House of Representatives would vote by states, or both. But any such effort would take a while, and the interim situation's influence on the presidency could be very great. On the other hand, it is quite possible that a move to abolish the Electoral College would fail, as all of the other numerous attempts have failed, because once a new party is established, any attempt to change the important rules of the game would be immediately seen as malevolent and grossly undemocratic. Manipulation of the electoral rules to determine the outcome of a specific contest almost always backfires, weakening the legitimacy of the government as well as the parties to the manipulation. Electoral manipulation helped bring down the Fourth Republic in France. Fear of such a plot backfiring would delay, perhaps even indefinitely, the abolition of the Electoral College. As soon as the move was made to blunt the influence of a third party by abolishing the Electoral College, however, there would have to be a confrontation with the entire electoral system, including the single-member district system of congressional elections. Why? Because the democratic rhetoric involved in Electoral College reform would spotlight the nonmajoritarian features of Congress. Nothing drastic like proportional representation in multiple-member districts would be required. The single-member district system could be left intact by simply changing the victory requirement from the present plurality to an absolute majority, which would require a second election, or run-off, between the two leading candidates. As I mentioned, such a majoritarian system requiring a run-off is highly accommodating to third parties.[15]

Any scenario involving a third party necessarily raises the question, if there is to be a third party, why not a fourth or fifth, or more? Why not? The specter of fragmentation is a variant of the myth of the

[15]My thanks to Walter Dean Burnham for the suggestion.

apocalypse. True, the potential for fragmentation is very great in the United States. What is to prevent many groupings from growing into political parties? Note has already been taken of the remarkable and generally mischievous spread of PACs—those interest groups that have been turning from conventional strategies of influencing government officials to the strategies of getting the officials elected.

We do not need, however, to set artificial limits. There is a natural limit to the number of real political parties, for at least two reasons. (1) The costs of transformation from organized group to serious political party are tremendous. This is why such transformations are so rare—city unions forming the American Labor/Liberal party in New York in the 1930s and labor, agrarian, and Progressive groups creating the Farmer/Labor party in Minnesota in the 1920s are the two strongest examples. Most new parties grow from scratch, out of some diffuse social movement. An issue-oriented group, on the other hand, forms around a relatively homogeneous interest. When it turns from lobbying to running its own candidates, it must change both its strategies and its structure. To win, it has to confront a much larger and more heterogeneous constituency, even if its goal is only a 20 percent plurality, and the group's main interest necessarily becomes seriously diluted. It is for that reason that the big PACs pick out candidates around the country who already share the interest of their group. (2) The influence of the direct election of chief executives is just as strong a deterrent against a fifth, tenth, or nth party as it is against a third party. If we counted all the present parties that every four years offer a presidential candidate, we already have a multi-party system. But, as I observed earlier, most of these are not serious parties but are using the election to advance a particular message, either a protest against the system or a programmatic point. A new party that is truly serious about being a practical, electorally oriented party would have to organize on a much larger scale, eventually from the bottom up, and it would not be able to sustain itself unless it could offer a meaningful contest for the chief executive spot as well as for a few legislative offices. Even if there had been no legal barriers to John Anderson's National Unity party in 1984 and its candidates had been able to get on to a significant number of state ballots, it would not have become a serious third party. Perhaps, however, it can do so in 1988, if it runs a presidential candidate a second time

206

and also offers candidates for a minimum number of congressional and state legislative seats. The natural barriers are high.

One more question occurs: If a serious third party formed in a few states in one section of the country and another formed in another section, we might reach a chaos of several such real parties at the national level, each with a strong local base and little incentive to bargain. What would happen then to the national system? Why, a couple of the parties might even be radical! This concern too is chimerical. First of all, several such parties would simply be more closely representative of the true makeup of opinion in the United States. With Gilbert's Private Willis in *Iolanthe*,

> I often think it's comical
> How nature always does contrive
> That every boy and every gal
> That's born into the world alive
> Is either a little Liberal
> Or else a little Conservative!

Moreover, because of the special pull of the presidency there would still be the same incentive as today to combine forces, though with parties, instead of the present factions, combination would take the form of "combining lists," as in France—a system under which several parties run candidates for assembly, mayor, and so on in the general election and then for the run-off election two or more parties get together and make up a joint list of their surviving candidates. These party combinations would be reflected in the choices of cabinet members and other top officials after the election. The victory would tend to go to that candidate with a broad—though admittedly minority—popular base plus the skill required to put together a coalition of parties with representation in Congress.

But that is precisely the skill and the popular relationship needed in the modern presidency. It is in this sense that a system of three, or even four or five, parties is in itself the reform most needed. The change of party system would give the presidency more of a party base than it has had in the modern era. It would also give the presidency a congressional base that it hasn't had for more than a century. And it would give the president a basis in organizational continuity or management through delegation to people he can trust

207

because he could know them and their private agendas long before the election.

Presidential Power: If Building It Up Won't Work Try Building It Down

America approaches the end of the twentieth century with an enormous bureaucratized government, a plebiscitary presidency, and apparent faith that the latter can impose on the former an accountability sufficient to meet the rigorous test of democratic theory. Anyone who really shares this faith is living under a happy state of delusion. Anyone who does not believe and argues it nevertheless is engaging in one of Plato's Noble Lies; that is to say, the leaders do not believe it but believe it is in the public interest that the rest of us believe it. Then there are others who don't believe it but would like to make it the truth by giving the president more and more help. Presidents have themselves tried nearly everything to build for themselves a true capacity to govern. Congress, with few exceptions, has cooperated. The Supreme Court, with two minor exceptions, has cooperated. The public seems willing to cooperate in making truth out of the noble lie by investing more and more power in the presidency. The intellectuals, perhaps most of all, have cooperated. If that's not enough, then it's possible nothing is enough.

Since building up the presidency has not met the problem of presidential capacity to govern, the time has come to consider building it down. Building down goes against the mentality of American capitalism, whose primary measure of success is building up. Buildings are so important to American corporate managers that they fake them if necessary, through anything from useless mergers to misrepresentation of profits.[16] Very few leaders have tried to succeed by making a virtue of building down. There was Bismarck, who perceived greater strength in a "smaller Germany." There may be a case or two of weekly magazines whose publishers have sought to strengthen their position by abandoning the struggle for a maximum mass subscription in favor of a smaller and more select but stable readership. But

[16]See, for example, the critique of "paper entrepreneurialism" in Robert Reich's *The Next American Frontier* (New York: Times Books, 1983), ch. 8.

most leaders, in commerce and government, are guilty of what Barry Goldwater popularized in the 1960s, "growthmanship." In many circumstances, building up is an illusory solution or, at best, a short-term gain.

The most constructive approach to building down the presidency would be the strengthening of political parties. If party organizations returned to the center of presidential selection, they would build down the presidency by making collective responsibility a natural outcome of the selection process rather than an alien intruder. Real parties build down the presidency in constructive ways by making real cabinets possible. The present selection process and the present relationship between the president and public opinion produced the star symbol that renders a president's sharing power almost inconceivable. The selection process with parties involved makes the star system itself hard to conceive of.

A three-party system comes into the picture in at least two ways. First, if a two-party system is indeed an anachronism in modern programmatic governments, a three-party system could be the only reasonable way to make real parties possible. Second, a three-party system might build down the presidency by making it more of a parliamentary office. This development would constitute something of a return to the original intent of the Founders' design, a selection process culminating in the House of Representatives. The French improved upon their system by mixing theirs with ours to create the Fifth Republic. It is time we consider mixing ours with theirs. The Fifth Republic established a better balance than we have by successfully imposing an independently elected president upon a strong parliament, giving the parliament the leadership lacking in the Fourth Republic but keeping the popularly elected president tied closely to it.

The crying need to impose parliamentary responsibility on our independently elected president can be accomplished without formally amending the Constitution. Just as the two-party system transformed the presidential selection system and thereby the presidency, so would a three-party or multiparty system transform the presidency, by bringing Congress back into the selection process. This transformation could, in addition, give Congress incentive to confront the real problems of the presidency. Although I admit that is unlikely, the probability could be improved as more of its members

209

came to realize that Congress's survival as an institution may depend upon depriving the presidency of its claim to represent the Great American Majority. The presidency must be turned into a more parliamentary office.

Presidents who are products of the present system are also unlikely to try to change it—unless they come to recognize its inherent pathologies. The first president to recognize these pathologies will want to build down the presidency, and his or her legacy will be profound and lasting. A president who recognizes the pathology of the plebiscitary presidency will demand changes that will ward off failure and encourage shared responsibility. At a minimum, a rational president would veto congressional enactments delegating powers so broad and so vague that expectations cannot be met. This step in itself would build down the presidency in a very special way: It would incorporate more of Congress into the presidency because the clearer the intentions and the criteria of performance written into a statute, the more responsibility for its outcomes would be shared by the majority in Congress responsible for its passage. Such a way of building down alone would not produce a third party, but it would make the presidency more parliamentary, and thus more accommodating to strong parties and to three parties or more. Put this way, the prospect does not seem so unrealistic. To accomplish it, the president must simply make an analysis of the situation roughly similar to the analysis in this book. A president must simply change his point of view.

That draws the entire book toward its conclusion. Institutional reform is desperately needed, but the struggle for reform must be sensitive to the probability that there are no specific and concrete solutions for the problems of the plebiscitary presidency. One of the mischievous consequences of mixing technology and democracy is *belief in solutions.*[17] Solutions are for puzzles. Big government is not a puzzle. The plebiscitary presidency is not a puzzle. Each is a source of important problems because, like all institutions, each is built on some basic contradictions. These contradictions will not go away, because they are the result of mixing highly desirable goals that don't mix well. There is, for example, a contradiction between

---

[17]Cf. Daniel J. Boorstin, *Democracy and Its Discontents: Reflections on Everyday America* (New York: Random House, 1971), p. 120.

representation and efficiency. There is a contradiction between specialization and humanization. There is a contradiction between the goal of treating everyone equally and the goal of giving special attention to individual variation. There tend to be contradictions wherever demand is intense and supply is limited. Problems in any institution are likely to grow in importance and danger whenever people lose their appreciation for the contradictions inherent in an institution and proceed to maximize one side of a contradiction at the expense of the other. These are the imbalances so often referred to in this book. For such contradictions and the problems of balance among desirable but contradictory goals, *coping* is a more realistic goal than *solving*. Successful coping comes mainly from understanding, and the chief barrier to understanding is ideology—the steadfast defense of existing practices and existing distributions of power.

On one point at least there is strong agreement between this book and Ronald Reagan: his observation that where once government was part of the solution it is now part of the problem. Since I have been arguing the same thing at least since 1969,[18] I celebrate Reagan's recognition of the truth and regret the fact he does not actually believe it. He embraced big government and embraced, nay, enlarged the plebiscitary presidency more than most of his predecessors. Why do all recent presidents and important presidential aspirants look back with such admiration to Harry Truman, a man of such ordinary character and talents? I think they do so because Truman was the last president who was made bigger by the office he occupied. This is not to say that recent presidents have made more mistakes than presidents of the past. It is to say that they have been diminished by having to achieve so much more than past presidents and by having to use so much more deception to compensate for their failures. Modern presidents blame their failures on everything but the presidency, when the fault is the presidency more than anything else. It is there that successful coping must begin, with a change of attitude toward the plebiscitary presidency that will enable presidents and presidential candidates to confront the contradictions in the modern presidency rather than by embracing the office as it is.

---

[18]"The crisis of the 1960s is at bottom a political crisis, a crisis of public authority. During the Depression, stability was regained after a spectacular but unrevolutionary turn to government. . . . But today government itself is the problem": *The End of Liberalism*, 1st ed. (1969), p. xiii.

George Bernard Shaw put his finger on an essential point in "Don Juan in Hell," the famous interlude in *Man and Superman*:

Don Juan. Señor Commander [The Statue]: You know the way to the frontier of hell and heaven. Be good enough to direct me.

The Statue. Oh, the frontier is only the difference between two ways of looking at things. Any road will take you across if you really want to get there.

Real reform in American presidential government will not come until there is real change in the points of view of powerful people. As in psychoanalysis, so in politics, coping is a solution, and it will be found not in techniques but in awareness of the nature of the problem. Techniques will follow.

It is appropriate to end *The Personal President* on a psychoanalytic note. And it is not inappropriate to give the last word to a famous fictional psychiatrist, who provided the very last line, freely translated, of *Portnoy's Complaint*: "And now we can begin the analysis."

Index

Abramson, Paul R., 92nn
Adamany, David, 123, 124nn
Adams, John, 29
Administrative Procedure Act, 54-55
Administrative skills, and presidency, 53-54
Afghanistan, Soviet invasion of, 173
Alexander, Herbert, 114n, 122, 125
Alliance for Progress, 172
American Commonwealth, The (Bryce), 29n, 38-39, 97, 98
American Enterprise Institute, 94n
American Labor/Liberal party (New York) 206
American Political Science Association, 195-96; report of Committee on Political Parties of, 68-70, 71, 195-96
American Revolution, 23, 51
Anderson, John, 2n, 116, 206-7
Andropov, Yuri, 17
Antitrust laws, 41-43
Articles of Confederation, 31, 35
Atomic Energy Commission, 5, 163
"Automatic majority" under two-party system, 198, 201

Baker, Howard, 11
Baker, Russell, 143
Balance of power. *See* Separation of Powers
Barber, James David, 135-36
Bayh, Birch, 106
Bay of Pigs, 16n, 17
Bean, Louis H., 15n
Behavior of presidents, predicting:

institutional models, 136-72; psychological models, 135-37
Beirut, terrorist bombing in, 16-17, 95
Bell, David, 118-19
Bismarck, Otto von, 208-9
Block, John R., 120
Bretton Woods international monetary structure, 163, 169
British government, 97, 99, 127, 199
Brock, William, 120
Broder, David, 74n, 75, 81
Brown, Roger G., 78n
Bryce, James Lord, 29n, 38-40, 97, 98, 99
Buckley v. *Valeo*, 123n
Budget Act (1974), 183, 185-88
Budget Bureau, 2, 56. *See also* Office of Management and Budget
Budget process, reform of, 156, 185-88
Burger Court, 50n
Burnham, Walter Dean, 2n, 36nn, 60n, 78, 80n, 81-82, 83, 102-3, 205n
Burns, James MacGregor, 3nn, 8n, 60n, 110n, 189
Burr, Aaron, 33
Bush, George, 106
Business: attitude of toward big government, 7-8; influence of on executive, 60; public's expectations of, 94; regulation of, 41-43

Cabinet: appointments to during transition period, 118-21; and Constitution, 98; lack of power of, 141, 142; under Nixon, 143, 144; proposals to

213

Cabinet (*cont.*)
strengthen, 194-96; and strong parties, 209
Caddell, Patrick, 116
Campaigns, presidential, 92, 112-17; federal funding of, 96, 105-6, 111; financial contributions to, 123-26, 131, 206
Camp David Accord, 172
Capitalist mentality, and reluctance to downscale presidency, 208-9
Caribbean Basin Initiative, 172
Carter, Jimmy, 4, 141, 147; cabinet of, 147; 1976 campaign of, 77, 106, 114-15, 116; 1980 campaign of, 114; and "crisis of confidence," 93; foreign policy of, 172-73; growth of government under, 4, 5 (table), 142, 146; and Iran hostage crisis, 17-18, 185; legislative ineffectiveness of, 129; in presidential transition period, 118, 119-20; public malaise under, ix, 10, 13, 14 (chart); and public relations, 122; mentioned, 81-82, 120, 136, 189
Casey, William, 77, 120
Caucuses, 36, 103, 105
Central Intelligence Agency (CIA), 4, 174
Chambers, William N., 35n, 36nn, 80n, 81n, 103n
Character, as basis for predicting presidential behavior, 135-37
Charisma, 19
Chernenko, Konstantin, 17
Chesterton, G. K., 134
Child Labor Act (1916), 43
Citizens for Eisenhower (CFE), 74
Civil Rights Act (1964), 50
Civil service, 2, 29, 39, 44, 54
Civil Service Act (1883), 29, 54
Civil Sevice Commission, 5, 54, 55
Civil War, 23, 26-27, 38, 68
Civil Works Administration, 44
Clawson, K. W., 7n
Clayton Antitrust Act (1914), 43
Cleveland, Grover, 38
Coalition building, 101-2, 112; and multiparty system, 201
Coalitions, 112, 198
Coattails, presidential, 83-85
Collective responsibility, 98-99, 182-83, 195, 201, 205; and strong parties, 209. *See also* Parliamentary government; Responsibility of the president

Committee to Reelect the President (CREEP), 76-77, 78-79
"Confidence gap," 92-95, 198
Confidence Gap, The (Lipset and Schneider), 93-94
Conflicts of interest, international, 170-71
Congress: constituency of, 82-86; delegation of power to executive, 45-46, 52-53, 157; delegation of power to president, 2-7, 20, 58, 179, 184, 208; position vis-à-vis president, 32-33, 66, 156, 188; and presidential nominating process, 32-34, 35-36, 202, 204-5; role of in traditional system, 30, 31
Congressional Budget and Impoundment Control Act (1974), 183, 185-88
Congressional Budget Office (CBO), 185-86
Congressional government, xi, 2, 28; envisaged in Constitution, 30, 32, 34, 40; erosion of, 52-58
Congressional Government (Wilson), 28
Congressional races, 82-86
Conservatism, vs. liberalism, 154-55, 159-60
Constituency of the president, 37-38, 82-83, 85 (chart), 86-87, 152-53; proposals for changing, 183, 204
Constitution, xi, 2, 22, 23-24, 25, 48, 58; and the cabinet, 98; and Congressional power, 30, 31, 33-34, 35; and constitutional crisis, 201-2; delegation of power of, 23-26, 30-33; and liberalism, 156; and presidential power, 30, 31, 32, 34, 121, 153; and presidential responsibility, 150; and presidential selection, 32-34, 204; regime of, 23-28. *See also* Federalism; Separation of Powers
Constitutional Convention, 188
Constitutional revolution under FDR, 49-50
Conventions: Eisenhower's changes of, 72-73; present function of, 108-11; in traditional system, 37, 38, 39. *See also* Nominating process
Convention system, proposals for restoring, 193-94
Coolidge, Calvin, 44
Corporate capitalism, 94
Corwin, E. S., 31n, 164n
Costikyan, Edward, 73, 103
Council of Economic Advisers, 51

Crane, Philip, 106
Crangle, Joseph F., 111
Crawford, William H., 37
Cronin, Thomas, 5n (with table), 166, 189n

Dahl, Robert A., 8, 9n
Daugherty, Harry, 109
David, Paul T., 108n
Davidson, Roger, 130n, 131-32
Davis, James W., 108n, 194n
Daynes, Byron W., 38n, 121n, 122n, 136n, 185nn
Deceit, of plebiscitary presidents, 2, 173-75, 181
Defense Department, in foreign affairs, 169
Delegates (convention): change in character of, 107-8, 111; growth in independence of, 72-73, 103-9; selection process for, 193
Delegation of power: by Congress to executive, 45-46, 52-53; by Congress to president, 2-7, 58, 147-49, 179, 184, 208; in Constitution, 23-26, 30-33; by president, 149-51. See also Responsibility of the president
Democracy, redefinition of, 8-9, 152
Democratic party, 71, 74; in Congress, 82-85, 127-29; and JFK, 75-76, 119; and liberalism, 158; in New York City, 88-91; in presidential elections, 91-92, 123; and presidential nominating process, 38, 104, 111-12; under FDR, 59-61, 101
Democratization of the presidency, 37-38, 82-83, 152-54, 182-83. See also Plebiscitary presidency
Depression, 43, 45, 52. See also New Deal
Dewey, Thomas, 110
Dillon, Douglas, 118
Diplomacy, presidents' distrust of, 168-69
Direct primary, proposals for, 192-93
Discretion, presidential, 6
Dole, Robert, 11
Dulles, John Foster, 166

Economic change, and presidential popularity, 13-15, 19
Edsall, Thomas, 131n
Einaudi, Mario, 49
Eisenhower, Dwight D., 189; campaigns

of, 71-74; and foreign policy, 166n; growth of White House Staff under, 4, 5 (table); and nominating process, 71-75; popularity of, 10, 14; and Republican party, 71, 74
Electoral College, 33-34, 36, 202, 204-5
Emergency powers, 6-7
Employment Act (1946), 51, 57, 67
Executive Office of the President (EOP), 142, 143
Executive privilege, 6
Executive Reorganization Act (1939), 3
Expectations, public, of business, 94
Expectations, public, of government, 52, 94-95, 96, 198
Expectations, public, of president: excessiveness of, 51-52, 99, 175, 178, 188; need for deflation of, 182-83; presidents' attempts to satisfy with appearances, 11, 20, 139, 149, 160, 175, 178; probable failure to satisfy, x, xii, 9-11, 20, 139-40, 175, 178, 181; reasons for, x, 20, 69, 96, 151-52; and weak party system, 195-96

Fahrenkopf, Frank, 77
Failure of presidents, 10-11. See also Expectations, public, of president
Fair Labor Standards Act, 50n
Fallows, James, 12n
Farley, James, 60
Farmer-Labor party, 206
Federal Bureau of Investigation (FBI), 4, 174
Federal Elections Campaign Act (1974), 122, 123
Federalism: and Constitution, 23-24; erosion of, 41-43, 45-51; and growth of federal government, 2-7; and liberalism, 156; and presidential nominating process, 32, 34; in traditional system, 24-28, 41
Federalist Papers, 33n, 134
Federalist party, 36, 37
Federal Labor Relations Authority, 6
Federal Reserve Act (1913), 43, 47
Federal Trade Commission Act (1914), 43
Ferraro, Geraldine, 150
Fireside Chats (of FDR), 65
First Constitutional Revolution, 49-50
First Party System, 35-36
Fluidity of presidential constituency, 91-92

Flux, vs. presidential coalition, 120, 126, 133, 193
Ford, Gerald: 1976 campaign of, 113-14; disregard of War Powers Resolution, 184-85; popularity of, 13, 14; and public relations, 122; mentioned, 4, 5 (table)
Foreign policy (U.S.): amateurish conduct of, 161-62; control of by president, 163-64, 165-67; lack of coordination of, 169-70; and nuclear weapons, 163, 170; presidents' overdramatizing of, 170-73; "traditional system" of, 161
Foreign relations, and presidential popularity, 15-20, 133, 168-69
Freed, Bruce F., 123n
French government, 97, 207, 209
Fugitive Slave Acts, 27
Fund for a Conservative Majority, 125

Gallup, George, 81n
Gallup Poll, 14n (with chart), 62
Gillette, Guy, 61
Ginsberg, Benjamin, 80n
Goldwater, Barry, 11, 209
Goodman, Allan E., 175n
Goodman, Robert, 17
Government, growth of, x-xi, 7, 67, 141-43, 182; under Carter, 4, 5 (table), 142, 146; under Reagan, 5 (table), 151-52, 158-59, 160; under FDR, 1, 44-48, 58, 101
Government jobs, 2, 28-30, 44. See also Cabinet; Civil service; White House Staff
Government powers, federal: growth of, 42, 45-52; in traditional system, 24-25, 26-28
Government powers, of states, 24-26, 41, 48, 50
Government revolution under FDR, 50-52
Grange, 42
Grant, Ulysses S., 38
Green, John, 123n
Greenstein, Fred, 166n
Grenada invasion, 17, 19, 167

Hahn, Harlan, 108n
Haig, Alexander, 147, 164, 167
Hamilton, Alexander, 33, 38, 134-35
Harding, Warren, ix, 109
Hargrove, Erwin, 135
Harr, John E., 162n

Harris, Louis, 116
Harris Survey, 14n (with chart), 18n (with chart)
Hart, Gary, 108
Hatch Acts (1938-39), 3, 54, 60
Heclo, Hugh, 98, 118n, 119, 121
Heineman Task Force, 4
Helvering v. Davis, 48n
Hepburn Act (1906), 43
Hoover Commission, 3-4
Hoover, Herbert, 4, 44, 59
Hopkins, Harry, 61
House of Representatives, ix, 33-34, 82, 202, 204-5. See also Congress
Hughes, Charles Evans, 53
Humphrey, Hubert, 10-11
Huntington, Samuel, 26

Ideology: and defense of status quo, 211; and presidential voting, 81, 82
Immigration and Naturalization Service v. Chadha, 50n
Imperial presidency, 177-78, 179-82; and plebiscitary presidency, 180
Imperial Presidency, The (Schlesinger), 7, 177
Income tax, x, 43, 47
Independents (voters), 82-83, 86-87, 113, 198
Initiative. See "Keeping the initiative"
Institutional reform. See Reform
Institutional revolution under FDR, 52-58
Insurgency, in political parties, 87-92
Interest group liberalism, 58-60
Interest groups, 42, 58-60, 69, 100, 123-26. See also Political action committees
International events, and presidential popularity, 15-20, 133, 168-69
Interstate Commerce Act (1887), 42-43
Iranian hostages, 16n, 17-19, 185
Isolation of plebiscitary presidents, 145
"Isolationism," 162

Jackson, Andrew, 29, 35, 36-38, 63
Jackson, Brooks, 106n, 125nn
Jackson, Henry, 10, 76, 106
Jackson, Jesse, 17
Jacobsen, Gary, 92n
Janowitz, Morris, 162n
Jefferson, Thomas, 22, 27, 29, 33, 34-35
Johnson, Andrew, 38
Johnson, Loch K., 108n
Johnson, Lyndon B., 158, 174; and

Johnson, Lyndon B. (*cont.*)
emergency powers, 7; foreign policy of, 166, 171, 181; popularity of, 11, 14; mentioned, 4, 5 (table), 13
Joint Chiefs of Staff, 4
Jones, Charles O., 132

Katzenbach v. *McClung*, 50
Kaufman, Herbert, 29n
Kearny, Edward, 77n
"Keeping the initiative," 138-40; in foreign policy, 165-67; in the White House, 139-51
Kelly, Alfred H., 42n
Kendall, Willmoore, 9n
Kennedy, Edward, 10, 114
Kennedy, John F., 4, 9, 116, 174; assassination of, 10, 182; and Democratic party, 75-76; foreign policy of, 16n, 17, 171; popularity of, 10, 14; and presidential transition period, 117, 118-19
Kennedy-Johnson Volunteers Association, 76
Kennedy, Robert F., 76
Key, V. O., Jr., 37n, 70-71, 76n, 90
King, Anthony, 120
King Caucus, 36, 103
Kirkpatrick, Jeane, 120
Kissinger, Henry, 166
Klain, Maurice, 199n
Korean Air Lines incident, 17

Ladd, Everett C., 81n
Landis Report, 4
Landon, Alf, 62
Lane, Robert E., 7-8
Laws of Politico-Dynamics, 11, 19-20, 178
Laxalt, Paul, 77-78
League of Nations, 163
Lebanese conflict, 16-17, 95
Legislative oversight, theory of, 6
Lengle, James, 105n
Lewis, Drew, 120
Liberalism: vs. conservatism, 154-55, 159-60; and Constitution, 156; "interest group," 58-60; and plebiscitary presidency, 154-60; and Supreme Court, 156-57
Libertarianism, vs. conservatism, 155
Liberty League, 60
Lincoln, Abraham, 23, 38, 109-10
Lindley, Ernest K., 48-49
Lipset, Seymour Martin, 93-94
Literary Digest, 62
Lubell, Samuel, 74, 102

McCarthyism, 163
McCormick, Richard, 36
McGovern, George, 10, 92, 116
McLuhan, Marshall, 114
McNamara, Robert, 118
Madison, James, 32, 34, 41, 156, 183
Malbin, Michael J., 106n, 123n
Management, and presidency, 55-56
Mann-Elkins Act (1910), 43
Marshall Plan, 163
Mass media: newspapers, 63-65; in presidential races, 105, 113-14, 116-17; radio and television, 63-65, 78, 113-14, 116-17, 132; use of by presidents to keep initiative, 11, 138-40, 178; use of by Reagan, 12; use of by FDR, 65. *See also* Polling
Mayaguez incident, 16n, 184-85
Meese, Edwin, 77
Military: amateurishness of, 162; control of by plebiscitary presidents, 4, 183-85
Mondale, Walter, x, 10, 84, 108, 150
Mosher, Frederick, 29n, 53n, 54n, 55-56
Moynihan, Daniel Patrick, 111
Multiparty system: and "building down" presidential power, 209-10; fears about, 196-204; with four or more parties, 205-7; likely effect on presidency of, 202-3, 204-8; vs. two-party system, 195-208
Muskie, Edmund, 10

Nathan, Richard P., 143-44, 145n
National Industrial Recovery Act, 6, 53
National Labor Relations Act, 47
National Labor Relations Board, 47-48
National Labor Relations Board v. *Jones & Laughlin Steel Corp.*, 47, 48n
National League of Cities v. *Usery*, 50n
National Recovery Administration, 58
National Security Act (1947), 165-66
National Security Council, 4n (with table), 165
National Unity party, 206-7
Nelson, Michael, 12n, 36n, 130n
Neustadt, Richard, 9, 56-57, 117n, 118n, 119-21, 139
New Deal, 1, 21, 44, 60, 62, 67, 179; break with traditional system, 48, 50-51, 58-59
New Frontier program, 9, 182
New Hampshire primary, 105, 106
Newland, Chester, 146nn

New York City, contested nominations in, 88-91
New York State, parties in, 200, 206
Nixon, Richard, 3, 10-11, 136, 189; attempts of to appropriate power, 143-46, 174; 1960 campaign of, 113; CREEP, 76-79; and emergency powers, 6-7; expansion of government under, 4, 5 (table), 158; foreign policy of, 16n, 166, 169, 171; and the imperial presidency, 180-81; misconceptions about, 143, 145, 179; popularity of, ix, 10, 14; and presidential transition period, 119; Watergate and, 176-79, 189
Nominating process: changes in, 72-73, 103-12; conventions in, 37, 38, 39, 72-73, 108-11; and Democratic party, 104; Eisenhower and, 71-75; as envisaged in Constitution, 32-34; and King Caucus, 36, 103; mass participation in, 79; and the media, 105; and party system, 35-40, 101; primaries in, 72-73, 103-6; public expectations as factor in, 105
Nuclear Regulatory Commission, 5
Nuclear weapons, 95, 163, 170, 175

O'Brien, Lawrence, 75-76
Office of Administration, 4n (with table)
Office of Management and Budget (OMB), 4, 56, 120, 138, 142, 146, 186
Office of Personnel Management, 6
Office of Policy Development, 4n (with table)
O'Neill, Thomas, 12
Ornstein, Norman, 187n
Ostrom, Vincent, 54n

Parker, Joseph, 77n
Parliamentary government, 34, 97-99, 191; and a multiparty system, 209-10. See also Congressional government
Participatory democracy, 100
Partisanship, decline of, 85-86, 91; in Congress, 126-30. See also Two-party system, decline of
Party's Over, The (Broder), 75, 81
Party system, U.S. See Two-party system; Two-party system, decline of
"Party unity scores" (measure of party discipline in Congress), 126-27, 128 (table)

Patronage: defined, 25; and job appointments, 29-30; and political parties, 61-62
Patronage state, 38, 42-45, 66; associated with unremarkable presidents, 34-35, 40; decline of, 41-43; policies of, 25-30, 46 (table)
Pentagon, 169
Personal presidency, xi, 20, 69-70, 81, 91-92, 115; advantages of, 153-54; development of, 62-65, 79-80; effects of on domestic policy, 155-60, 173-75; effects of on foreign policy, 161-75; Eisenhower and, 71-72. See also Constituency of the president; Expectations, public, of president; Plebiscitary presidency
Pierce, Franklin, 39
Pious, Richard, 31, 79, 141
Plebiscitary presidency, 97-133, 180-82; consistency of with imperial presidency, 180; dangers of, 20, 133, 145; decline of party system and, 79; and foreign policy, 165-73; pathology of, x-xii, 20, 133, 145, 147, 210; and FDR, 62, 65. See also Expectations, public, of president; Personal presidency
Plumbers, 178
Police power. See Regulatory policies
Political action committees (PACs), 123, 126, 131, 188, 206
Political revolution under FDR, 58-66
Politics, Parties, and Pressure Groups (Key), 70-71, 90
Polk, James K., 39
Polling, 105, 115-16; in 1976 campaign, 113-14; in 1984 campaign, 78; and "confidence gap," 92-94; and direct representation in government, 100; of Gallup, Roper, Fortune, and the New York Times, 62; and Reagan's popularity, 12-20, 95; used by incumbent presidents, 152
Polsby, Nelson, 91, 105n, 111n, 194n
Pomper, Gerald, 107
Power, of state and federal governments. See Federalism; Government powers, federal; Government powers, of states
Power, presidential: ambivalence of presidents and public toward, 189; attempts of plebiscitary presidents to accrue, 138-51, 178, 180-82; Congressional delegation of, 5-7; growth of,

Power, presidential (*cont.*)
3-7, 56-58; lack of restraints on, 67-68; need for restraints on, 7, 135, 159; proposal for reducing, 208-10; reasons for presidents' attempts to accrue, 147-51; and Supreme Court, 1, 6, 20, 179, 208; theoretical justifications of, 8-9, 20-21, 57, 71
Presidency, change in concept of, 8-9, 56-58, 134-35
Presidential Character, The (Barber), 135-36
Presidential discretion, enlargement of, 6
Presidential government, xi-xii, 2, 99, 151, 182. *See also* Power, presidential
Presidential Power (Neustadt), 9, 56-57, 118-20, 139
President's Committee on Administrative Management (FDR), 1-3, 4, 6, 55-56, 68
Press conferences, presidential, 182
Press secretary, presidential, 121
Pressure groups. *See* Interest groups; Political action committees
Primaries, 72, 73; and decline of party system, 75, 88-91, 105, 106-7; proposals for direct primary, 192-93. *See also* Nominating process
Progressives, 201
Promises, of presidential candidates, 12, 115
Proposition 13 (California, 1978), 94
Public Opinion, 92n, 94n
Public relations, 178
Public Works Administration, 44
Pure Food and Drug Act (1906), 43

Ranney, Austin, 88
Reagan, Ronald, 11, 26, 141; and the budget process, 159, 186-87; economic improvement under, ix-x, 13-15; 1980 election of, 81-82, 83, 86, 106; 1984 election of, ix-xii; expansion of domestic surveillance under, 174-75; expansion of government under, 5 (table), 151-52, 158-59, 160; foreign policy of, 16-19, 166-67, 169, 171-72; growth of plebiscitary presidency under, 211; legislative leadership of, 129, 139; popularity of, ix-x, 12-20, 133; presidential campaigns of, 77-78, 150; and presidential transition period, 120; and Republican solidarity in

Congress, 130; and running mate selection, 150; strategy of for keeping initiative, 145-47, 149
Reconciliation Bill (1981), 187
Redistributive policies. *See* Welfare state policies
Reedy, George, 134, 135, 139, 140
Reform: of budget process, 156, 185-88; of campaign process, 122, 126, 150-51; of civil service, 53n; feasibility vs. effectiveness of, 195; of government structure, 130, 132, 156. *See also* Reform of the presidency
Reform of the presidency, 182-212; Congressional Budget Impoundment and Control Act, 185-88; criteria for effectiveness of, 182-83; proposal for a multiparty system, 195-208; proposal for a six-year term, 188-91; proposals for a direct primary, 192-93; proposals for restoring convention system, 193-94; proposals to strengthen cabinet, 194-95; War Powers Resolution, 183-85
Regulatory policies, 26, 42-43, 45-48, 50, 157-58
Reich, Robert, 208n
Reiter, Howard, 107n, 111n
Representation by district, 198-200
Republican party, 36, 71, 74, 91, 109, 123, 131-32; in Congress, 82-85, 127-30
Republican party, Jeffersonian, 35, 36, 37
Responsibility, collective, 98-99, 183, 195, 201, 205. *See also* Parliamentary government
Responsibility of the president, 69, 147-51, 178, 180, 181, 204; proposal for distributing, 150-51. *See also* Delegation of power
Reston, James, 132
Rhetoric, inflated, of plebiscitary presidents, 115, 170-73
Ripley, Randall, 98n, 129n
Rogers, William, 166
Rollins, Edward J., 78
Roosevelt, Franklin D., 1, 3, 38, 44-66; and decline of party system, 59-62, 65-66; and mass media, 62-65; and plebiscitary presidency, 61-62, 65; mentioned, ix, 5 (table), 12
Roosevelt coalition, 101-2
Roosevelt Revolution, The (Einaudi), 49
Roosevelt, Theodore, 38, 57, 80
Rosenstein, Steven J., 86n

Rosenthal, Alan, 199n
Rossiter, Clinton, 9, 34n, 38n, 156n
Rusk, Dean, 118, 166

Salamon, Lester, 130n, 132n, 138n, 187n
Schattschneider, E. E., 162n
Schechter Poultry Corporation v. United
    States, 6n, 53
Schick, Allen, 130n, 138n, 187-88
Schlesinger, Arthur, Jr., 7, 176-77, 178n,
    179, 180
Schneider, William, 93-94
Schneier, Edward, 60n, 128n
Schweiker, Richard, 120
Second Constitutional Revolution, 49n
Second Hoover Commission, 4
Second Party System, 36-37
Second Republic (U.S.), xi, 11n, 21, 96,
    97, 99, 116, 117, 133
Secretary of state, weakness of, 118, 147,
    164, 166-67, 169
Sectionalism, decline of, 68
Separation of Powers, 1-6, 28; attempts to
    restore, 156, 183-88; dominance of
    Congress in traditional system of, 31,
    37; erosion of, xi, 52-58, 66; and
    liberalism, 156; as set forth in
    Constitution, 23-26, 30-33; stability of
    traditional system of, 26-27. See also
    Delegation of power
Service delivery, as criterion of good
    government, 51, 94-96, 99, 139. See also
    Expectations, public, of president
Shafer, Byron, 105n
Shefter, Martin, 53n
Sherman Antitrust Act (1890), 42
Shultz, George, 16, 167
Single-member district system, 198-200,
    205
Six-year term, presidential, 188-91
Skowronek, Stephen, 36n
Smith, William French, 120
Social security, 46-47, 158
Split-ticket voting, 80-86, 113
"Spoils system," 28
"State building" period, 28, 32, 35, 36
State Department, weakness of, 144, 163,
    169
States, powers of, 24-26, 41, 48, 50. See
    also Federalism
Steel seizure case, 179
Stein, Herbert, 45n
Stevenson, Adlai, 75, 84, 110
Steward Machine Co. v. Davis, 48n

Stockman, David, 146
Straw polls, 105
Sullivan, Mark, 109
"Super secretaries" (under Nixon), 144-45
Supreme Court, 6, 58; and First Consti-
    tutional Revolution, 49-50; and growth
    of executive power, 1, 6, 20, 52-53, 157,
    179, 208; and growth of federal power,
    41-42, 43, 47-50; and liberalism, 156-
    57

Taft, Robert, 71-73
Tammany Hall, 88, 90
Tatalovich, Raymond, 38n, 121n, 122n,
    136n, 185n
Tehran hostages, 16n, 17-19, 172-73, 185
Tenth Amendment, 50n
Three Laws of Politico-Dynamics, 11, 19-
    20, 178
Ticket splitting. See Split-ticket voting
Tillman, Seth P., 175n
Tocqueville, Alexis de, 22-23, 36
Tonkin Gulf Resolution, 173-74, 175, 181
Traditional system, 21, 22-43, 101, 121;
    patronage basis of, 25-30, 38, 42-45,
    46 (table)
Transition period, presidential, 117-21
Treasury Department, 31; in foreign
    affairs, 164, 169
Truman, Harry, 4, 8, 14, 71, 128, 147, 179,
    189, 211
Trust in government, public, 92-95, 198
Turner, Julius, 60n, 128n
Twelfth Amendment, 33, 103, 202
Twentieth Amendment, 117-18, 189
Twilight of the Presidency (Reedy), 134,
    135, 139, 140
Two-party system (U.S.), 40, 103;
    "automatic majority" and, 198, 201;
    early influence of, 33, 209; golden age
    of, 35, 101-2; longevity of, 196-97; vs.
    multiparty system, 195-208; myths
    about, 196-204; in nominating process,
    35-40; and voter turnout, 197-98;
    Woodrow Wilson on, 54. See also Two-
    party system, decline of
Two-party system (U.S.), decline of, xi,
    68-92, 103, 111, 121; APSA Committee
    on Political Parties report, 68-70, 195-
    96; and campaign reforms, 123, 132-
    33; and decline of national committees'
    influence, 73-79, 113; and decline of
    party discipline in Congress, 126-30;
    and decline of party leaders' control of

Two-party system, decline of (*cont.*)
delegates, 72-73, 109, 110; and
declining control of nominations, 87-
92; implications of for reform attempts,
194, 195; Independents and, 87; and
parties' role in presidential elections,
123; proposals for correcting, 193-94;
and proposals for nonrepeatable terms,
190-91; under FDR, 59-62, 65-66; split-
ticket voting and, 81-82

Udall, Morris, 106
Unification Act (National Security Act),
165-66
Unilateralism, in U.S. foreign policy, 162
United Nations, 163

Vance, Cyrus, 166
Vanocur, Sander, 116-17
Veto: congressional, 2-3; presidential,
37-38
Vice president, 5n (with table), 33, 150
Vietnam war, 7, 16n, 181
Vocational Rehabilitation Act (1973), 129
Voter turnout, and two-party system,
197-98

*Wabash, St. Louis and Pacific Railroad
Company* v. *Illinois*, 41-42
Wallace, George, 191
War Powers Resolution, 183-85
Warren Court, 49

Washington, George, 34, 161, 163
"Wasted votes," 199, 200-201
Watergate scandal, 7, 105, 122, 173-74,
176-79, 181, 189
Watt, James, 120, 147
Wayne, Stephen J., 113n
Weinberger, Caspar, 120
Welfare state policies, 46 (table), 47-48,
50-51, 157-58
Wheeler, Burton, 60
White, Byron, 76
White House Staff, 141, 143-44, 148-49
(table); under Carter, 4, 142; under
Nixon, 4, 143-44
White, Leonard D., 40n, 121n
White, Theodore H., 76, 77n, 115, 117n
Wickard v. *Filburn*, 49-50
Wildavsky, Aaron, 105n
Willkie clubs, 73-74
Wilson, Woodrow: *Congressional
Government*, xi, 2, 28; departures of
from patronage state policies, 42-43;
foreign policy of, 163; on politics and
government, 54; on the single six-year
term, 189; mentioned, 27, 29, 38, 56
Wirthlin, Richard, 116
Wolfinger, Raymond E., 86n
Works Progress Administration, 44, 61

Young, James Sterling, 91n, 111n, 194n
Youngstown Sheet & Tube Co. v. *Sawyer*,
179

Also by Theodore J. Lowi

At the Pleasure of the Mayor
The Pursuit of Justice, with Robert F. Kennedy
Private Life and Public Order, editor
The Politics of Disorder
Poliscide, with Benjamin Ginsberg
Incomplete Conquest: Governing America
Legislative Politics U.S.A., editor with Randall B. Ripley
The End of Liberalism
Nationalizing Government, editor with Alan Stone

Library of Congress Cataloging in Publication Data

Lowi, Theodore J.
   The personal president.

   Includes index.
   1. Presidents—United States. I. Title.
JK516.L89   1985   321.8′042′0973   84-45804
ISBN 0-8014-1798-8